T0295695

WEAPONS

OF

THE RICH

Strategic Action of Private Entrepreneurs
in Contemporary China

WEAPONS

—— OF ——

THE RICH

Strategic Action of Private Entrepreneurs
in Contemporary China

Thomas Heberer
University Duisburg-Essen, Germany

Gunter Schubert
Eberhard Karls University Tübingen, Germany

 **World Scientific**

NEW JERSEY · LONDON · SINGAPORE · BEIJING · SHANGHAI · HONG KONG · TAIPEI · CHENNAI · TOKYO

Published by

World Scientific Publishing Co. Pte. Ltd.
5 Toh Tuck Link, Singapore 596224
USA office: 27 Warren Street, Suite 401-402, Hackensack, NJ 07601
UK office: 57 Shelton Street, Covent Garden, London WC2H 9HE

Library of Congress Cataloging-in-Publication Data
Names: Heberer, Thomas, author. | Schubert, Gunter, 1963–   author.
Title: Weapons of the rich : strategic action of private entrepreneurs in contemporary China /
    Thomas Heberer, University Duisburg-Essen, Germany,
    Gunter Schubert, Eberhard Karls University Tübingen, Germany.
Description: New Jersey : World Scientific, [2020] | Includes bibliographical references and index.
Identifiers: LCCN 2020001849 | ISBN 9789811212796 (hardcover) |
    ISBN 9789811212802 (ebook) | ISBN 9789811212819 (ebook other)
Subjects: LCSH: Entrepreneurship--China. | Businesspeople--China. | Privatization--China.
Classification: LCC HB615 .H3379 2020 | DDC 338/.040951--dc23
LC record available at https://lccn.loc.gov/2020001849

British Library Cataloguing-in-Publication Data
A catalogue record for this book is available from the British Library.

For any available supplementary material, please visit
https://www.worldscientific.com/worldscibooks/10.1142/11624#t=suppl

Desk Editors: Balasubramanian/Shreya Gopi

Typeset by Stallion Press
Email: enquiries@stallionpress.com

About the Authors

Thomas Heberer is Senior Professor of Chinese Politics & Society at the Institute of Political Science and the Institute of East Asian Studies, University Duisburg-Essen.

Gunter Schubert is Chair Professor of Greater China Studies at the Department of Chinese Studies, Eberhard Karls University Tübingen.

Acknowledgments

This book would not have been possible without the support of many individuals and institutions. We would like to express our heartfelt appreciation for the manifold support of our Chinese colleagues who spared no effort in helping us to open doors and set up interviews, discussing with us our observations and sharing with us as much joy as hardship when navigating in China's tricky political system. Without their guidance, we would not have been able to conduct our fieldwork on all administrative levels nor to properly understand the many hidden rules and mechanisms of Chinese local politics. We are particularly grateful to Prof. Yu Keping and Prof. He Zengke from Peking University; to Prof. Yu Jianxing and Prof. Shen Yongdong from Zhejiang University; to Dr. Yang Xuedong, Dr. Chen Jiagang, Dr. Ding Kaijie, Dr. des Chen Xuelian, Dr. Li Yuejun, Dr. Liu Shengli, and Dr. Bao Chuanjian, our colleagues at the Central Translation and Compilation Bureau: to Prof. Chang Xinxin from the Central Party School; Prof. Yu Xianyang from Renmin University; Prof. Yu Junbo from Jilin University; Prof. Chen Baosheng from Wenzhou University; Prof. Han Guangming (Zhongshan University, Guangzhou) and Dr. Yu Xiuling as well as Prof. Zhou Yuhao from Zhengzhou University. We are further grateful to Hao Yi, Wang Weimin, Wang Jianmin, and Zhao Hui who organized and supported our research in Beijing, Qingdao, Jimo, Shenzhen, and Xuzhou; and the large number of officials and entrepreneurs who, through their personal efforts and networks, facilitated the success of this research. We would also like to thank our colleagues Prof. Zhou Xueguang from Stanford University and Prof. Björn Alpermann from the University of Würzburg for the time they spent to read through chapter drafts of this book and making valuable comments and suggestions.

Further thanks goes to Abbey S. Heffer for her meticulous proof-reading and to Mario Hauter who patiently checked our chapter bibliographies.

This project has been generously supported by the *German Federal Ministry of Education and Research* and the *German Research Foundation* (DFG).

Thomas Heberer and Gunter Schubert
Duisburg and Tübingen
August 20, 2019

Contents

List of Figures

List of Tables

Introduction

China's private sector economy is in transition, as is the Chinese economy
as a whole. The success of the officially pursued objective to change from
an export- and investment-driven growth model to a development strategy
based on domestic consumption, underpinned by a parallel drive for technological innovation in China's manufacturing and service industries, will
not only decide about the future of the country's economic trajectory but
also of its political system. The ambitious goal of becoming a leading
world power and modern economic entity by 2050 was announced at the
19th Party Congress of the Chinese Communist Party (CCP) in October
2017. To do so requires an innovative and flexible private sector.
Structural change within the Chinese economy is of paramount importance to regime survival. This implies that the private sector will become
increasingly important for sustaining growth, even though the central
government under Xi Jinping has made it clear that it will protect and
develop the state sector as well. China's state-owned enterprises (SOEs),
particularly those destined to become 'national champions', have already
made considerable headway to become powerful players in the global
economy. Despite this, the Chinese Communist Party (CCP) needs to support even a strong public sector to drive home the argument that China is
(still) socialist.

Nevertheless, when Xi Jinping came to power in 2012 (and this project started), the party state embarked on a program of reform to strengthen

the private sector economy. Private sector reform was not explicitly mentioned in the 'Decision of the Central Committee of the Communist Party of China on Some Major Issues Concerning Comprehensively Deepening the Reform', adopted at the 3rd Plenum of the 18th CCP Congress in November 2013,[1] the central policy document of the Xi Jinping era between the 18th and the 19th Party Congresses. However, in the immediate aftermath of the 3rd Plenum, three reform packages were introduced to strengthen the economic system: a program for streamlining local government finances by divorcing them from corporate 'local government funding vehicles'; a program for institutionalizing transferable land management rights; and a program for new Pilot Free Trade Zones (*shiyan ziyou maoyiqu*) — initially set up in Tianjin, Shanghai, Guangdong, and Fujian — to spur high technology and service sector development (Naughton, 2015). When the central government introduced so-called 'supply-side structural reforms' in late 2015 — an attempt by the central government to streamline its policy approach to economic refurbishment — measures were brought on track to cut excess capacity in the industrial and real estate sectors, restructure public debt, reform the credit sector, and 'reduce costs' by lowering taxes and expenses for public services (Naughton, 2016a, 2016b). 'Supply-side structural reforms' have also been designed to boost state enterprise reform, since the curtailing of overcapacity and public-corporate debt is clearly linked to the further transformation of SOEs via 'mixed ownership' and 'investment funds', hence opening them up for more private capital. Each of these reforms is highly relevant to private sector development.[2] Moreover, on many occasions since the 3rd Plenum, the Chinese leadership has publicly reassured private entrepreneurs that it would further support the private sector, by expanding its position in the Chinese economy and

---

[1]*Zhonggong zhongyang guanyu quanmian shenhua gaige ruogan wenti de jueding* (Decision of the Chinese Communist Party and the Central Government on Some Issues Concerning Comprehensively Deepening Reforms: Chinese version), http://cpc.people.com.cn/n/2013/1115/c64094-23559163.html (accessed 3 January 2019).

[2]There have been more specific economic policies initiated by the central government after the 3rd Plenum which are highly relevant for the private sector, for example, VAT reform, the reform of the *hukou*-System and the promotion of microfinance, just to name a few.

improving its efficiency and international competitiveness.[3] This confirms the fact that the future of 'Socialism with Chinese characteristics' depends on the economic success of China's private entrepreneurs in domestic and global markets. Against this background, the quest for ensuring both cooperation and control of their private entrepreneurs forces China's leaders to walk a tightrope, arguably making state–business relations politically more sensitive than they have been at any point in the last two decades of reform.

In his seminal book *Weapons of the Weak*, James C. Scott analyzes everyday forms of resistance by socially weak groups and argues that a history of the *Weapons of the Rich* remains to be written (1985: 172). With this book, we want to re-stimulate the debate on China's private entrepreneurs[4] by making the argument that they have *sharpened their weapons* over the last decade and become influential political players — we call them a 'strategic group' (see below) — within the Chinese polity. Hence, our study is about the political consequences of current structural and institutional change in the Chinese economy and polity for state–business relations, or more precisely, for relations between the state and China's private entrepreneurs. As political scientists, we are interested in the question if, and to what extent, China's rising dependence on a flourishing private sector translates into maneuvering space for private entrepreneurs to strategically safeguard and expand their interests *vis-à-vis* the party state and to trigger institutional change. While they do not openly challenge the

---

[3]In early 2016, for instance, Xi Jinping expressed his strong support of private sector development in order to calm down growing apprehensions among Chinese entrepreneurs that private businesses might be more strictly constrained in the future. See http://finance. sina.com.cn/roll/2016-03-09/doc-ifxqafrm7345622.shtml (accessed 10 March 2016).

[4]In this study, we define 'private entrepreneurs' as the owners of large companies (including the presidents or CEOs of business conglomerates) and those of smaller and medium-sized firms to the exclusion of small-scale, self-employed business owners with only a few workers and staff members (*getihu*). Large entrepreneurs are those with an annual turnover of more than 100 million RMB, and medium-sized ones account for more than 30 million. According to a decree of the Chinese government from 2009, there is no general definition that applies to all types of private enterprises. Generally speaking, they are differentiated according to the number of employees, revenue and total assets, but the categorization varies across different business fields (Zhonghua Renmin Gongheguo Gongye He Xinxihua Bu, 2011).

current regime, their weapons have altered the power balance within the current regime coalition, which connects private entrepreneurs to the party state at all administrative levels. It is hard to predict what will come of this 'hidden horizontalization' of power relations within the coalition. Obviously, the specter of 'crony capitalism' looms already large in contemporary China (Pei, 2016), and entrepreneurial (mis)behavior has been put under close scrutiny by the government of Xi Jinping. At the same time, the future of 'Socialism with Chinese characteristics in the new era' depends on the sound development of the private economy and, therefore, the promotion of private entrepreneurship. It can thus be expected that entrepreneurial influence in the regime collation will rise, with inevitable consequences for regime legitimacy and stability.

Research on the political influence of China's private entrepreneurs for regime survival has been conducted since the 1990s. However, by applying 'strategic group' analysis, we have chosen a different approach for tracing and investigating this evolving relationship compared to most of our colleagues who have written on this subject over the last two decades or so. Hence, we believe that our analysis, which draws on qualitative data gathered over several years (see below), offers a number of new insights and observations which will enrich the existing literature and state of knowledge in the field.

In the past, China scholars have consistently described private entrepreneurs as allies of the Communist Party. Allegedly satisfied with the regime's promise to establish a 'socialist market economy' and its related private sector policies since the end of the Maoist era, private entrepreneurs have been found to be loyal and acquiescent supporters of the party state. Looking at their very different social backgrounds and limited 'political voice', China scholars described them as largely co-opted by the regime which successfully kept private entrepreneurs in a state of structural dependency, mostly via official control by the party state over the institutions and resources necessary to build and maintain a private enterprise. This book takes an analytical perspective that differs from this viewpoint, by which we hope to provide a more nuanced interpretation of the role and significance of private entrepreneurs in Chinese society and politics. Based on our empirical findings, we argue that far from being 'domesticated' and 'atomized' regime supporters who engage in corrupt behavior to secure political protection of their businesses, *private entre-preneurs pursue manifold strategies to pursue their interests, which go far beyond parochial rent-seeking or individual protection by party state cadres.* As their common 'field position', in Bourdieuan terms, pro-duces similar lifestyles, a social group-awareness and identical political demands to strengthen the private sector (by regulatory measures, finan-cial assistance or participation in economic policy-making), private entre-preneurs collectively strive for political recognition by the party state and for meaningful political influence in national and local policy-making.

Our core hypothesis is that *private entrepreneurs are a 'strategic group' in China's polity that display increasing political agency and influ-ence within the party state.* As we will show, private entrepreneurs employ an arsenal of strategies to protect their economic interests *vis-à-vis* both the party–state bureaucracies and state-owned enterprises across the coun-try, though there is (as yet) not much coordinated action which would connect them geographically across space. Nevertheless, by working nationwide through multidimensional networks that crisscross different party state units, administrative tiers, formal institutions such as (local) parliamentary bodies — People's Congresses (PCs) and People's Political Consultative Conferences (PPCCs) — and business associations, both formal and informal — such as entrepreneurial networks — private entre-preneurs do indeed act *collectively.* At the same time, identical exposure to the party state's control of major economic resources and to the institu-tional constraints of China's political system — 'positional closeness', as we call it — produces identical complaints and demands on the part of private entrepreneurs directed at the party state all over China. This results in similar strategic action by private entrepreneurs which, as we hypoth-esize from our findings, increasingly strengthens their collective identity as a social group and collective political agency, hence further contribut-ing to their formation of a 'strategic group'. We also contend, and will show, that, as a strategic group, private entrepreneurs substantially influ-ence policy-making and institutional change in contemporary China, though they do not (as yet) challenge the current regime.

This book particularly looks at the government–business nexus in China's local state in order to understand the formation of private entre-preneurs as a 'strategic group'. It is based on fieldwork conducted by the authors for 4–6 weeks each year between 2012 and 2017 in Beijing and different localities (cities and counties) in the provinces of Fujian, Guangdong, Hainan, Hubei, Jiangsu, Jilin, Shandong, Sichuan, Yunnan, and Zhejiang, with additional control interviews conducted in Fujian, Henan, Jiangsu, and Zhejiang in 2018. We talked to some 150 entrepreneurs operating middle-sized and large companies or conglomerates of both traditional and modern business sectors, including automobile components, furniture, lighting, houseware, sports apparel, biotechnology, chemical upstream products, solar cells, optical machinery, cosmetics, health care products, yacht manufacturing, real estate, private hospitals, nutrition, etc. We also interviewed entrepreneurs in the service sector, e.g. in the tourist and leisure industries. Our respondents were foremost the owners, board of directors or CEOs of these companies with 100 to several thousand employees, though there were also a number of respondents from small internet start-ups. Moreover, we interviewed numerous cadres at township, county, city, and provincial level responsible for private sector development, entrepreneurial chambers of commerce, industry and trade organizations, and members of entrepreneurial networks. Our interviews followed semi-standardized questionnaires and took between 1 and 2 hours each. We mostly visited our respondents in their companies and talked on-site, but in some cases met them in hotels or cafes on their request. Identification of respondents was supported by local scholars, who the authors knew from earlier research, and colleagues from two research centers affiliated to the Beijing-based Central Compilation & Translation Bureau under the Chinese Communist Party. Moreover, we had support from the Central Party School, from the College of Public Administration at Zhejiang University, and from befriended individual entrepreneurs. Each interview was either recorded and later transcribed or memorized by individual note-taking which we exchanged and compared after the interview was completed. Additionally, we have collected and analyzed countless Chinese media reports on private sector development and state–business relations which have complemented our understanding of the topic.

The book is structured as follows: We first give a brief overview of the history and current state of China's private sector development (Chapter 1) before summarizing major insights of the scholarly literature on state–business relations and the significance of private entrepreneurs in the Chinese polity (Chapter 2). We then introduce our theoretical framework, which conceptualizes private entrepreneurs as a 'strategic group' (Chapter 3). Our empirical work employs 'strategic group' analysis to illustrate how private entrepreneurs engage in different forms of formal and informal strategic collective action (Chapters 4 and 5). Finally, we present our conclusions and probe an outlook into the nearer future of state–business relations in China.

References

Naughton, Barry. (2015). Is there a "Xi Model" of economic reform? Acceleration of economic reform since Fall 2014. *China Leadership Monitor* 46, 1–13.

Naughton, Barry. (2016a). Supply-side structural reform: Policy-makers look for a way out. *China Leadership Monitor* 49, 1–13.

Naughton, Barry. (2016b). Supply-side structural reform at mid-year: Compliance, initiative, and unintended consequences. *China Leadership Monitor* 51, 1–11.

Pei, Minxin. (2016). *China's Crony Capitalism: The Dynamics of Regime Decay.* Harvard: Harvard University Press.

Scott, James C. (1985). *Weapons of the Weak: Everyday Forms of Peasant Resistance.* New Haven and London: Yale University Press.

Chapter 1

The Rise and Current State of China's Private Sector

Brief Overview of Private Sector Development after 1949

After the Communist Revolution succeeded in 1949, China's private entrepreneurs were politically exposed and were soon targeted by the new leaders. Although most of them were identified as belonging to the 'National Bourgeoisie'[1] and, as such, accepted as allies of the Communist government in the early years of the new regime, the tide had already changed by 1952. In the 'Five-Anti Campaign' launched that year, large-scale entrepreneurs were accused of tax evasion and other economic wrongdoing. In 1953, the regime announced a new 'general line for the transition to socialism' and the socialization of industry and commerce. In 1956, the private sector in urban China was eradicated and all entrepreneurial assets taken over by the state. At roughly the same time, private enterprises in rural areas were abolished as well. For the rest of the Maoist period (1949–1976), China's economy was state-controlled, although some petty businesses were able to survive in the countryside (Dickson,

---

[1] The 'National Bourgeoisie' consisted of indigenous entrepreneurs not allied with foreign investors, multinational corporations, foreign banks, or the military.

2007: 831; Dickson, 2008).[2] By the time of the groundbreaking reforms promulgated at the 3rd Plenum of the 11th CP Central Committee in December 1978, no more than 140,000 officially counted 'household enterprises' existed in China (Gold, 2017: 464).

After 'reform and opening-up' was formally introduced in the years following the 3rd Plenum, China's private sector soon reemerged and quickly gained steam. Its starting point was the development, in the mid-1970s, of a private shadow economy and illegal market activities in many of China's poverty-stricken areas which were tolerated at the time due to the economic crisis in the countryside. In other words, China's private sector development was initiated by spontaneous local action as peasants returned to household-based agricultural production.[3] As a consequence, markets emerged which were officially illegal at the time. Over the course of the economic crisis, which hit the country in the second half of the 1970s, pressure on the rural areas became unbearable. In response, some poorer provinces (Anhui, Sichuan) tolerated the rise of local markets. Taking note of the ensuing rapid recuperation of the rural economy resulting from these local markets, the central leadership gradually legalized and eventually permitted the establishment of small-scale individual businesses. In fact, the reform policies of the late 1970s, including private sector reforms, must be regarded as a belated legalization of collective action on the part of the peasantry and not merely as a political turn initiated by the Communist Party, even though the role of the party leadership was critical (see Figure 1).[4]

---

[2]For the situation of private entrepreneurship in the Maoist era, see Solinger (1984) and Heberer (1989). For more recent historical accounts of the rise of the private economy in post-Mao China, see, e.g. Zheng and Yang (2011), Coase and Wang (2013), Chen (2015), Wu and Ma (2016), and Lin (2017). See also Chen and Naughton (2017), who have proposed a sequence of three generations of a 'China model' of economic development.

[3]Since undisguised resistance would have been laden with risk, the peasants developed a strategy of permanent though limited fence-breaking by, for instance, ignoring legal restrictions of private economic activities, something James C. Scott has classified as 'everyday forms of peasant resistance' (Scott, 1985, 1989, see Chapter 3).

[4]The process of de-collectivization in agriculture was typical for later developments in the industrial and service sectors as well: Limited transgressions of laws or regulations which were tolerated by the regime induced copycat effects leading to an extensive practice of

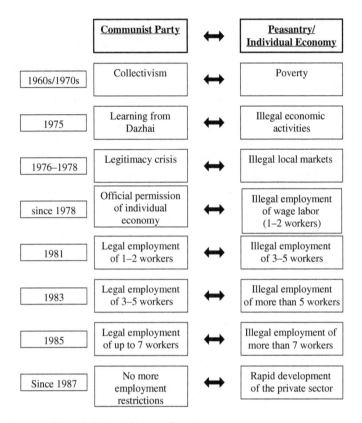

Figure 1:   The Rise of China's Private Sector
Source: Compiled by the authors.

The return to family-based commercial agriculture eventually led to some 150–200 million rural workers being made redundant, with no access to the labor market in the urban state-owned sector. The only way to absorb them was through incorporation into the informal sector, i.e. self-employment in petty trade and craft-based activities. As this was initially forbidden for ideological reasons, these individually owned

'fence-breaking', first at the grassroots and soon across all administrative tiers (Fforde and de Vylder, 1996: 1). The success of the private shadow economy in solving supply-side shortages and creating jobs discouraged suppression by party leaders, once again inducing new transgressions of the law, to the extent that reforms in areas other than the economy were soon brought about as well.

companies (*getihu*) employed paid 'family members' or 'relatives'. Though hesitantly, the state accepted this practice and, since the beginning of the 1980s, gradually liberalized employment of up to seven workers as wage labor.[5] Until 1988, when the above-mentioned regulation allowing for the registration of individual companies with more than seven employees came into force, private entrepreneurs operated in a gray area.[6] Although they had enjoyed constitutional protection since the end of 1982,[7] the social reputation of private entrepreneurs was low and they remained politically stigmatized. Only when Deng Xiaoping, the Communist Party's paramount leader at the time, remarked in 1985 that it was good if some people became rich first did the perception of private entrepreneurs in Chinese society begin gradually to change (Yang and Li, 2008; Li, 2013).[8]

Overall, developments on the ground were always one step ahead of ideological adaption and political decision-making, indicating that the party state was neither willing nor able to control the dynamic of the private sector with its undeniable advantages in creating employment, reinvigorating production, and generating new income. Moreover, the political leadership was under significant pressure from the rural population, reinforcing internal differences on the future trajectory of China's economic transformation and enabling reform-minded party leaders to push ahead with market-oriented reforms.

---

[5]This was a somewhat arbitrary limit taken from a comment of Karl Marx made in Chapter 9 of the third volume of *Capital* according to which a capitalist enterprise with eight and more employees would appropriate the workers' surplus value, hence committing capitalist exploitation.

[6]In 1988, the Chinese State Council enacted the 'Provisional Regulations for Private Enterprises of the PR of China' (Zhonghua Renmin Gongheguo siying qiye zanxing tiaoli), see Heberer (1989: 400–412) and, for the full text in Chinese, *Renmin Ribao*, 29 June 1988.

[7]The state constitution, which was amended in December 1982, stated in Article 11 that the individual economy was a supplement to the socialist public economy and was protected by the state.

[8]'Let some become rich first' (*Rang yi bufen ren xian fuqilai*), statement made by Deng Xiaoping on 23 October 1985, when meeting a delegation of U.S. entrepreneurs. http://cpc.people.com.cn/GB/34136/2569304.html (accessed 30 March 2018).

In an interview with one of the authors, Hu Yaobang, who was the General Secretary of the Chinese Communist Party (CCP) at the time, argued that the private sector was, on the one hand, an 'absolutely indispensable supplement to the socialist economy' (*bi bu ke shao de buchong*); however, on the other hand, he stated that it should not exceed (*bu neng chaoguo*) the collective and state-owned economy (Hu, 2011: 30).[9] This assessment shows that, at that time, the Chinese leadership did not imagine that private entrepreneurship would once again become the dominant economic force in China's economy. After Zhao Ziyang, then the Communist Party's General Secretary, announced in 1987 that China was in the 'primary stage of socialism', implying that more elements had to be taken from capitalism to develop the socialist economy, the 'green light' was finally given for private sector development. During the 1st Session of the 7th National People's Congress in spring 1988, the constitution was amended by declaring the private sector to be a supplement to the socialist public economy, resulting in the formal legalization of individual companies with more than seven employees as private enterprises (*siying qiye*).[10] In August of that year, the 'Provisional Ordinance on the Administration of Self-Employed Individuals in Urban and Rural Industry and Commerce' was promulgated by the State Council, the legal basis for the individual economy until 2011 (Lin, 2017: 32).[11] Some 225,000 private enterprises with more than seven employees, which were registered as individual, collective, or cooperative companies at the end of 1987, could now gain the new status of 'private enterprise' by registering organizationally in terms of 'sole proprietorship', 'partnership', or 'limited liability company' (Heberer, 2003a: 18). This was an

---

[9]The full text of the interview conducted by Thomas Heberer (in German) in *Die Welt*, 17 November 1986. Hu Deping's book contains its Chinese part on private sector development.

[10]Article 11 of the 1982 constitution was revised as follows: 'The State permits the private sector of the economy to exist and develop within the limits prescribed by law. The private sector of the economy is a supplement to the socialist public economy. The State protects the lawful rights and interests of the private sector of the economy, and exercises guidance, supervision, and control over the private sector of the economy.'

[11]It was then replaced by the 'Ordinance of Urban and Rural Industrial and Commercial Self-Employment' (Lin, 2017: 32).

important confirmation of the party state's reform course and its rising support for the private sector. However, private entrepreneurs were soon targeted by conservative regime forces which accused them of subverting socialism, allegedly proven by their support of the Tiananmen protests of 1989.[12] They were banned from becoming members of the Communist Party and politically stigmatized in the aftermath of the 1989 events, despite the fact that the Chinese economy, and thus the Communist Party, benefited hugely from the stamina and economic prowess of the country's private entrepreneurs, who were critical for driving forward market reforms in what had become a 'dual-track' economy[13] since the early 1980s.[14]

The number of private companies dropped significantly in the aftermath of the 1989 crackdown of the protest movement. Only after Deng Xiaoping had embarked on his famous 'Southern Tour' (*nanxun*) in early 1992 (Baum, 1994) and pushed back the opponents of market reform in the party was China's private sector politically rehabilitated and could dynamically expand.[15] The CCP's 14th Congress in 1992 introduced the concept of a 'socialist market economy', implicitly making the private sector an integral component of the national economy. A year later,

---

[12]The extent to which the 1989 protest movement was supported by private entrepreneurs is estimated as low by most scholars. There was financial and material support by a number of them, but in general private entrepreneurs abstained from becoming entangled in the protests and displayed much ambivalence in taking a stance on them (Wank, 1995).

[13]'Dual-track' means the pursuance of market reforms under the auspices of a command economy protected by the state.

[14]One of the most comprehensive and telling studies on the rise of the private sector in post-Mao China is Nee and Opper's *Capitalism from Below* (2012), which meticulously traces the interplay of state institutions and informal agency on the part of entrepreneurial actors which resulted in institutional adaptation and change by shifts in market competition, entrepreneurial action bringing about institutional innovation, mutual monitoring and enforcement in cross-cutting networks and mimicking, i.e. copying effects caused by successful private entrepreneurs which led to increasing collective action for further changes in the overall institutional setup of the Chinese economy.

[15]However, Deng's ideological 'victory' remained contested in the party throughout the 1990s and it was only thanks to his personal authority that the 'reform and opening up' was not attacked with more serious consequences as market reforms went into rough water periodically during that decade.

the 3rd Plenum of the 14th Central Committee of the CCP replaced the term 'commodity economy' with 'market economy' in the official ideological speak, underlining that, henceforth, enterprises with different ownerships would compete on equal terms in the Chinese market (Gold, 2017: 468). From here, the private sector developed dynamically. As a result, in 1995, the Party leadership released a statement explaining that all forms of ownership should develop in parallel and with equal rights. The prospering provinces in the eastern part of the country termed the private sector the 'motor' of the 'socialist market economy' (Jiang Zemin, 1995).

In 1997, the 15th Party Congress declared that although the public sector was to remain the backbone of the national economy, non-public sectors were 'important constituents of the socialist market economy' (Heberer, 2003b: 19). This formula was constitutionally codified in 1999 in Article 16 (Liang Chuanyun, 1990; Qin and Jia, 1993).[16] In his speech at the founding date of the CCP on 1 July 2000, the then CCP general secretary Jiang Zemin stated that, like workers, peasants, intellectuals, cadres, and soldiers, private entrepreneurs were also 'builders of socialism with Chinese characteristics'.[17] The 5th Plenum of the 15th Central Committee then announced in October 2000 that self-employed and privately owned businesses would be further strengthened. Finally, by including the 'Three Represents' (*sange daibiao*)[18] into the party Charter at the 16th National Congress in 2002, private entrepreneurs were officially allowed to join the Communist Party as members of the 'advanced productive forces' (He Yiting, 2001; Dickson, 2007: 833).[19] These

---

[16]During roughly the same time frame, there was a complete restructuring of the public sector economy (see below).

[17]Jiang Zemin, 'Qi yi jianghua da tupo' (Big breakthrough by Jiang Zemin's July 1st talk). http://talk.163.com/06/0323/16/2CTNGB5600301IJI.html (accessed 22 June 2018).

[18]The 'Three Represents' were officially mentioned for the first time by General Secretary Jiang Zemin in 2001 in a keynote speech at the occasion of the 80th anniversary of the founding of the Communist Party. According to this formula, the Party represents China's 'advanced social productive forces' (i.e. economic development), the 'progressive course of China's advanced culture' (i.e. cultural development), and 'the fundamental interests of the majority of the Chinese people'.

[19]This was no less than a revolutionary change in the party constitution: Private entrepreneurship, the epitome of mankind's exploitation, was now defined as a major pillar of

Table 1: **The Development of China's Private Sector (1989–2004)**

	1989	1994	1999	2004
Number of private enterprises (in million)	0.091	0.432	1.509	3.651
Number of workers and staff (in million)	1.430	5.695	16.992	40.686
Average registered capital (in million RMB)	0.093	0.335	0.681	1.313
Average output value (in thousand RMB)	107	264	509	631

Note: The 'individual sector' (*geti jingji*) with less than eight workers and staff is not included in these figures.
Source: Dickson (2007: 833).

ideological adjustments captured what had been happening on the ground over the years. As Dickson (2007: 832) noted, after 1992, the number of private enterprises grew by 35 percent every year and the number of employees rose to almost 17 million by 1999 (see Table 1).

It needs to be noted that in the early 1990s, more than two-thirds of China's registered private companies (but also more than a third of registered individual firms) were still located in rural areas. However, by 1997, the urban percentage of all private companies exceeded 60 percent (62.1 percent) for the first time, while the rural percentage dropped under 40 percent (37.9 percent).[20] The increase of private economic activity in the urban areas was the result of a process by which an increasing number of rural entrepreneurs moved to urban areas expecting to expand their entrepreneurial activities more smoothly with closer proximity of markets, easier access to raw materials, and less bureaucratic control.[21] In the 1990s, many collectively and state-owned firms were transformed into

---

socialist development instead of, as in the early years of the People's Republic, being considered only a transitory means in the struggle to bring about socialist transformation.
[20] *Zhongguo Gongshang Bao* (accessed 20 March 1998).
[21] Chinese firm development confirms the theory of Hayami and Kawagoe (1993), among others, according to which a productive upswing in agriculture entails entrepreneurship specializing in industrially processing agricultural produce. In this way, the agricultural sector is connected with modern industry and urban markets. Traditional village and clan communities facilitate this process as they help to keep costs at a minimum. Rural industrialization generates increases in income for both urban and rural areas. Consequently, rural–urban migration is calibrated and limited at a tenable level.

shareholding companies or companies with limited liability, or they were sold to private entrepreneurs, many of them former managers of collectively owned enterprises who 'jumped into the sea' (*xiahai*) to survive and prosper during China's capitalist transformation. This gave a strong push to private sector development, as did China's WTO entry in December 2001 which provided private entrepreneurs with access to world markets, a legally more advantageous framework and, overall, new opportunities for growth and development.[22]

Two years into the new government of Hu Jintao and Wen Jiabao in 2004, Article 11 of the Chinese constitution was revised again, now explicitly stipulating that 'the state encourages, supports and guides the development of the private sector, and exercises supervision and administration over the sector according to law'. Article 13 explicitly protects the legal rights of private enterprises by the stipulation that 'the lawful private property of citizens shall not be encroached upon'. In February 2005, the State Council issued 'Guidelines on Encouraging, Supporting, and Guiding the Development of Self-employed, Private, and Other Non-Public Entities' in order to facilitate access for private capital — both domestic and foreign — to sectors so far monopolized by state-owned enterprises (SOEs), like power, telecommunications, railway, air transport, oil, public utilities, etc. (Lin, 2017: 35). After another 3 years, a Property Rights Law was finally promulgated in 2007 by the National People's Congress. By now, the party state had fully embraced private entrepreneurship, recognizing its contribution to 'Socialism with Chinese Characteristics' and its future significance for the country's economic well-being.[23]

The rise of the private sector was closely connected to the privatization of China's rural township-and-village enterprises (TVEs)[24] and the

---

[22]For an interesting example of structural, institutional, and social change induced by ethnic entrepreneurs in an ethnic minority area in China as well as their competition with Han entrepreneurs — an issue which, however, cannot be addressed in this volume — see Heberer (2007).

[23]As a Chinese entrepreneur noted, the private sector was developed by giving it freedom (*fang*) and not by means of a bureaucratic steering (*guan*) (Sun, 2018: 55).

[24]The history of China's TVEs, which developed out of the old communes and production brigades after the household contract responsibility system had been installed in rural China, is well accounted for by Oi (1999), Naughton (2007), and Huang (2008).

vast majority of medium- and small-sized SOEs between the mid-1990s and early 2000s. Many TVEs were private undertakings anyway, as entrepreneurs colluded with local governments for mutual benefit by giving TVEs a 'red hat', i.e. registering them as collective enterprises to ensure ideological acceptability (Wang, 2016).[25] In the late 1990s, when the TVEs, most of which were producing labor-intensive goods like textiles, machinery parts, tools, or fertilizer, faced increasing market competition because of low entry barriers and, subsequently, falling product prices, large-scale privatization set in. In just a few years, over 90 percent of TVEs became officially registered private enterprises (Oi, 2001; Li and Rozelle, 2003). The privatization of SOEs, which commenced in the mid-1990s, was a more protracted process as a vast majority were located in urban areas and responsible for the social well-being of millions of workers on the state's payroll. Politically hedged by a decision adopted by the 15th Party Congress in 1997 to 'hold on to the large and let go off the small' (*zhuada fangxiao*), some 50,000 small- and medium-sized SOEs were privatized between 2001 and 2006 (Dickson, 2007: 836–837).[26]

---

[25] Huang Yasheng (2012) has argued that China's capitalist takeoff was predominantly due to the success of its TVEs. On the development of TVEs and other rural ownership forms, see Fan *et al.* (2015: 65–160). In 1985, according to data published by the Chinese Ministry of Agriculture, there were 12 million TVEs of which 10.5 million were registered as private and only 1.57 million as collective (!). In the same year, the official data started to divide TVEs into three categories, namely (1) collective, (2) privately run, and (3) household businesses. The growth of TVEs in the following years until 1993 occurred entirely in the second category. This means that the government was not only well aware of the private character of most TVEs, which had meanwhile registered as collective enterprises, but also accounted for them as such statistically. Huang also points at another interesting aspect of private sector development in China's countryside during the 1980s: the liberalization of informal finance (via rural credit cooperatives and so-called rural cooperative foundations) as a substitute for formal finance to help private enterprises solidify their operations. However, starting in the early 1990s, the central government reverted its former policies and attempted to wipe out informal finance schemes in order to regain full control over the credit sector and the private sector economy. Since then, private companies have suffered from a structural 'credit crunch'.

[26] Dickson cites a survey conducted by the All-China Federation of Industry and Commerce (*gongshanglian*) and the Chinese Academy of Social Sciences in 2002 which also showed that 25 percent of all officially registered private enterprises at the time had originally been part of the state sector.

Since then, the number of officially registered private enterprises has continuously risen. At the end of 2017, there were up to 65,794 million individual enterprises and 27,263 million private enterprises with a combined labor force of 341 million (see also Table 2).[27] Though no detailed data are available, according to official and academic sources, private enterprises today contribute more than 50 percent of China's tax income, more than 60 percent of its GDP, more than 70 percent to innovation, and more than 80 percent to urban and 90 percent to rural employment. More than 90 percent of all enterprises in contemporary China are private (Wang and Yang, 2018).[28] A fair number of them have become huge conglomerates and global players, with top positions in the Forbes Global 2000 and 500 lists.[29] Over the years, party leaders have consistently argued for a strengthening of both the private and public sector economy in order to underline the importance of a balanced relationship between the two as the foundation of 'Chinese socialism'. However, the future of the Chinese economy relies on the healthy development of the country's private entrepreneurship, no matter how much the party state protects and nurtures the public sector and its most important SOEs, which are now labeled 'national champions'.[30]

---

[27] *Wo guo shi you geti gongshanghu he siying qiye zhan quanbu shichang zhuti 94 percent* (Individual and private enterprises constitute 94 percent of all market players), *Xinhua News Net*, 22 January. http://www.xinhuanet.com/fortune/2018-01/22/c_1122297394.htm (accessed 9 August 2018).

[28] Some reports, however, argue that these data do refer to small and medium enterprises only. See, e.g. '*Wei xiaowei qiye shutuan, xu shichang 'zhichi' genshang*' (A bailout for small enterprises requires 'support' for their survival in the market), *Xin Jing Bao* (New Capital Newspaper), 31 August 2018; *Zhongda lihao* (Major advantages), *Zheng, shang xuejie jiti xingdong, minqi xinde de chuntian yao laile* (Collective action of politics, business and scientists, the new spring for private enterprises is arriving). https://465557. kuaizhan.com/11/45/p5516239418a8bf (accessed 1 September 2018).

[29] Well-known 'national champions', which have ranked among the top 10 on the Forbes' Global 500 list of 2017, are *State Grid* (2), *Sinopec* (3), and *China National Petroleum* (4).

[30] 'National champions' are companies which a government has identified as major driving forces of its overall economic development strategy. They have easier access to credit, are given preferential treatment in government contract bidding, and sometimes gain monopoly or oligopoly status in certain sectors of a country's economy. China's biggest companies, most of them state-owned, are called 'national champions', among which are the

Table 2:   The Development of China's Private Sector (2005–2017)

	2005	2010	2015	2016	2017
Number of private enterprises (in million)[*]	4.3009	12.5386	19.0823	23.0920	27.2628
Number of employees (in million)[*]	58.241	91.760	163.949	179.971	198.817

Note: [*]Excluding individual companies (*getihu*).
Source: National Bureau of Statistics, http://data.stats.gov.cn.

Stages and Models of Private Sector Development

China's 'capitalist transformation' and private sector development have been through several distinct stages since the start of 'reform and opening up' (*gaige kaifang*) in 1978. Wang and Yang describe these stages as follows: (1) the initial stage stretching from 1978 to 1988; (2) a period of decline from 1989 to 1991 following the suppression of the urban protest movement in June 1989; (3) a period of recovery and adjustment between 1992 and 2001; (4) rapid economic development from 2002 to 2012; (5) a period of sectoral differentiation between 2008 and 2012; and finally (6) a turn to upgrading and innovation since 2013. However,

world's three largest companies: Industrial and Commercial Bank of China (ICBC), China Construction Bank (CCB), and Agricultural Bank of China (ABC). Huawei, the world's largest producer of smartphones, is probably the most prominent example for a private 'national champion', though a vast majority of them are SOEs. The establishment of the State-Owned Assets Supervision and Administration Commission (SASAC) in 2003 marks the starting point of China's 'national champion' policy, as SASAC was assigned the task of enacting industrial policies to transform China's top 40 companies into such giants (Graceffo, 2017). Today, in accordance with the state's call to promote so-called 'Strategic Emerging Industries', which was written into the 12th Five-Year Plan (2011–2015) and further refined in the 13th Five-Year Plan (2016–2020), China's 'national champions' play a major role in developing an 'innovation economy' in sectors like information technology, biotechnology, robotics and intelligence systems, high-efficiency energy storage, new-energy vehicles, etc. For a long time, the promotion of 'national champions' has been criticized by both foreign and Chinese experts as they threaten to 'crowd out' the domestic private sector and shut out international competitors from the Chinese market. For an early study on China's 'national champion' policy, arguing that this policy can be traced back to the 1970s, see Nolan (2001).

this categorization is rather heuristic. From a regional and local perspective, the time sequence of private sector development differed considerably across the country and is perhaps better defined by distinguishing between different trajectories or models of economic transformation in the reform era (see also Schubert and Heberer, 2015; Shen and Tsai, 2016):

(1) The **Pearl River Delta** model (*Zhusanjiao moshi*) of Guangdong province is characterized by economic growth based on foreign investment. This model stood closest to what Deng Xiaoping had in mind when he ordered the establishment of the first Special Economic Zones in Guangdong and Fujian in the early 1980s. Local governments cooperated closely with foreign (including Hong Kong and Taiwanese) enterprises by providing a sound business infrastructure with cheap land and labor and efficient transportation, while foreign investors retained full control of their companies. This model has often been identified with local state entrepreneurialism, which of course also materialized in other parts of China and was not related only to foreign investment.

(2) The **Southern Jiangsu** model (*Sunan moshi*) saw early private sector development based on the privatization of former collectively owned TVEs during the 1990s and early 2000s, and tight connections between local enterprises and governments. Many private entrepreneurs had previously been managers of TVEs and were hence party members in a position to 'jump into the sea' (*xiahai*) by taking over TVE assets and commercializing their operations. Local governments, for their part, delivered policies most favorable for private sector development and protected native enterprises from external competition, leading to what has been called local state developmentalism or even corporatism (Shen and Tsai, 2016; Oi, 1999).

(3) The **Wenzhou** model (*Wenzhou moshi*) refers to Wenzhou municipality, a prefectural-level city in Zhejiang province, where private sector development was originally based on low-tech and labor-intensive export production by native entrepreneurs, informal finance, and tight marketing networks throughout China. In the early years, the Wenzhou government took a laissez-faire approach toward the private sector and did not intervene much in the local economy, other than

providing basic public goods financed by a rising tax income. Wenzhou became a model for national emulation in the 1990s, but its private sector ran into serious problems even before 2008/2009, when the global financial crisis set in and Wenzhou's export economy collapsed. The low quality of many of its products in conjunction with the family-based structure of many of its companies induced the local government to push for industrial restructuring and upgrading — with moderate success thus far.[31]

(4) The **Jinjiang** model (*Jinjiang moshi*) in Fujian province stands for the rise of native entrepreneurship without the opportunities stemming from the decline and transformation of TVEs like in Southern Jiangsu. Jinjiang's early generations of private entrepreneurs were not party members but nevertheless worked closely with local governments, relying on kinship ties and 'localism', i.e. the invocation of a joint mission to develop the local economy. The local government of this county-level city took responsibility for fostering private sector responsibility early on, making use of Jinjiang's close proximity to the coast which helped to build up regional trade networks. In that sense, Jinjiang followed the logic of local state entrepreneurialism and corporatism, and many of its enterprises were small and medium sized. However, their economic outreach did not go far beyond the immediate environment in Fujian and hence differed substantially from its Wenzhou counterpart.

---

[31] Our fieldwork in Wenzhou in 2013 and 2017 brought to the fore the manifold problems of the private sector in this prefecture-level city. Private entrepreneurs complained strongly that the local government does too little to help them survive the rough-and-tumble of economic adjustment due to necessary structural change. In a particularly telling interview with local entrepreneurs and business associations on September 23–24, 2017, the local government was asked, among other things, to shield the local economy from external investors, reduce taxes, facilitate access to credit, provide for skilled labor from outside Wenzhou, engage in more communication between private enterprises and government cadres, and reduce the pressures put on the private sector to adjust to environmental guidelines. Whereas many Wenzhou entrepreneurs did not care for the government in the early years of 'reform and opening up', they now call for the state's help and guidance. This was confirmed by an interview with a former policy advisor to the Wenzhou government, 12 April 2018.

(5) In addition to the four models mentioned thus far, we would also add rural private sector development as a special variant and call it the **Enshi** model (*Enshi moshi*), after a county-level city within Enshi Tujia and Miao Autonomous Prefecture in Western Hubei Province where we conducted fieldwork in 2013. In places like Enshi, very few industrial enterprises exist and most of them operate in the processing of agricultural products. Tourism is also an important economic sector. Private entrepreneurs have little capital and depend strongly on the support and guidance of the local government for identifying and accessing markets or building a sound management structure within their companies. The local government tries hard to stimulate internal and external investment and clearly steers the building up of a private sector economy. It offers numerous subsidy schemes for that purpose, though its fiscal maneuvering space is limited. Enshi's lack of qualified cadres who know how to drive forward economic modernization and its isolated geographic location with difficult transport conditions make it an inevitable latecomer in terms of private sector development in China.

No matter which model best summarizes the specific trajectory of private sector development across China, in most places, local governments have played multiple, critical roles as gatekeepers, enablers, and steering subjects. They have done so by improving the local infrastructure, ensuring access to land, labor, and credit, granting tax rebates and subsidies for product innovation and branding, providing for vocational education and market information, enforcing industrial upgrading and environmental compliance, and empowering business associations to serve as transmission belts for entrepreneurial concerns and demands. It is the objective and obligation of local governments everywhere in China to improve the competitive capacity of private enterprises in their respective jurisdictions in domestic and international markets around the world and to establish a more effective administration system. Private entrepreneurs, for their part, strive to closely cooperate with local governments because of their control of critical resources and information badly needed for market success, and the power of local bureaucracies to protect 'their' enterprises from external competition. At the same time, the private sector has become

increasingly significant for local development and positive cadre evaluation over the years, entailing a relationship of mutual dependence between
local governments and private entrepreneurs that has shaped state–
business relations since the beginning of private sector development in
the 1980s. As we have argued elsewhere (Schubert and Heberer, 2015),
this relationship gradually changed throughout the Hu–Wen era and the
early years of the Xi Jinping administration, when the local state was
ordered to scale back its developmentalist and entrepreneurialist activities
and become more of a regulator — a shift of function from immediate
'leadership' (*lingdao*) to 'guidance' (*yindao*) and mere service provision
(*fuwu*).[32]

The Private Sector in the Xi Jinping Era

In his report to the 18th Party Congress in 2012, the outgoing CCP general
secretary Hu Jintao explicitly mentioned the private sector only twice by
postulating that private financial institutions and private hospitals should
be rapidly developed (Hu Jintao, 2012). Also, in 2013, the CCP's Central
Committee decision on further deepening reforms, thus setting out Xi
Jinping's comprehensive policy agenda for China's future, addressed
the private sector only marginally.[33] Rather, it emphasized the party state's
intention to facilitate private investment in SOEs and better access for
private entrepreneurs to markets so far controlled by SOEs, but the overall impression from the document text was that the party leaders, most

---

[32]We have defined this shift as the rise of 'local state corporatism 2.0'. In traditional local
state corporatism ('local state corporatism 1.0'), local governments and private enterprises
were conceptualized as components of a larger entity (a corporate firm) with the goal of
maximizing the profits of the local corporate state. In this concept, the state figured as an
entrepreneur itself, establishing and operating collective-owned enterprises (TVEs) in
order to develop a locality. Under the conditions of 'local state corporatism 2.0', however,
the local state no longer figures as a 'corporate head' but increasingly acts as an 'interested
facilitator' and regulator of private sector development.

[33]*Zhonggong zhongyang guanyu quanmian shenhua gaige ruogan wenti de jueding*
(Decision of the Chinese Communist Party and the Central Government on Some Issues
Concerning Comprehensively Deepening Reforms). Chinese version: http://cpc.people.
com.cn/n/2013/1115/c64094-23559163.html (accessed 3 January 2019).

importantly Xi himself, had second thoughts about the government's former commitment to more leeway for the private sector. Many private entrepreneurs were alarmed. This compelled party leaders, most notably Xi Jinping himself, to reassure private entrepreneurs that their worries were groundless and the regime ready to further support and develop the private sector.[34]

In fact, between 2012 and 2018, no important policies targeting the private sector were launched, though the Chinese leadership concerned themselves with reassuring private entrepreneurs that this sector would still be supported politically and that it was crucial for China's further development and innovation drive.[35] Hence, private sector policies were addressed in very general terms concerning content. It seems as though, during this period, the party leadership foremost intended to clarify the future role of the private sector for China's further economic transformation and its relationship with the state-owned sector before any new policies were defined. As such, in the following paragraphs, we focus on a discursive level to pinpoint the party state's stance on private sector development.

When Xi Jinping came to power in 2012, he called for greater efforts to incorporate private entrepreneurs into the political system. In May 2016, he sought to strengthen party work within the 'new social classes' (*xin shehui jieceng*),[36] particularly among young entrepreneurs in the private sector, people returning to China after studying abroad, and professionals working in the new media. He demanded that these new classes should be represented in organizations such as the CCP and other political

---

[34] See, e.g. 'Xi Jinping tan minying qiyejia: dajia dou you tou you lian yao weihu hao xingxiang' (Xi Jinping on private entrepreneurs: All are respected people who should safeguard their image). http://finance.sina.com.cn/roll/2016-03-09/doc-ifxqafrm7345622. shtml (accessed 10 March 2016).

[35] An extensive Chinese study on the innovation potential of China's private entrepreneurs is provided by Liu Dan (2017).

[36] 'New social classes' refers to four groups of people: private entrepreneurs and leading managing and technical personnel of private enterprises and foreign joint ventures; leading figures of intermediate and social organizations; self-employed persons; and leading figures in the new social media (see also Luqiu and Liu, 2018). An overview of the 'New social classes' is provided by Zhang Linjiang (2018).

parties, in People's Congresses (PCs), People's Political Consultative Conferences (PPCCs), etc.[37] In September 2016, Yu Zhengsheng, while on an inspection tour in Tianjin as a member of the CCP's Politburo Standing Committee and Chairman of the National PPCC, declared that people of the 'new social strata', particularly entrepreneurs in the non-public economic sectors, should be fully respected, and party state authorities should help them to 'unite around the CCP and the government' (Yu Zhengsheng, 2016). The United Front Departments (*tongzhanbu*) of the CCP were called upon to take care of this new social segment and offer training courses to bring private entrepreneurs closer to the party and strengthen their entrepreneurial and 'patriotic' spirit,[38] a task which had already been written into the Charter of the CCP United Front Department in 2015.[39] A national conference of leading 'United Front' cadres held in early 2018 again supported the decision to reinforce party work within these 'new social classes'.[40]

In the context of the anti-corruption campaign initiated in 2014 China's political leadership also targeted private entrepreneurs. Many of them were involved in major corruption cases. Interestingly, in autumn 2016 *Renmin Ribao* published an article on the private sector calling for a 'new relationship' between private entrepreneurs and leading cadres in

---

[37] A specific bureau was established to consult representatives from these new social classes. See '*Zhongyang tongzhanbu shige 11 nian zai she xinju zhuanmen fuze xinde shehui jieceng renshi tongzhan gongzuo*' (After 11 years the United Front Department of the CCP has established a new bureau targeting the new social classes). http://epaper. jinghua.cn/html/2016-07/05/content_316162.htm (accessed 1 October 2016).

[38] See '*Shaanxi xin shengdai qiyejia he xinde shehui jieceng renshi lingting 19da jingshen xuanchuan*' (The new generation of entrepreneurs and new social classes in Shanxi listen to the propagation of the spirit of the 19th Party Congress). http://news.sina.com.cn/o/2017-12-08/doc-ifypnyqi2272507.shtml (accessed 1 May 2018).

[39] See *Zai jie '*xindeshehui jieceng renshi*'* (Newly understanding the 'new social classes'). http://www.zytzb.gov.cn/tzb2010/zcjd/201703/f2cd5f2c04b64e8a95e5ab7e6f378a81.shtml (accessed 2 May 2018).

[40] '*Quanguo tongzhanbuzhang huiyi: Jinnian yao jiaqiang xinde shehui jieceng renshi tongzhan gongzuo*' (National conference of the heads of United Front Departments: From this year onwards the United Front work with new the social classes shall be reinforced). http://money.163.com/18/0118/15/D8EOOPUB002580S6.html (accessed 4 May 2018). On private entrepreneurs as a new social class, see also Huang Dongya (2014).

order to combat corruption. Such a statement had originally been made by Xi Jinping during a meeting of entrepreneurial delegates to the National PPCC in March of that year. Xi emphasized that the government–business relations (*zhengshang guanxi*) should be 'intimate' (*qin*) and 'clean' (*qing*), meaning just and honest. He called on both government officials and entrepreneurs to create a new atmosphere of cooperative relations in which corrupt practices, exchange of power and money, as well as predatory behavior on the part of cadres and entrepreneurs had no place. Although governments at all levels and entrepreneurs should keep a distance from each other, the former should treat private enterprises like relatives, frequently communicate with them, take care of them, and support them in solving problems. Entrepreneurs in turn should contribute to local development and refrain from corrupt and illegitimate practices (Zou, 2016). In his report to the 19th National Congress of the CCP, Xi Jinping reiterated that constructing new *qin* and *qing* relations between politics and business would be the right way to create a 'healthy' private economy and sound entrepreneurship (Xi Jinping, 2017). Interestingly, a provincial party publication emphasized that the core responsibility to accomplish this objective was on the side of the government, not on the side of private entrepreneurs (Xia, 2018).

For his part, Premier Li Keqiang underscored in his work report presented at the annual session of the National PC in 2016 the Chinese government's intention to resolutely promote private sector development.[41] Li had emphasized several times before that 'mass entrepreneurship' and 'entrepreneurial innovation' (*dazhong chuangye, wanzhong chuangxin*) would be fostered in order to achieve China's ambitious development goals.[42] In fact, judging by numerous official statements made by the Premier in recent years, China's private entrepreneurs are conceived of as a crucial force for initiating and maintaining a process of

---

[41] See http://house.china.com.cn/apple/fullview_823253.htm (accessed 28 March 2016).

[42] See, e.g. Mass entrepreneurship and innovation as new growth engine. http://english.gov.cn/premier/news/2016/03/03/content_281475300571752.htm (accessed 24 April 2018). See also http://guoqing.china.com.cn/word-en/2016-05/10/content_38430378.htm (accessed 24 April 2018).

continuous technological innovation, an important precondition of China becoming a globally competitive economy (Li Keqiang, 2017).[43]

In September 2017, shortly before the 19th Party Congress of the CCP, a joint statement issued by the CCP's Central Committee and the State Council reemphasized the state's willingness to put new policies on track to assist private entrepreneurs and protect their legal rights. The new policies sought to ensure that their innovative capacity, patriotism, and 'entrepreneurial spirit' (*qiyejia jingshen*)[44] be further developed, and that they consistently act in the interest of the nation, their businesses, and their employees.[45] Private entrepreneurs were expected to advance patriotism and professionalism, as well as innovation and social responsibility (Zhonggong Zhongyang Guowuyuan, 2017). Official documents like this one have repeatedly reiterated the party state's invocation of private entrepreneurs as both loyal regime supporters and an innovating force bearing a major responsibility for China's modernizing program until 2050.

Interestingly, Xi Jinping's report to the 19th National Party Congress of the CCP in October 2017, however, addressed the private sector only marginally. He emphasized that its development should be supported (*zhichi fazhan*) and guided (*yindao*) and that the 'entrepreneurial spirit' should be further promoted and protected (Xi, 2017). The same holds true for the Working Report of the Government at the 2018 session of the

---

[43] See, e.g. *'Rang minying qiye chengwei chuangxin zhuti'* (Let private enterprises become the main force of innovation) (2017). *Qinghai Ribao (Qinghai Daily)*, 24 November. http://news.ifeng.com/a/20171124/53544625_0.shtml (accessed 2 May 2018). A 2018 report published by the European Chamber of Commerce in Beijing revealed that in 2017 the expenses of private enterprises for research and development were 13 percent higher than in 2016. The report noted that these figures are comparable to those in industrialized countries. See *Frankfurter Allgemeine Zeitung*, 21 June 2018.

[44] In 2018, a forum organized by private entrepreneurs defined 'entrepreneurial spirit' as the determination to contribute to the nation no matter how big the difficulties are (Wang Meng, 2018: 77). For the party, 'entrepreneurial spirit' means to be creative and innovative so that they can pave the way for China's turn from being a production base for traditional industries to a high-tech and knowledge-based economy (Wang Meng, 2018).

[45] For an early academic conceptualization of 'entrepreneurial spirit' with the help of indicators to measure entrepreneurship as well as innovation and leadership capacity, see Wu *et al.* (2014) and Hu (2018). Xi Jinping, for his part, added patriotism and social responsibility to the concept of 'entrepreneurial spirit'.

National People's Congress, delivered by Prime Minister Li Keqiang, which only mentioned the government's intention to 'solve the crucial problems of private enterprises' (Li Keqiang, 2018). Nevertheless, even these limited references to the private sector induced the All-China Federation of Industry and Commerce (ACFIC/*Gongshanglian*) and its local branches to proclaim the implementation of new private sector policies.[46] To what extent these initiatives will translate into the implementation of concrete policies over the coming years remains to be seen, but party and government leaders have made it very clear that China's future depends on the success of its private entrepreneurs in an increasingly competitive global economy.

For instance, the vice-president of the Federation of Industry and Commerce of Anhui Province and a member of the People's Political Consultative Conference called for assisting the private sector to overcome the 'three difficulties' facing this sector: lack of capital, shortage of manpower, and insufficient support of local governments to initiate and finance innovations.[47] In his speech at the World Economic Forum in Davos in 2014, Prime Minister Li Keqiang announced the above-mentioned promotion of 'mass entrepreneurship and mass innovation' to boost the Chinese economy and entrepreneurial innovation,[48] which was followed in 2015 by the promulgation of the 'Opinion of the State Council on Some Issues and Measures for Boosting Mass Entrepreneurship' (Guowuyuan, 2015). In mid-2017, the Chinese State Council adopted detailed guidelines for promoting 'mass entrepreneurship' in order to

---

[46] In April 2018, for instance, the National Federation of Industry and Commerce organized a meeting in Beijing attended by government representatives and private entrepreneurs to discuss new policies to strengthen private enterprises such as downscaling administrative procedures and costs, as well as introducing new tax reduction incentives. See *9 bumen wei minqi zhuanchang jiedu youhua yingshang huanjing* (Special meeting with 9 government bureaus to interpret the optimization of the business environment), http://www.xinhuanet.com/politics/2018-04/03/c_1122628747.htm (accessed 3 April 2018).

[47] *Liu Mingping weiyuan huyu zhuoli pojie minying qiye 'san nan'* (PCC member Liu Mingping urges to solve the 'three difficulties' of private entrepreneurs). *Jiangzhun Shibao* (*Jiangzhun Times*), 8 March 2018.

[48] For his speech, see http://www.qnr.cn/waiyu/yiwen/eng/201501/1039326.html (accessed 4 May 2018).

open up new avenues of employment, optimize China's economic structure, and foster sustained growth. According to these guidelines the state shall facilitate business registration procedures, set up new credit channels and financial services for start-ups and promising enterprises, nurture collaboration between enterprises and research institutes in order to assist private enterprises in identifying and employing skilled workers and professionals, open new industries for private investment, and enact measures to strengthen the protection of property rights, intellectual property, and the legal status of private businesses (Guowuyuan, 2017). Prime Minister Li Keqiang reiterated the same points in September 2018, emphasizing the need to 'intensify mass entrepreneurship' and further facilitate businesses start-ups.[49] This would suggest that private investment and the role of private enterprises in generating economic growth and new job opportunities had become increasingly urgent. The fact that Li had to repeat the official line announced in 2017 revealed how difficult it was to implement new private sector policies.

To support private enterprise development, in early 2018, the 'Central Political and Legal Work Conference', organized by the powerful 'Central Political and Legal Work Commission' (*Zhongyang zhengfawei*) under the Central Committee of the CCP, called for taking further measures to protect individual property rights to make private entrepreneurs feel safer in their business operations and to trigger entrepreneurial innovation. Concurrently, Guo Shengkun, head of the commission and member of the Political Bureau of the CCP, emphasized the need to handle the legal cases of entrepreneurs properly in accordance with the law. In fact, several court verdicts based on false accusations and flawed trials in recent years had been abrogated and the respective victims rehabilitated.[50] This has made observers speculate on the beginning of a new era in state–business relations.[51]

---

[49] Nation to boost entrepreneurship innovation, *China Daily*, 7 September 2018.

[50] *'2018 nian zhongda lifa, anli quanmian shuli'* (Significant legislation in 2018, comprehensively sort out specific cases). http://www.chinalawinfo.com/Feature/FeatureDisplay1.aspx?featureId=602&year=2018&data=2018/2/5 (accessed 4 May 2018).

[51] A prominent example of those private entrepreneurs recently acquitted is Zhang Wenzhong, founder of the Wumart chain stores, who was declared innocent of charges of fraud, embezzlement, and corporate bribery in May 2018, after spending nine of his

Indeed, there is evidence that the Chinese leadership is facilitating private sector investment and development, for instance, in the defense industry, which is so far closely monopolized by public sector investment. This should foster more competition, trigger innovation, and reduce costs since the private sector may offer lower prices for defense and more dual-use products than SOEs are usually able to provide (Nouwens and Béraud-Sudreau, 2018). In fact, the Chinese leadership has shown a lot of trust in the private sector's ability to spur innovation, which is badly needed in order to accomplish the party state's modernization objectives.

Arguably, the party state believes that the high-tech sector is paramount to materializing China's 'China 2025' development blueprint, according to which China intends to become the world's leading nation in ten high-tech industries by the year 2025. A study at the MERICS Institute in Berlin has highlighted that without the private sector, particularly small and medium high-tech enterprises, it will be hard to achieve this goal. Likewise, the Chinese leadership has identified SMEs as critical for its 2025 objectives. Generally, private enterprises should help to improve the performance of state-owned firms, if necessary by 'mega-mergers' between them. In addition, party organizations in private enterprises shall assist entrepreneurs to pursue technological upgrading and innovation (Zenglein and Holzmann, 2019).

Challenges of Private Sector Development

Despite all assurances by the central leadership, the private sector is still not treated on an equal footing with the public sector. For instance, as was reported in 2018 in the context of China's debt-cutting efforts, private companies are perishing due to bond defaults, whereas state-owned firms, in spite of heavy debts amounting to more than 70 percent of China's total corporate debt, are surviving due to massive state subsidies.

12-year sentence in jail. In fact, close connections to high-ranking officials may prove to be either a blessing or an existential danger for China's private entrepreneurs, as their fortune becomes intrinsically linked to the destiny of their political patrons, a destiny which has become unpredictable in Xi Jinping's China. See Wang (2018a).

This shows that, even now, the party state has not yet come to a conclusion on what kind of mechanisms must be implemented to solve the tremendous cash flow problems of Chinese enterprises. The recent crackdown on shadow banking and 'illegal borrowing' has only aggravated this problem (Tang, 2018).

In June 2018, the Central Committee of the CCP and the State Council ordered that polluting enterprises should be technically upgraded, transferred to other areas in interior China, or simply be closed (Zhonggong Zhongyang Guowuyuan, 2018). All administrative levels were ordered to take immediate steps to implement this directive, and implementation would become an indicator of cadre performance evaluation. In August 2018, entrepreneurs and business associations complained that a large number of small and medium enterprises (the overwhelming majority of them private) were ordered to stop production or had even been closed. They pointed to the economic importance of the private sector and argued that they were interested in solving the environmental problems of their enterprises themselves. However, nobody would give technical advice or come up with transparent criteria or standards for those technologies considered environmentally friendly or not. The outcome of this would be that local authorities arbitrarily closed down companies, a large number of workers became unemployed, and social stability was negatively impacted.[52]

The rigid implementation of environmental policies restricts the private sector significantly. Obviously, the party state targets polluting industries, i.e. the more traditional sectors of the Chinese economy, to cease production. At the same time, it fosters high-tech enterprises to push for a modern, innovation-oriented private sector. The discussion on the future

---

[52] '*Gongchang tingle! Dapi gongren shiye! Huanbao Zhongya xia, hai tan shenme fazhan*' (Factories stop production! Many workers are jobless! How to talk about development under strong pressure of environmental protection). https://www.xuehua.us/2018/08/10/ 工厂停了%EF%BC%81大批工人失业%EF%BC%81环保重压下%EF%BC%8C还谈 什么/zh-tw/ (accessed 15 February 2020) A respondent told us that in his hometown alone (a prefectural city) hundreds of enterprises had been officially closed, though many of them continued to operate clandestinely and with the silent approval of the local government. Interview, Chinese entrepreneur, Duisburg, 8 August 2018.

development of the private sector was also fueled by an investigative report published in 2016 which predicted that more than 95 percent of China's private enterprises were going to vanish within the next 5 years, particularly those founded during the 1970s and 1980s. These entrepreneurs, it was argued, wanted to make money but were unwilling to learn how to be innovative. According to the report, the number of private enterprises running losses had increased tremendously, from 41,000 in 2011 to 59,000 in 2015 alone (Shui, 2016).[53]

In fact, the slowdown of China's economic growth hit the private sector particularly hard, primarily small- and medium-sized enterprises. In order to support this important pillar of the Chinese economy, which also suffered due to a systemic credit crunch and high tax rates, a State Council executive meeting in August 2018 chaired by Premier Li Keqiang decided that smaller enterprises should enjoy better access to affordable loans. It was argued that financial institutions should be incentivized to be more supportive of smaller businesses, and regulatory oversight should be improved to ensure that credit services are made available for small- and medium-sized private companies. At the same time, it was suggested that taxes for these enterprises should be reduced. Li explained that small businesses play a critical role in creating jobs and that the well-known problems of credit access have to be solved as soon as possible (Guowuyuan, 2018). A few days later the 'State Leading Group for Promoting the Development of Small and Medium Enterprises' (*Guowuyuan cujin zhong xiao qiye fazhan gongzuo lingdao xiaozu*) admitted that small- and medium-sized enterprises in particular are still discriminated against in favor of SOEs and that the 'Law on Promoting Medium and Small-sized Enterprises' (*Zhong xiao qiye cujin fa*) promulgated in 2017 had so far not been properly implemented. A package of measures to solve the most urgent problems of private companies concerning access to bank loans and excessive taxes was then brought on

---

[53]An article in *Renmin Ribao* noted in 2013 that the average lifespan of 50 percent of all private enterprises in China is less than five years (Cheng, 2013).

track (Caxin Zhoukan, 2018).[54] To underscore the government's determination to improve the credit situation for small and medium enterprises Li Keqiang visited the Nantong branch of the Bank of Jiangsu in November 2018, praising it as a model for providing such enterprises with low-interest loans.[55] A meeting of the Standing Committee of the State Council in December 2018 reiterated this determination.[56]

In his report on the work of the government during the second session of the 13th National People's Congress in March 2019, Prime Minister Li Keqiang emphasized that improvement of the business environment of small and medium enterprises is a must, that the bank loan problem must be solved under any conditions, and that private banks should be permitted and fostered.[57] Shortly thereafter, the political leadership reiterated measures to be taken in order to raise the confidence of private entrepreneurs, most notably an improvement of market access for private enterprises, facilitation of access to bank loans, simplification of administrative procedures, and the strengthening of market supervision and regulation. The prime minister also emphasized the significance of competition and of equal treatment of private and SOEs which must be guaranteed by the

---

[54] See also '*Zhongda li hao. Zheng, shang xuejie jiti xingdong, min qi xinde de chuntian yao laile*' (Major advantages. Collective action of politics, business and scientists, the new spring for private enterprises is arriving). https://465557.kuaizhan.com/11/45/p5516239418a8bf (accessed 1 September 2018).

[55] *Li Keqiang kaocha Jiangsu — xia feiji weihe zhiben zheli*? (Why did Li Keqiang go straight there after getting the aircraft during his inspection tour of Jiangsu?). http://www.gov.cn/xinwen/2018-11/29/content_5344449.htm (accessed 7 June 2019).

[56] *Li Keqiang zhuchi zhaokai Guowuyuan Changwu huiyi, bushu jiada dui minying jingji he zhongxiao qiye zhichi deng* (Li Keqiang presides over a meeting of the Standing Committee of the State Council deploying increased support for middle and small enterprises, etc.). http://www.gov.cn/xinwen/2018-12/24/content_5351724.htm (accessed 7 June 2019). A female entrepreneur from Jiangsu noted during an interview in Duisburg on 26 May 2019 that this gave rise to great hopes for Chinese entrepreneurs.

[57] Li Keqiang, 2019 nian guowuyuan zhengfu gongzuo baogao (2019 Report of the State Council on the Work of the Government). https://news.sina.com.cn/c/xl/2019-03-05/doc-ihsxncvf9915493.shtml (accessed 12 April 2019); English version: http://english.gov.cn/premier/speeches/2019/03/16/content_281476565265580.htm (accessed 12 April 2019). Xi Jinping also emphasized these points during a meeting with the People's Congress delegation from Fujian Province, see Beijing Qingnianbao (*Beijing Youth Daily*), p. A3.

state.[58] China's supreme judge Zhou Qiang promised that the rights of private entrepreneurs would be better protected,[59] the first time the private sector was ever mentioned in a work report of the Supreme Court. In mid-July 2019, the National Development and Reform Commission decided upon measures to better protect private enterprises' intellectual property rights, to guarantee their equal market access and fair treatment regarding public bids and government procurement, and to punish infringements upon private enterprises.[60]

As a matter of fact, the Chinese government has for years tried to solve these issues, but with limited success. Against the backdrop of the recent economic slowdown and the US–China trade war, small and medium enterprises are facing increasing risks, all the more since private enterprises in 2017 accounted for more than 90 percent of Chinese exports. The number of Chinese entrepreneurs on the Hurun lists's 2 billion RMB threshold fell by 237 in 2018 from 1,893 in 2017 (Hancock, 2019).

With regard to taxation by private entrepreneurs, Changdong Zhang (2017) argues that due to high tax rates (value added tax 17 percent, corporate tax 33 percent) almost all private entrepreneurs try to avoid or evade taxes by looking for patrons within the party state to protect them, which leads to hiding business income from the tax authorities and out-right bribery of officials. The party state, according to Zhang, is not inter-ested in remedying these practices since it allows maintenance of effective political control over private entrepreneurship: In the case of (political)

---

[58] Zhonggong Zhongyang bangongting, guowuyuan bangongting yinfa, Guanyu cujin zhongxiao qiye jiankang fazhan de zhidao yijian (General Office of the Central Committee of the Communist Party of China and General Office of the State Council: Guidelines for the Promotion of a Healthy Development of Medium and Small Enterprises) 7 April 2019. http://www.xinhuanet.com/2019-04/07/c_1124335674.htm (accessed 12 April 2019).

[59] Zhou Qiang, Zuigao Renmin Fayuan gongzuo baogao (Work report of the Supreme People's Court). http://www.xinhuanet.com/politics/2019-03/19/c_1124253887.htm (accessed 12 April 2019).

[60] Minying qiye xiaowei qiye fazhan zai ying zhengce hongli (Policy dividends for the development of small private firms), 15 July 2019. http://www.xinhuanet.com/fortune/2019-07/15/c_1210196054.htm (accessed 29 July 2019).

'misbehavior', entrepreneurs could at any time be arrested by being accused of 'tax evasion'. At the same time, as Zhang further argues, the party state has a 'strong incentive to keep a large SOE sector for both ideological and instrumental reasons' (Zhang, 2017: 49). In fact, there is some evidence on this. In September 2018, Li Yang, Chairman of the National Institute for Finance & Development, a think tank of the Chinese government, argued that investment in and the takeover of private enterprises by SOEs had increased substantially. This observation, which has been shared by a number of our respondents in the later stages of our fieldwork, points to a more recent trend in China's ongoing economic transformation formula which may be called 'oligopolization under SOE leadership'. State-owned companies at all administrative levels are 'encouraged' by local governments to invest in private enterprises to control a majority of shares or buy them out, if possible. From their perspective, this makes sense: SOEs become, arguably, more modern and competitive, which facilitates access to bank loans and helps local economic development. Li warned that this might discourage and negatively impact private sector development (Han, 2018). However, the current 'oligopolization trend' is hard to stop given the vulnerability of China's small- and medium-sized private enterprises, the powerful resources most SOEs have at their disposal, and the cadre evaluation system which still regards economic development as the major indicator of performance and, thus, personal promotion.

A Core Problem: Getting Access to Capital

A major obstacle to private sector development is a severe shortage of investment capital. Particularly in times of economic crisis, banks are rather reluctant to lend credits to enterprises; and if they do, they would rather serve state-owned companies which can rely on official collateral or big private conglomerates who usually meet their loan performance targets more quickly than small- and medium-scale enterprises. Even if the government demands that banks lower their lending standards to support private enterprises, change is unlikely as long as the state does not back up credits for the private sector in some way — for instance, by loosening capital requirements for banks or providing guarantees on private sector loans to reduce the lending risk (Orange Wang, 2018). Moreover, the granting of loans is selective. As Quan and Leng (2018) have shown, in many places local governments decide which company is qualified to receive a loan and which is not, giving priority to high-tech businesses and obstructing loans to small- and medium-sized firms of the manufacturing sector which have been the principle driving force of economic development in recent decades (Chan and He, 2019). On top of this, if an enterprise is unable to win contracts from public offers it might be unable to get any credit at all.

A large number of private enterprises, acting as guarantors for other firms, are also facing insolvency. Since private entrepreneurs as a rule need proper collateral or guarantors in order to acquire a bank loan, private enterprises frequently act as mutual guarantors for other businesses. This 'cross-guaranteeing of debt' is dangerous for financial systems and new lending (Shu, 2019). In addition, delayed payments of government authorities and SOEs to private enterprises (for completed tasks) are a further issue which negatively impacts cash flow of enterprises (Hu, 2019).

Due to the above-mentioned significance of small- and medium-sized firms, the central government seems determined to undertake efforts to find a solution for all these problems. Accordingly, in February 2019, the CCP's Central Committee and the State Council ordered that all Chinese banks increase lending to private enterprises in order to support the private sector and to avoid a further slowdown of the economy. Also in 2019, large commercial banks are expected to increase the number of loans offered to small- and medium-sized enterprises by more than 30 percent (Jinrong fuwu 18tiao, 2019). Since banks have still been reluctant to provide loans to small- and medium-private enterprises due to higher credit risks, China's Banking and Insurance Regulatory Commission (CBIRC) in February 2019 again urged state-owned commercial banks to facilitate and increase lending to these enterprises and reduce lending rates in order to avert an economic slowdown.[61]

---

[61] *Zhongguo yinbao jianhui guanyu jinyibu jiaqiang jinrong fuwu minying qiye youguan gongzuo tongzhi* (China's Bank and Insurance Regulatory Commission on further strengthening credit service for private enterprises), Document No. 8/2009. http://www.cbrc.gov.cn/chinese/newShouDoc/C7BD7955D9E448189297FBB859BAFA8A.html (accessed 12 April 2019).

Although the central government repeatedly promised to provide more loans to private enterprises, in reality no major change was observed until the end of 2018 (Yao, 2018). However, due to the importance of the private sector, the central government has, historically, at least endeavored to find further solutions for these recurring problems. For example, in 2008, soon after the central government had launched the '4 trillion economic package' in response to the outbreak of the world financial crisis, the People's Bank of China (PBOC) released credits through China's banking system. It also encouraged the sub-branches of commercial banks to increase their lending by administrative incentives such as promotions or demotions. This induced the banks to draw up so-called 'implicit contracts' with local enterprises, i.e. establishing a system of mutual guarantees between local enterprises to extend their ability to apply for loans and then force the banks into lending, so that official targets for overall credit expansion could be met. However, when inflation and unsustainable investments reached unbearable levels, the government soon turned to fiscal contraction, leading to a severe credit crunch in the private sector beginning in the late 2000s without an end in sight so far (Chen Ye and Guan, 2018; see also Wang and Tong, 2018). To this day, a relaxation of lending policies on the part of China's banks is hampered by high levels of public and private debt, making it politically risky for the People's Bank of China — or the central government, for that matter — to force the banking system to expand its credit lines for private enterprises.[62]

In reality, there is contradictory information on solving the credit issue. In April 2019, it was reported that state-owned commercial banks such as the Bank of Communication had increased the credit volume for private enterprises and concurrently reduced interest rates.[63] Moreover, in June 2019, China's State Council decided to further reduce real interest rates on loans for small and medium enterprises, cap lending surcharges, support corporate finance, facilitate intellectual property pledge financing,

---

[62]Evidently, the same does not hold true of the public sector, as state-owned enterprises are equipped with huge credit to invest in China's grand geoeconomic schemes, most notably the 'Belt-and-Road Initiative'. See, e.g. Zou Lei (2018).

[63] *Fuwu minying jingji, bai nian jiaohang zhuli qianwan xiaowei qiye fazhan* (Serving the private sector, the 100-year-old Bank of Communication assists in the development of millions of small enterprises). *Caixin Zhoukan* (Financial News), 8 April 2019. http://promote.caixin.com/2019-04-08/101400602.html (accessed 12 April 2019).

and improve financial services in general for the private sector.[64] A report of the Standing Committee of the National People's Congress, however, revealed that the effects of these policies have been far from being satisfactory. Banks are still risk-averse, set high thresholds for loans, are hesitant to grant them to small and medium enterprises, and demand high interests.[65] Obviously, it is difficult for the central government to implement private sector policies on a national scale since local banks are reluctant to support them. One major reason is related to conflicting bank policies. On the one hand, the central bank has several times cut banks' reserve requirement ratios in order to facilitate liquidity and loan provision for private enterprises. On the other hand, the central government has requested that banks reduce lending risks, thus strengthening the banks' perception of small private firms as the riskiest group of borrowers.

In order to counterbalance this dilemma, Chinese banks introduced a worldwide accepted measure of lending: discounting of bankers' acceptances. When a company buys something from a supplier, it can pay using a so-called bankers' acceptance, which is issued by a bank on behalf of the buyer. When the acceptance matures, the supplier exchanges it for

---

[64] *Li Keqiang zhuchi zhaokai Guowuyuan Changwu huiyi queding jinyibu jiangdi xiaowei qiye rongzi shiji lilü de cuoshi deng* (Li Keqiang presides over a meeting of the State Council to ascertain, among other things, the further lowering of financial interest rates), 26 June 2019, http://www.gov.cn/guowuyuan/2019-06/26/content_5403503.htm (accessed 10 July 2019). As a consequence, to fulfill the quota requirements by the central government, some major banks reinterpreted the term 'small enterprises' in order to inflate related statistics. See an investigative report of the Standing Committee of the National People's Congress: '*Wei zhongxiao qiye jiankang fazhan "bamai kaifang"*' (For a healthy development of small and medium enterprises 'feel the pulse to extract a square root' [the latter meaning to treat them according to specific needs]), *Renmin Ribao*, 29 June 2019. http://www.npc.gov.cn/npc/c30834/201906/1c7aa48d24fc488bafc3a67e0daae602.shtml (accessed 10 July 2017). A report of the People's Bank of China noted that in May 2019 the total balance sheet of renminbi credits for small and medium enterprises amounted to more than 10.3 trillion yuan (ca. 1.5 trillion US-$), with an average interest rate of 4.6 percent. See Renmin Yinhang (2019).

[65] '*Wei zhongxiao qiye jiankang fazhan "bamai kaifang"*' (For a healthy development of small and medium enterprises 'feel the pulse to extract a square root' [the latter meaning to treat them according to specific needs]), *Renmin Ribao*, 29 June 2019. http://www.npc.gov.cn/npc/c30834/201906/1c7aa48d24fc488bafc3a67e0daae602.shtml (accessed 10 July 2017).

cash from the bank for the amount of the sale. The bank then seeks payment from the company on whose behalf it issued the acceptance. If the company needs money before the acceptance is due, it can go to any bank and exchange the acceptance for cash, albeit at a discount to the value of the acceptance which is cashed in by the bank. That's the reason why many private businessmen are reluctant to turn to this method as it reduces further the already small profit margins of private businesses.[66]

Discourses on Private Entrepreneurship

As mentioned earlier, self-employed individuals reemerged with the onset of economic reforms at the end of the 1970s, which were followed by the gradual legalization of private entrepreneurship in the 1980s. Since then, the term 'entrepreneur', which has always been ideologically problematic in a socialist system, has been hotly debated in China. Figure 2 summarizes the change in the official assessment and terminology of entrepreneurship until its reinterpretation as 'traditional Chinese' or 'socialist' in the 1990s. In the early 1990s, the term 'peasant entrepreneurs' (*nongmin qiyejia*) was employed to describe successful managers of rural enterprises who were seen as 'representatives of the advanced productive forces in the countryside' (e.g. Wang and Chen, 1985). Since the mid-1990s, Chinese academics have discussed the Schumpeterian idea of the entrepreneur. Not only them, even Chinese officials later admitted that an entrepreneurial stratum had once again come to the fore in China (Xu, 1997; Zhang and Li, 1998).

Figure 2 illustrates the change in the assessment and official conceptualization of 'entrepreneurs' up until the 1990s. In the 1950s, the characterization as 'capitalists' or 'bourgeois' attributed an anti-socialist character to entrepreneurship and thus placed them outside society. As of the mid-1950s, entrepreneurs effectively ceased to exist. The leading personnel of (state-owned) enterprises were officially nominated SOE directors, often acting as party secretaries at the same time. With the beginning of the reform policies in the late 1970s 'individual businesses' and, eventually, 'private entrepreneurs' (in rural areas initially called 'peasant

---

[66]For details, see McMahon (2019).

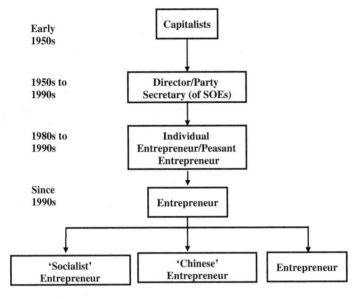

Figure 2: The Chinese Entrepreneur as a Discursive Category

Source: The authors.

entrepreneurs') finally came into existence once more. Only in the 1990s was the term 'entrepreneur' in its 'correct' usage discussed among both scholars and policy advisors, but with different attributes such as 'socialist', 'Chinese', or simply speaking of 'entrepreneurs'.

Throughout the 1990s, the entrepreneurial stratum was labeled the 'most valuable' resource of the economy, which thus had to be supported and further developed by granting private entrepreneurs equal economic, political, and legal status within Chinese society. It was argued that intellectuals should be encouraged to become entrepreneurs, and the state sector should no longer be favored one-sidedly (Wei and Sun, 1994). It also became apparent that innovative or 'scientific entrepreneurs' would be needed (Zhao, 1998). Being an entrepreneur was qualified as an 'honor' (*rongyaode*), and operating a company was portrayed as a kind of 'heroism' (*yingxiong zhuyi*) (Yu Shaowen, 1994). As the 'most valuable' resource (Zhao, 1998), entrepreneurs were created in the course of China's social transformation as a product of the market economy, which they then subsequently nurtured (Mi and Gao, 1997: 42–44). By the end of the 1990s, entrepreneurship was finally classified as a 'profession' and no longer had political overtones (Zhang and Liu, 1996; Li, 1999).

At the same time, the Chinese entrepreneur was treated as a culturally specific type. It was argued that this type was different from its Western counterpart through its 'distinct Chinese qualities' (*Zhongguo tese*) as a 'reformer' (*gaigejia*) and a 'hero' (*yingxiong*), working in the interests of society and for the benefit of its overall prosperity (Liu, 1997). This discussion was continued in the more recent discourse on the 'Confucian entrepreneur' (*rushang*, see Chapter 3). Other authors have declared, in an apologetic fashion, Chinese entrepreneurs to be 'socialist' as they contribute to the building up of a 'material' and 'intellectual culture of Socialism'. In contrast to their Western counterparts, 'socialist entrepreneurs' fulfilled two central requirements: they were innovators (*chuangxinzhe*) and at the same time possessed 'political qualities', i.e. they supported the CCP and the socialist system (Yuan, 1997). They belonged after all to the 'avant-garde of the economic revolution' (Zhang and Liu, 1996) and were called to be patriots, to behave in a 'morally superior' way, display a 'good ideology' and a good working style, and to constantly improve themselves (Zhongguo qiyejia diaocha xitong, 1998).

Overall, the role and function of private entrepreneurs in China's economic transformation had been seen as widely positive within domestic discourse, and at the end of the Hu–Wen era, their 'profession' was socially and politically accepted. Under Xi Jinping, the private sector was called important for further economic reform at various occasions, and domestic discourse focused on their potential as 'innovators' and drivers of high-tech development (see, e.g. Liu, 2017). Particularly larger private enterprises were praised as a 'leading force' in promoting corporate social responsibility and public charity (see, e.g. Cao, 2018). Nevertheless, in recent years, private entrepreneurs have had to face much criticism, too. The 2018 vaccine scandal which exposed the criminal behavior of a large private drug producer, Changchun Changsheng Biological Technology Co Ltd,[67] various incidents on construction sites for which private firms were

---

[67] It was reported in July 2018 that Changchun Changsheng Bio-technology and the Wuhan Institute of Biological Products had sold faulty DPT (diphtheria, whooping cough, and

held responsible, and numerous corruption cases involving private entrepreneurs have together triggered a discussion on the future of the private sector in China.[68] Being aware of the political danger caused by such negative reporting for the private sector, Pan Shiyi, a celebrity blogger and chairman of SOHO China company, one of the most prominent real estate developers in China, wrote on his Weibo blog that private entrepreneurs should not only strive for profit but must also be role models in Chinese society and be committed to the social well-being of their employees (Pan, 2018). In September 2018, Wu Xiaoping, a veteran financial entrepreneur, published a short essay on social media in which he made the following surprising claim:

in the progress of China's great history of reform and opening up, the private economy has tentatively completed its important historical task to assist the public economy in making a developmental leap forward. In the next step, the private economy should not be expanded blindly, but in a completely new fashion become a more centralized, solidaric and extensive public–private mixed system, so that in the course of the new development of a society based on a socialist market economy a new gravity will steadily come to the fore.[69]

Put differently, China's private sector economy should be phased out to the benefit of a mixed system in which the public sector would be leading. Although this statement was criticized by most netizens, it coincided with a mood among some leftist intellectuals and a popular undercurrent within

---

tetanus) vaccines that were given to children as young as three months old under official health programs in Chongqing, Shandong, and Hebei provinces. Changsheng Bio-tech had also systematically forged data in the production of rabies shots. See 'China's lawmakers consider 'strictest' rules on vaccine industry after scandals', *South China Morning Post*, 24 December 2018, https://www.scmp.com/news/china/politics/article/2179357/chinas-lawmakers-consider-strictest-rules-vaccine-industry-after (accessed 5 January 2019). Xie (2018) provides an overview on the problems of product quality of private enterprises taking Hunan Province as an example.

[68] Pei Minxin's book on China's Crony Capitalism (2016) is the most comprehensive Western publication on corruption by private entrepreneurs, covering the early years of the Xi Jinping era as well.

[69] Wu (2018); see also Wang (2018b).

certain sections of the population critical of private entrepreneurs' wide association with corruption and unclean behavior. For years, scholars such as Zhou Xincheng (see, e.g. Zhou, 2018), the former head of the School of Marxism at Renmin University, or Chen Zhonghua, the Dean of the International Academy of Politics and Law, demanded the elimination of the private sector, which they saw as contrary to Marxist theory. On the other side, at the 'Forum of 50 People' (50 *ren luntan*), a meeting of influential economists and senior officials held in September 2018, a majority of participants strongly criticized the slogan 'Let the state sector come in and the private sector withdraw' (*guojin mintui*) and all demands of abolishing the private sector (An, 2018). Moreover, few of the respondents with whom we spoke after Wu's essay had been published seemed particularly worried. Still, the debate caused uneasiness among many entrepreneurs that private sector policies might change during the coming years of the Xi Jinping era. Prominent figures such as Hu Deping (2018), the influential son of the late party general secretary Hu Yaobang, warned of tendencies to cut down private sector development. The government has since tried to reassure the country's private entrepreneurs that this was not going to happen. A *Renmin Ribao* editorial reiterated that the private sector was indispensable to China's development and modernizing process and that government policies would help to improve, not limit, it (Li Zheng, 2018). Premier Li Keqiang reassured attendees at the 'Tianjin World Economic Forum', also held in September 2018, that the private economy would be further promoted and that all obstacles to development should and would be removed from this crucial and promising sector of the Chinese economy (Li Yanli, 2018). Finally, Xi Jinping declared at the 'Conference on Private Enterprises' (*Minying qiye zuotanhui*) held in November 2018 that private entrepreneurs 'can feel reassured'. Policies toward the private sector would not change, and the private economy would be further promoted and supported. Entrepreneurs are, as Xi argues, 'our own people' (*women zijide ren*) (Xi Jinping, 2018a, 2018b). In the weeks that followed, the problems of the private sector and possible solutions were widely discussed, and many party state organizations at the central and provincial level assiduously expressed their support and assistance to that sector.[70]

---

[70] See, e.g. the Minister of Justice Wei Zhezhe (2018) who, however, expressed his support in a very general way, seemingly paying mere lip service to the official line. The People's

However, in his speech, Xi Jinping also emphasized that SOEs still are the main force (*zhuti*) in the Chinese economy (Xi Jinping, 2018a). The renowned economist Cheng Enfu from the Chinese Academy of Social Sciences explicitly underlined this position in the Party's daily *Renmin Ribao* (Cheng, 2018). Economist Sheng Hong thus interpreted the expression of political support of the private sector by Chinese leaders and the media as a 'tranquilizer' (*dingxinwan*) and 'speech therapy' (*hualiao*) and noted that Xi's formula of entrepreneurs being 'our own people' would make the latter feel rather uneasy as they would not understand the meaning of this wording (Sheng, 2018).

Despite all reassurances by the Chinese leadership that private sector policies would not change, it was recently reported that listed private companies are forced to sell significant stakes to SOEs (Hancock, 2019). In fact, there is huge pressure on private enterprises to become part of investment companies (*touzi gongsi*), in which representatives of state authorities, SOEs, and private enterprises have shares. Membership in these companies facilitates access to public procurement contracts and access to bank loans (Li Gengnan, 2018). The same is true if SOEs invest in private enterprises (Lu, 2018). An entrepreneur told us that this trend was very serious. In many cases, local governments would only trust private enterprises that closely collaborated with state-owned firms or if these state-owned firms held a significant share in them. Many entrepreneurs had no other alternative but to follow this path. Government officials would play a leading role in investment firms, e.g. leading figures of the 'State-owned Assets Supervision and Administration Commission' (*Guoziwei*). The same interviewee emphasized, however, that these policies were not only a control instrument of the party state but also a measure to help major

---

Bank of China (Li Jie, 2018) or Fujian's provincial party secretary, who was the first major political figure on the provincial level to express strong support for private sector development (Jiang Shengyang, 2018), took a more pronounced position. See also the speech given by the party secretary of Zhejiang Province (Che Jun, 2018). Probably different from most other provinces, Zhejiang Province commenced to help private enterprises to reduce their production costs (Tian Yu, 2018). At local level, all provinces and cities organized meetings with entrepreneurs in order to explain the party's policies to them. Some local governments such as the government of Shenyang published open 'letters of thanks' in which they thanked private entrepreneurs for their significant contributions to economic development in their jurisdictions (see, e.g. Zhi quan shi, 2018).

private enterprises improve their efficiency and their national and international competitiveness.[71] In 2019, it was reported that private solar power and energy firms which faced a debt crisis in recent years were increasingly taken over by publicly subsidized state-owned companies (Chen and Kirton, 2019), for many entrepreneurs a further sign of the retreat of the private sector.[72]

In addition, promises by the leadership and reality frequently differ. Take, for instance, the case of entrepreneur Zhao Faqi who fought against the arbitrary cancellation of a government contract for coal exploration rights and therefore campaigned online and also turned to the courts for suing this government. Winning his case, celebrated as a hero among private entrepreneurs, and supported by many liberal economists and lawyers, he suddenly disappeared, probably after being arrested. Many entrepreneurs took this story as a litmus test for the legal system and the official claim that the Chinese leadership would support the private sector against predatory officials. *The New York Times* quoted Zhao a few weeks before his disappearance, saying that he faced a lot of risks and pressure because of this lawsuit, and that Chinese entrepreneurs would yearn for the rule of law to replace arbitrary power: 'You can't say someone is protected one day, and take away protection the next day.'[73]

A larger number of corporate scandals related to private enterprises in recent years have strongly affected trust in the party state's private sector policies. Not a few entrepreneurs were held in criminal custody, some of them later released and rehabilitated due to wrongful verdicts. Such verdicts, an entrepreneur told us, might be motivated by increasing prejudices *vis-à-vis* private entrepreneurs, social discontent with the widening gap between rich and poor, and a sentiment in society that the wealth of most entrepreneurs originates from criminal behavior.[74] Zhang Wenzhong, founder of the Wumart chain stores who had been held in prison for seven years due to a flawed prosecution and was released and rehabilitated in 2013 told the annual *Yabuli China Entrepreneurs Forum* in February 2018

---

[71] Interview, entrepreneur, Fujian, 22 September 2018.
[72] Talk with Chinese entrepreneurs of the second generation, Duisburg, 16 July 2019.
[73] On the details of this story, see Buckley (2019).
[74] *Talk, Duisburg*, 16 July 2019.

that what had happened to him could happen to every entrepreneur in China at any time and that without the intervention of political leaders this unjust and mistaken judgement would have never been revoked. He urged that the legal rights of private entrepreneurs should be better protected.[75] Cases such as Zhang's have strongly undermined confidence in China's private sector policies among private entrepreneurs. Many entrepreneurs do not buy recent official statements of the Chinese leadership in support of the private sector anymore, which have been made in relation to the China–US trade conflict or the overall importance of the private sector to stabilize and modernize the economy.[76]

Recently, Chen Tianyong, a (private) Chinese real estate developer in Shanghai, who left China in early 2019 and settled down in Malta, published an article on the social media explaining the reasons for his emigration. He argued that many entrepreneurs have lost confidence in China's future, that the Chinese leadership has mismanaged the economy, and that the level of economic and political liberalization has decreased. He called upon his fellow entrepreneurs to leave China as soon as possible (Chen, 2019; Li Yuan, 2019). A recent survey by Hurun, a research institute located in Shanghai, seems to confirm Chen's pessimism. According to this survey, only one-third of China's rich people are very confident with regard to China's economic prospects.[77] If private entrepreneurs are indeed losing confidence in government policies, this will have negative effects on both private sector development and the strategic acting of private entrepreneurs.

The recent debate on private entrepreneurship in conjunction with the mixed signals sent by China's leaders, who emphasize the importance of both the public and private sector while abstaining from clarifying their

---

[75] See *Cong Zhang Wenzhong yuan'an kan Zhongguo qiyejia qunti de daoyi yu dandang* (From the wrong charges towards Zhang Wenzhong understand righteousness and justice as well as the responsibility of China's group of entrepreneurs), 28 February 2018. http://finance.sina.com.cn/meeting/2018-02-28/doc-ifwnpcns4523251.shtml (accessed 15 July 2019).

[76] *Talk: Duisburg*, 16 July 2019.

[77] See 'Business Insider', 14 March 2019, https://www.scmp.com/magazines/style/news-trends/article/3001616/have-chinas-super-rich-lost-faith-countrys-embattled (accessed 12 April 2019).

relationship in terms of consistent policy-making, has unsettled private entrepreneurs and may, over time, mean that the younger generation is far less willing to 'jump into the sea'.[78] The call of the party state for public–private mergers and for SOEs at all administrative levels to invest in private enterprises, combined with increasing debt ratios on the part of private companies facing discrimination within the current credit system (Wu and Fran, 2018), serves to reinforce the skepticism of many private entrepreneurs concerning their future in an evolving Chinese economy. Official encouragement of state enterprises to attract private investment is read by many as a state-sponsored takeover operation and not as a promise of new opportunities for gaining access to markets so far dominated by the state sector (Sun and Lin, 2018). The announcement of Alibaba's charismatic Chairman Ma Yun in 2018 of withdrawing from his company and focusing on his charity foundation, and an increasing reideologization of state and society pushed by the current leadership have further fueled the concerns of private entrepreneurs that the political climate might gradually turn against them. Strategic action to defend their economic interests, the major topic of this book, might become more difficult in the coming years.

References

An, Delie. (2018). *Beijing 50ren luntan da chidu fayan piping guojin mintui* (The 50 People Forum in Beijing comprehensively criticized the slogan 'let the state-owned enterprises come in and the private ones retreat'). http://www.aboluowang.com/2018/0919/1176558.html (accessed 24 September 2018).

Baum, Richard. (1994). *Burying Mao: Chinese Politics in the Age of Deng Xiaoping*. Princeton: Princeton University Press.

Buckley, Chris. (2019). Chinese entrepreneur takes on the system, and drops out of sight, *The New York Times*, 9 March. https://www.nytimes.com/2019/03/

---

[78] In February 2019, in a keynote address delivered shortly after the debate on the future of the Chinese private sector at the annual 'Yabuli China Entrepreneurs Forum', a high-level event organized by private entrepreneurs as a discussion forum with the Chinese leadership, the director of the 'State-owned Asset Supervision and Administration Commission' (SASAC) said, in a non-committal fashion, 'in the face of economic globalization… strengthening cooperation [between the public and private sectors] is the general trend.' See Huang and Kirton (2019).

09/world/asia/china-scandal-xi-jinping-private-business.html (accessed 12 April 2019).

Cao, Xu. (2018). *Di 15jie Zhongguo cishan bang jiemu zaiji qiyejia yiran shi shehuide juanzeng zhudao liliang* (Opening announcement of the 15th China charity meeting: Entrepreneurs are the leading force of social donations). *Jingji wang* (Economic network). http://www.ceweekly.cn/2018/0329/221123.shtml (accessed 24 September 2018).

Caxin Zhoukan (*Finance Weekly*). (2018). *Cujin zhengce de zuihao caipan shi zhong xiao qiye* (The best proof for advancing policies are small and medium enterprises), Issue 34, 27 August, 4.

Chan, Elaine and He, Huifeng. (2019). China's private firms in traditional low-tech sectors struggling without government support. *South China Morning Post*, 21 April. https://www.scmp.com/economy/china-economy/article/3006995/chinas-private-firms-traditional-low-tech-sectors-struggling (accessed 16 July 2019).

Che, Jun. (2018). *Yi shiji xingdong tuidong minying jingji zai chuang huihuang jifa minying qiyejia zai li xingong* (By practical actions triggering new great achievements of private entrepreneurs). *Jing-Chu Zheshang* (Zhejiang businessmen in Hubei and Hunan), 12, 51–53.

Chen, Ling and Naughton, Barry. (2017). A dynamic China model: The co-evolution of economics and politics in China. *Journal of Contemporary China* 26(103), 18–34.

Chen, Tianyong. (2019). *Wo weishenme likai Zhongguo. Yige qiye jingyingzhe de linbie zhengyan* (Why I am leaving China. An entrepreneur's farewell admonition). https://botanwang.com/articles/201901/%E6%88%91%E4%B8%BA%E4%BB%80%E4%B9%88%E7%A6%BB%E5%BC%80%E4%B8%AD%E5%9B%BD%EF%BC%9F.html (accessed 12 April 2019).

Chen, Xuewan and Kirton, David. (2019). State Sector Gobbles Up Private Solar Firms Reeling From Slashed Subsidies. *Caixin*, 20 July. https://www.caixinglobal.com/2019-06-20/state-sector-gobbles-up-private-solar-firms-reeling-from-slashed-subsidies-101429496.html (accessed 12 July 2019).

Chen, Yufeng, Ye, Zhipeng and Huang, Guan. (2018). The Financial crisis in Wenzhou: An unanticipated consequence of China's "four trillion stimulus package". *China: An International Journal* 16(1), 152–173.

Chen, Zongshi. (2015). *The Revival, Legitimation, and Development of Private Enterprises in China: Empowering State Capitalism*. New York: Palgrave Macmillan.

Cheng, Enfu. (2018). *Guoyou qiye zuoyong bu ke tidai* (The role of state-owned enterprises cannot be replaced). *Renmin Ribao*, 29 November.

Cheng, Hui. (2013). Banshu qiye 'nianling' bu dao wu sui (The life span of half of the enterprises amounts to less than five years). *Renmin Ribao* (People's Daily), 31 July.

Coase, Ronald and Wang, Ning. (2013). *How China Became Capitalist*. London: Palgrave MacMillan.

Dickson, Bruce J. (2007). Integrating wealth into power: The communist party's embrace of China's private sector. *The China Quarterly* 192, 827–854.

Dickson, Bruce J. (2008). *Wealth into Power: The Communist Party's Embrace of China's Private Sector*. Cambridge: Cambridge University Press.

Fan, Jie, Heberer, Thomas and Taubmann, Wolfgang. (2015). *Rural China. Economic and Social Change in the Late Twentieth Century* (new edition). London and New York: Routledge.

Fforde, Adam and de Vylder, Stefan. (1996). *From Plan to Market: The Economic Transition in Vietnam*. Boulder: Westview Press.

Gan, Nectar. (2018). China sends message to the private sector as tycoon Zhang Wenzhong exonerated. *South China Morning Post*, 1 July. https://www.scmp.com/news/china/policies-politics/article/2148924/china-sends-message-private-sector-exonerating-tycoon (accessed 15 July 2019).

Gilley, Bruce. (2011). Paradigms of Chinese politics: Kicking society back out. *Journal of Contemporary China* 20(70), 517–533.

Gold, Thomas B. (2017). Normalizing private business in China. *Journal of Chinese Political Science* 22(3), 461–472.

Graceffo, Antonio. (2017). China's national champions: State support makes Chinese companies dominant. *Foreign Policy Journal* (May), https://www.foreignpolicyjournal.com/2017/2005/2015/chinas-national-champions-state-support-makes-chinese-companies-dominant/ (accessed 2 April 2018).

Guowuyuan. (2015). *Guowuyuan guanyu dali tuijin dazhong chuangye wanzhong chuangxin ruogan zhengce moshi de yijian* (Opinion of the State Council on some policy models to promote with great force mass entrepreneurship and entrepreneurial innovation). http://www.gov.cn/zhengce/content/2015-06/16/content_9855.htm (accessed 4 May 2018).

Guowuyuan. (2017). Jin yibu tuijin dazhong chuangye wanzhong chuangxin shenru fazhan (One further step to foster the development of mass entrepreneurship and entrepreneurial innovation). *Renmin Ribao (People's Daily)*, 28 July.

Guowuyuan. (2018). *Suoduan xiaowei qiye daikuan shenpi zhouqi* (Cut down the time for approval of credits for smaller enterprises). http://finance.people.com.cn/n1/2018/0823/c1004-30245588.html (accessed 1 September 2018).

Hancock, Tom. (2019). Xi Jinping's China: Why entrepreneurs feel like second-class citizens. Strong support for state-owned companies is weighing down on the dynamic private sector. *Financial Times*, 13 May. https://www.ft.com/content/fcb06530-680a-11e9-9adc-98bf1d35a056 (accessed 2 August 2019).

Hayami, Yujiro and Kawagoe, Toshihiko. (1993). *The Agrarian Origins of Commerce and Industry.* New York and Basingstoke: MacMillan Press/St. Martin's Press.

He, Yiting (Ed.). (2001). *Xuexi Jiang Zemin 'qi yi' jianghua fudao wenda* (Supporting material for the study of Jiang Zemin's 'July 1st' speech). Beijing: Dangjian duwu chubanshe/Yanjiu chubanshe.

Heberer, Thomas. (1989). *Die Rolle des urbanen Individualsektors für Arbeitsmarkt und Stadtwirtschaft in China* (The Role of the Urban Individual Sector for the Labor Market and the Urban Economy in China). Bremer Beiträge zur Geographie und Raumplanung. Bremen: Universität Bremen.

Heberer, Thomas. (2003a). Strategic groups and state capacity: The case of the private entrepreneurs. *China Perspectives* 46, 4–14.

Heberer, Thomas. (2003b). *Private Entrepreneurs in China and Vietnam. Social and Political Functioning of Strategic Groups.* Leiden: Brill.

Heberer, Thomas. (2007). *Doing Business in Rural China. Liangshan's New Ethnic Entrepreneurs.* Seattle and London: University of Washington Press.

Hu, Deping. (2011). *Zhongguo weishenme yao gaige. Siyi fuqin Hu Yaobang* (Why must China reform. In memory of my father Hu Yaobang). Beijing: Renmin chubanshe.

Hu, Deping. (2018). Jingyi dazhe gongxiang de qihao gao xinde gongsi heying (Be vigilant against flaunting the banner of going for new public-private joint ventures). *Zhongguo Minshang Zazhi* (China's Journal for Entrepreneurs), 28 September 2018. https://boxun.com/news/gb/pubvp/2018/09/201809280018.shtml (accessed 20 December 2018).

Hu, Jintao. (2012). *Report to the 18th Party Congress.* (2012). http://www.china-embassy.org/eng/zt/18th_CPC_National_Congress_Eng/t992917.htm (accessed 18 June 2018).

Hu, Kun. (2018). Liu Yonghao: Minying qiye jintian zhongyu dedaole rentong (Liu Yonghao: Today private enterprises are finally acknowledged). *Zhongguo Qiyejia* (China's entrepreneurs), 6 March, pp. 78–81.

Hu, Yongqi. (2019). Private firms get postponed payments. *China Daily*, 26 February.

Huang, Dongya. (2014). Siying qiyezhu yu zhengzhi fazhan. Guanyu shichang chuangxin zhong siying qiyezhu de jieji xiangxiang ji qi fansi (Private entre-preneurs and political development. A reflection on class imagination of pri-vate entrepreneurs in market innovation). *Shehui* (*Chinese Journal of Sociology*) 34(4), 138–164.

Huang, Rong and Kirton, David. (2019). State firm overseer says mixed-ownership can help fix the economy. *Caixin* (English), 18 February. https://www.caixinglobal.com/2019-02-18/state-enterprise-supervisor-says-mixed-ownership-can-help-fix-the-economy-101380925.html (accessed 12 April 2019).

Huang, Yasheng. (2008). *Capitalism with Chinese Characteristics*. Cambridge: Cambridge University Press.

Huang, Yasheng. (2012). How did China take off? *Journal of Economic Perspectives* 26(4), 147–170.

Jiang, Shengyang. (2018). Tuidong minying jingji zai gao zhiliang fazhan luoshi ganchao zhong fahui gengda zhicheng zuoyong. Zhuanfang Fujian shengwei shuji Yu Weiguo (Promote the private economy under conditions of developing and implementing high quality, thus developing still greater support and functional significance. Interview with Yu Weiguo, party secretary of Fujian Province). *Renmin Ribao*, 19 November.

Jiang, Zemin. (1995). *Zhengque chuli shehuizhuyi xiandaihua jianshe zhong de ruogan zhongda guanxi* (Correctly handle some crucial relationships during the construction of socialist modernization). http://cpc.people.com.cn/GB/64162/64168/64567/65446/4441712.html (accessed 14 August 2019).

Jinrong fuwu 18tiao rang minqi 'bu cha qian' (The 18 clauses of financial services shall ensure that private enterprises do not lack money). (2019). *Renmin Ribao*, 16 February. http://www.gov.cn/zhengce/2019-02/16/content_5366152.htm (accessed 7 March 2019).

Li, Gang. (1999). Rang qiyejia chengwei yizhong zhiye (Let entrepreneurship become a profession). *Zhongguo Qiyejia* (Chinese Entrepreneurs), July, 49.

Li, Gengnan. (2018). *Minying qiye jiujing zai nali?* (Where at all are private enterprises?). *Xinlang caijing yijian lingxiu zhuanlan* (Xinlang finance and economy opinion leaders' forum), 18 December. http://finance.sina.com.cn/zl/china/2018-12-18/zl-ihqhqcir7921217.shtml (accessed 27 December 2018).

Li, Hongbin and Rozelle, Scott. (2003). Privatizing rural China: Insider privatization, innovative contracts and the performance of township enterprises. *The China Quarterly* 176, 981–1005.

Li, Huaqun. (2013). History and development of entrepreneurship in China. In Zhang, Ting and Stough, Roger R. (Eds.), *Entrepreneurship and Economic Growth in China*. Singapore: World Scientific, 13–33.

Li, Jie. (2018). Minqi rongzi you 'zhushou' (Assistant for loans to private enterprises). *Renmin Ribao*, 27 October.

Li, Keqiang. (2017). *Dui 2017nian quanguo dazhong chuangye wanzhong chuangxin huodong zhou zuochu zhongyao pishi* (Important comment on the national week of 'mass entrepreneurship and mass innovation' in 2017. http://www.xinhuanet.com/fortune/2017-09/15/c_129705309.htm (accessed 12 March 2018).

Li, Keqiang. (2018). *2018 nian guowuyuan zhengfu gongzuo baogao* (State Council Government Work Report 2018). http://www.gov.cn/premier/2018-03/22/content_5276608.htm (accessed 29 July 2019).

Li, Yanli. (2018). *Li Keqiang: Jianjue xiaochu zai minying jingji fazhan de gezhong bu heli zhang'ai* (Resolutely remove all kinds of unreasonable obstacles of private economic development). http://finance.sina.com.cn/china/gncj/2018-09-19/doc-ifxeuwwr6033722.shtml (accessed 24 September 2018).

Li, Yuan. (2019). China's entrepreneurs are wary of its future. *The New York Times*, 23 February. https://www.nytimes.com/2019/02/23/business/china-entrepreneurs-confidence.html (accessed 7 March 2019).

Li, Zheng. (2018). Renmin Ribao, renmin shipping. Tatashishi ba minying jingji bande geng hao (People's Daily people's discussion: Let us make the private sector better steadily). *Renmin Ribao*, 14 September. http://opinion.people.com.cn/n1/2018/0914/c1003-30292215.html (accessed 18 September 2018).

Liang, Chuanyun. (1990). *Zhongguo siren qiye jingying guanli zhinan* (Introduction to the management of Chinese private enterprises). Beijing: Beijing daxue chubanshe.

Liu, Dan. (2017). *Zhongguo minying qiyejia. Chuangxin shengtai xitong de chengshudu pingjia yanjiu* (Research on maturity evaluation of private entrepreneurs' innovation eco-system in China). Beijing: Zhongguo caijing chubanshe.

Lin, Yi-min. (2017). *Dancing with the Devil: The Political Economy of Privatization in China*. Oxford University Press: New York.

Liu, Yong. (1997). *Zhongguo qiye shounao* (Leading Chinese entrepreneurs). Zhuhai: Zhuhai chubanshe.

Lu, Meicheng. (2018). Zhongguo duojia minying qiye bei guoqi tunbing (Many Chinese private enterprises are absorbed by state-owned ones). *Jinrong Shibao* (*Financial Times*), 27 September. http://economics.dwnews.com/news/2018-09-27/60087684.html (accessed 27 December 2018).

Luqiu, Luwei R. and Liu, Chuyu. (2018). A 'new social class' or old friends? A study of private entrepreneurs in the National People's Congress of China. *Journal of East Asian Studies* 18(3), 389–400.

McMahon, Dinny. (2019). Why China Can't Get Its Economy Moving. Weak growth numbers are a sign that the most efficient companies still aren't getting the kind of credit they need to expand. *Bloomberg Opinion*, 15 July.

https://www.bloomberg.com/opinion/articles/2019-07-15/china-s-private-companies-still-aren-t-getting-enough-credit (accessed 29 July 2019).

Mi, Jianning and Gao, Dexiang. (1997). Qiyejia jieceng de shehuixue hanyi (The sociological meaning of an entrepreneurial stratum). *Shehuixue Yanjiu* (Sociological Studies) 4, 42–47.

Naughton, Barry. (2007). *The Chinese Economy: Transitions and Growth.* Cambridge: MIT Press.

Nee, Victor and Opper, Sonja. (2012). *Capitalism from Below.* Cambridge: Harvard University Press.

Nolan, Peter. (2001). *China and the Global Economy: National Champions, Industrial Policy, and the Big Business Revolution.* New York: Palgrave MacMillan.

Nouwens, Meia and Béraud-Sudreau, Lucie. (2018). Xi looks to China's private sector as he pursues a slimmer, smarter private sector into its defence-industrial base. *War on the Rocks,* 23 February. https://warontherocks.com/2018/02/xi-looks-chinas-private-sector-pursues-slimmer-smarter-pla/ (accessed 11 May 2018).

Oi, Jean C. (1999). *Rural China Takes Off: Institutional Foundations of Economic Reform.* Berkeley: University of California Press.

Oi, Jean C. (2001). The role of the local state in China's transitional economy. *The China Quarterly* 144, 1132–1149.

Pan, Shiyi. (2018). *Yimiao shijian, jianzhu tanta shijian gei mei yige qiye dou qiaoxiangle jingzhong* (The vaccination and the construction site collapse incidents are ringing alarm bells among every enterprise). https://www.weibo.com/ttarticle/p/show?id=2309404267925589604027&mod=zwenzhang (accessed 24 September 2018).

Pei, Minxin. (2016) *China's Crony Capitalism. The Dynamics of Regime Decay.* Harvard: Harvard University Press.

Qin, Shaoxiang and Jia, Ting. (1993). *Shehui xin qunti tanmi — Zhongguo siying qiyezhu jieceng* (On the new social stratum of Chinese private entrepreneurs). Beijing: Zhongguo fazhan chubanshe.

Quan, Yue and Leng, Cheng. (2018). In depth: Rags to riches entrepreneurs head for inglorious fall. *Caixin* (*Financial News,* English), https://www.caixinglobal.com/2018-11-26/rags-to-riches-entrepreneurs-head-for-inglorious-fall-101352140.html (accessed 15 February 2020).

Renmin Yinhang. (2019). *Yinbao Jianhui 'Xiaowei qiye jinrong fuwu youguan qingkuang' xinwen fabuhui wenzi shilu* (Written news release of the People's Bank and the Banking and Insurance Regulatory Commission on 'The situation of financial services for small-scale enterprises'), 24 June. http://www.nifa.org. cn/nifa/2961652/2961656/2982615/index.html (accessed 12 July 2019).

Schubert, Gunter and Heberer, Thomas. (2015). Continuity and change in China's 'local state developmentalism'. *Issues & Studies* 51(2), 1–38.

Scott, James C. (1985). *Weapons of the Weak. Everyday Forms of Peasant Resistance*. New Haven and London: Yale University Press.

Scott, James C. (1989). Everyday forms of resistance. *Copenhagen Journal of Asian Studies* 4, 33–62.

Shen, Xiaoxiao and Tsai, Kellee S. (2016). Institutional adaptability in China: Local developmental models under changing economic conditions. *World Development* 87, 107–127.

Sheng, Hong. (2018). *Ruhe rang minying qiyejia xiangxin zhengfu* (How to make private entrepreneurs believe the government), 5 December. http://www. ftchinese.com/story/001080522?full=y&archive (accessed 27 December 2018).

Shu, Zhang. (2019). Debt guarantee tangle: China's private firms hit by default contagion. *Reuters Business News*, 12 February. https://www.reuters.com/ article/us-china-economy-debt/debt-guarantee-tangle-chinas-private-firms-hit-by-default-contagion-idUSKCN1Q107W (accessed 5 March 2019).

Shui, Muran. (2016). *Zhongguo 90 percent siqi jiang daobi, yichang pohuaishi de liansuo fanying jiu zai yanqian!* (90 percent of private enterprises are going to collapse, a destructive chain reaction just before our eyes), http:// finance.sina.com.cn/roll/2016-04-05/doc-ifxqxcnr5331369.shtml (accessed 14 August 2018).

Solinger, Dorothy. (1984). *Chinese Business under Socialism: The Politics of Domestic Commerce in Contemporary China*. Berkeley: University of California Press.

Sun, Gang. (2018). Chen Jiancheng: Qiyejia bu neng dang 'yingxiong' (Chen Jiancheng: Entrepreneurs cannot be 'heroes'). *Zheshang* (*Zhejiang Businessmen*) 294, September, 52–55.

Sun, Lizhao and Lin, Jinbing. (2018). Big state firms urged to bring in private capital at highest corporate level. *Caixin* (Financial News), 19 September. https://www.caixinglobal.com/2018-09-19/big-state-firms-urged-to-bring-in-private-capital-at-highest-corporate-level-101328246.html (accessed 24 September 2018).

Tang, Frank. (2018). China's debt-cutting efforts are sinking private companies, while debt-ridden state firms float on. *South China Morning Post*, 6 June 2018. http://www.scmp.com/news/china/economy/article/2149408/chinas-delever-aging-efforts-are-sinking-private-sector-while-debt (accessed 22 June 2018).

Tian, Yu. (2018). Zhejiang zai tui 35 tiao qiye jiangcheng chengben zhengce (Zhejiang's policy to assist 35 enterprises to reduce production costs). *Jing-Chu Zheshang* (Zhejiang businessmen in Hubei and Hunan) 12, 66–68.

Wan, Jing and Tong, Sarah Y. (2018). Shadow banking and China's monetary puzzle. *China: An International Journal* 16(2), 151–169.

Wang, Junmin. (2016). Taking the 'red hat' off Chinese private entrepreneurs. Institutional dependents, innovative collaborators, and political opponents. *Sociology of Development* 2(3), Fall, 293–321.

Wang, Meng. (2018). Shenme shi qiyejia jingshen de shidai tezheng? (What are the peculiarities of the entrepreneurial spirit in this period?). *Lilun wang* (Theory net). http://www.qstheory.cn/2018-01/12/c_1122251727.htm (accessed 9 August 2018).

Wang, Orange. (2018). Brother, can you spare a dime: China's small firms can't get loans even with the government's push. *South China Morning Post*, 29 August. https://www.scmp.com/business/china-business/article/2161759/brother-can-you-spare-dime-chinas-small-firms-cant-get-loans (accessed 13 September 2018).

Wang, Xiangwei. (2018a). Beijing's tight grip on economy leaves tycoons on a tightrope, *South China Morning Post*, 10 June 2018. http://www.scmp.com/week-asia/opinion/article/2149935/beijings-tight-grip-economy-leaves-tycoons-tightrope (accessed 18 June 2018).

Wang, Xiangwei. (2018b). China must take urgent action to push its private sector past a crisis of confidence. *South China Morning Post*, 15 September. https://www.scmp.com/week-asia/opinion/article/2164204/china-must-take-urgent-action-push-its-private-sector-past-crisis (accessed 18 September 2018).

Wang, Haibing and Yang, Huixin. (2018). Zhongguo minying jingji gaige yu fazhan 40 nian: huigu yu zhanwang (40 years of reform and development of China's private economy: Retrospect and outlook). *Jingji Yu Guanli Yanjiu* (Research on Economy and Management) 39(4), 3–14.

Wank, David. (1995). Private business, bureaucracy, and political alliance in a Chinese city. *The Australian Journal of Chinese Affairs* 33, 55–71.

Wei, Zhanrong and Sun, Aozhou. (1994). Lun wo guo qiyejia jieceng de peiyu (On the cultivation of an entrepreneurial stratum in our country). *Jingji Wenti Tansuo* (Discussion of economic problems) 10, 25–27.

Wei, Zhezhe. (2018). Wei minqi fazhan yingzao lianghao fazhi huanjing (Building a well-ordered legal system to protect the private sector). *Renmin Ribao*, 12 November.

Wu, Jinglian and Ma, Guochuan. (2016). *Whither China? Restarting the Reform Agenda.* New York: Oxford University Press.

Wu, Xiaobo, Yuan, Yue, Feng, Xi and Chen, Ling. (2014). 2014 *Zhongguo qiye jiankang zhishu baogao* (2014 Index for Healthy Chinese Business). Hangzhou: Zhejiang daxue chubanshe.

Wu, Xiaomeng and Wang, Fran. (2018). What Deleveraging? Private Companies' Debt Ratios Jump. *Caixin*, 19.9. https://www.caixinglobal.com/2018-09-19/what-deleveraging-private-companies-debt-ratios-jump-101328233.html (accessed 24 September 2018).

Wu, Xiaoping. (2018). *Siying jingji yi wancheng xiezhu gongyou jingji fazhan ying zhujian lichang* (The private economy has completed its task in assisting the public sector and should now gradually step aside). http://wemedia.ifeng.com/77918883/wemedia.shtml (accessed 20 September 2018).

Xi, Jinping. (2017). Zai Zhongguo Gongchandang di 19ci quanguo daibiao dahuishang de baogao (Xi Jinping's Report at the 19th National Congress of the Communist Party of China). http://www.gov.cn/zhuanti/2017-10/27/content_5234876.htm (accessed 15 February 2020).

Xi, Jinping. (2018a). Zai minying qiye zuotanhuishang de jianghua (Speech at the conference on private enterprises). *Renmin Ribao*, 2 November.

Xi, Jinping. (2018b). Suoyou minying qiye he minying qiyejia wanquan keyi chixia dingxinwan (All private enterprises and private entrepreneurs can completely feel reassured). *Renmin Ribao*, 2 November.

Xie, Heng. (2018). *Hunan minying jingji fazhan yanjiu* (Study on the development of Hunan's private economy), Chengdu: Xinan Caijing Daxue Chubanshe.

Xu, Zhijian. (1997). Chuangxin lirun yu qiyejia wuxing zichan (Innovation profits and invisible assets of entrepreneurs). *Jingji Yanjiu* (Economic Studies) 8, 47–50.

Yang, Jing Yu and Li, Jiatao. (2008). The development of entrepreneurship in China. *Asia Pacific Journal of Management* 25(2), 335–359.

Yao, Kevin, Zhang, Shu and Qiu, Stella. (2018). China calls for more small-business loans. *Japan News*, 18 October.

Yu, Shaowen. (1997). Qiyejia yu quanli zhihuihua (Entrepreneurs and the wisdom of power). *Zhongguo Gongshang Bao*, 6 November.

Yu, Zhengsheng. (2016). Fahui shehui ge jieceng ge qunti youshi he zuoyong wei quanmian jiancheng xiaokang shehui ningju qiangda liliang (Developing the advantages and functions of all social classes and groups in order to build a comprehensive society with a modest living standard and bringing them together to build a great force). *Renmin Ribao*, 7 September. http://cpc.people.com.cn/n1/2016/0907/c64094-28696233.html (accessed 9 August 2018).

Yuan, Baohua. (1997). Yingzao shehuizhuyi qiyejia chengzhang de lianghao huanjing (Create favorable conditions for the rising socialist entrepreneurs). *Qiye Guanli (Enterprise Management)* 192, 5–8.

Zenglein, Max J. and Holzmann, Anna. (2019). Evolving made in China 2025. China's industrial policy in the quest for global tech leadership. *Merics Papers on China*, No. 8, July. Berlin: Mercator Institute for China Studies.

Zhang, Changdong. (2017). A fiscal sociological theory of authoritarian resilience: Developing theory through China case studies. *Sociological Theory*, 35(1), 39–63.

Zhang, Honglin and Liu, Xinhua (Eds.). (1996). *Zenyang dang ge qiyejia* (How to become an entrepreneur), Beijing: Qiye guanli chubanshe.

Zhang, Linjiang. (2018). Xinde shehui jieceng xingqi jiqi dui dangdai Zhongguo de yingxiang (The emerging of new social classes and their impact on contemporary China). *Zhongguo Shehuizhuyi Xueyuan* (China's College for Socialism), 29 May. http://www.zysy.org.cn/a1/a-XCXP4I283FD1C41B57E518 (accessed 8 January 2019).

Zhang, Wanding and Li, Dan. (1998). Qiyejia zhineng, juese yu tiaojian de tantao (Discussion of the function, role and conditions of private entrepreneurs). *Jingji Yanjiu* (Economic Studies) 8, 29–33.

Zhao, Pozhang. (1998). Zhongguo xuyao shijieji qiyejia (China needs world standard entrepreneurs). In: Zhongguo qiyejia diaocha xitong (Research Net of Chinese Entrepreneurs) (Ed.), *Zhongguo qiyejia duiwu chengzhang yu fazhan baogao* (Report on growth and development of China's entrepreneurial contingent). Beijing: Jingji kexue chubanshe, 524–536.

Zheng, Hongliang and Yang, Yang. (2011). Development of the Chinese private sector over the past 30 years. In: Shujie Yao, Bin Wu, Stephen L. Morgan and Dylan Sutherland (Eds.), *Sustainable Reform and Development in Post-Olympic China* (pp. 1–12). London and New York: Routledge.

Zhi quan shi minying qiyejia de yifeng xin (A letter to all the city's private entrepreneurs). (2018). Shenyang Ribao (*Shenyang Daily*), 13 December. http://epaper.syd.com.cn/syrb/html/2018-12/13/content_210456.htm?div=-1 (accessed 27 December 2018).

Zhongguo qiyejia diaocha xitong (Research Net of Chinese Entrepreneurs) (Ed.). (1998). Zhongguo qiyejia duiwu chengzhang yu fazhan baogao (Report on growth and development of China's entrepreneurial contingent). Beijing: Jingji kexue chubanshe.

Zhonggong Zhongyang Guowuyuan (2017). Yingzao qiyejia jiankang chengzhang huanjing, hongyang youxiu qiyejia jingshen geng hao fahui qiyejia zuoyong de yijian (Central Committee of the CCP and State Council on creating an environment for the healthy growth of entrepreneurs, promoting a spirit of outstanding entrepreneurship so that they can play a still better role). *Renmin Ribao*, 26 September. http://cpc.people.com.cn/n1/2017/0926/c64387-29558638.html (accessed 3 April 2018).

Zhonggong Zhongyang Guowuyuan (2018). *Guanyu quanmian jiaqiang shengtai huanjing baohu jianjue dahao wuran fangzhi gongjian zhande yijian* (Opinion of the CCP Central Committee and the State Council on strengthening ecological and environmental protection and resolutely prevent and fight pollution). http://www.gov.cn/zhengce/2018-06/24/content_5300953.htm (accessed 12 August 2018).

Zhou, Xincheng. (2018). *Gongchandang ren keyi ba ziji lilun gaikuo wei yijuhua: xiaomie siyouzhi* (Communists can put their own theory in a nutshell: Eradicate the private ownership system). http://m.kdnet.net/share-12592200.html?sform=club (accessed 20 September 2018).

Zou, Lei. (2018) *The Political Economy of China's Belt and Road Initiative.* Singapore: World Scientific.

Zou, Yating. (2016). Xinxing zhengshang guanxi. 'Qin' 'qing' zai xin ge you suo zun (Xi Jinping zhiguo li zhengguan jianci) (New state-business relations. 'Intimate', 'just and honest', everybody has to bear that in mind and to comply with it). *Renmin Ribao haiwaiban* (People's Daily Overseas Edition), 5 August.

Chapter 2

Private Sector Development and State–Business Relations in Post-Mao China: The State of the Field

Before introducing our theoretical framework and getting into our empirical data, it is necessary to bring some order to the social science literature on private entrepreneurship and the evolution of state–business relations in post-Mao China. This literature is vast and any review of it needs a specific focus. In this chapter, we summarize major findings of recent studies conducted by China scholars on (1) the rise of China's private sector since the late 1980s, (2) the different mechanisms for politically incorporating private entrepreneurs into the party state, and (3) efforts to conceptualize and theorize state–business relations. This state-of-the-field review[1] seeks to highlight continuities and changes in scholarly perspectives on China's private entrepreneurs, their political agency and their significance for regime survival. In doing so, we seek to make clear where our own research ties in and what it contributes to the field.

---

[1] We focus predominantly on the literature published in Western languages but where relevant or where new arguments and insights are provided, we also incorporate Chinese sources. Generally speaking, the Chinese literature on the topic is abundant but does not deviate from the findings of Western scholars and often enough echoes them.

State–Business Relations and the Political Incorporation of Private Entrepreneurs

Observing the rise of China's private sector, many China scholars, especially those working in the field of political science teaching at Western universities, have become very interested in the political agency of private entrepreneurs and their relationship with the party state. This interest seems more or less driven by the implicit assumption (or hope) that the formation of a new social constituency of private entrepreneurs, allegedly belonging to the most modern strata of Chinese society, would challenge the authoritarian rule of the CCP and help to bring about political liberalization, if not democratization — at least in the long run. But it soon became clear that, given the short history of private sector reform after the end of the Maoist era and the party state's unchallenged supremacy over the process of opening up for private entrepreneurship, those 'jumping into the sea' (*xiahai*) of Chinese capitalism would be closely watched and 'guided'. The following literature review focuses on studies that have analyzed private entrepreneurs' political incorporation into the party state from different angles and how this incorporation has affected state–business relations. As will be seen, most scholars assume that private entrepreneurs have little voice *vis-à-vis* the party state which has been very cautious in making allies of private sector actors within a regime coalition dominated by the cadre elites. Against this background, our own research highlights a dimension which has so far been under-researched by China scholars, i.e. the strategic action on the part of private entrepreneurs below the level of political incorporation.

As private sector development accelerated and increasingly gained in importance for the Chinese economy at the beginning of the reform era, the party state's relationship with private entrepreneurs quickly became a contentious issue within the Communist leadership. It was important to 'domesticate' this social constituency, which posed a challenge to regime legitimacy ideologically. Many private entrepreneurs who 'jumped into the sea', i.e. gave up their cadre position and turned to business, in the early days of 'reform and opening up' had been senior cadres at the local level before taking the leap. These former cadres often benefited from a murky process of TVE-privatization in the absence of sound regulatory institutions, making huge fortunes in the process. Others were peasants, craftspeople or petty traders who either started their own small business or registered their 'individual companies' (*getihu*) as private enterprises when this option became available.[2]

Obviously, many entrepreneurs were closely connected to the Communist Party. Later on, when the private economy started to flourish and the country saw the rise of big private enterprises and conglomerates, the social background of its entrepreneurs gradually changed and professionalized. However, the party state's grip remained firm, as the Communist Party struggled, throughout the first two decades of reform, with its decision to develop a private sector economy under the umbrella of 'Chinese socialism'. For their part, China's private entrepreneurs had to be cautious to not arouse suspicion in a highly sensitive political environment. At the same time, they were totally dependent on the party state's provision of the necessary resources and institutional environment to allow their businesses to operate successfully. As demonstrated in Chapter 1, there were different trajectories of private sector development — the most prominent of which are the 'Sunan model' of state-led TVE privatization, the 'Wenzhou model' of small- and medium-sized businesses rising 'autonomously' from the bottom up, and the 'Pearl River Delta model' of foreign-invested enterprises[3] — entailing very different experiences of private entrepreneurship across China. These models

---

[2]The percentage of people from former 'bad' or 'black' families (offspring of capitalists, large land-owners, people with a background in the former Guomindang administration or in the armed forces, so-called 'counter-revolutionaries', etc.) was relatively high among new entrepreneurs. In addition, disabled persons or previously-convicted people found employment in the private sector (Heberer, 1989).

[3]Besides political science research on private entrepreneurs' individual and collective agency, which stands at the center of this brief review, political economists became interested in the diverging pathways of China's 'capitalist transformation' on the one hand and in China's contribution to the 'varieties of capitalism debate' on the other. Hence, as mentioned above, different local development models were identified, as were corresponding models of local state–business relations, for instance, 'local state corporatism'. At the macro-level, scholars discussed China's specific brand of 'state-led capitalism' and compared it to other capitalisms around the globe. For an overview of research on models of local private sector development and local state developmentalism, see Schubert and Heberer (2015); for the connection between local state capacity and institutional

became key terms in explaining China's spectacular economic development of the 1990s and 2000s as generated by the non-state economy, and suggested the rise of an entrepreneurial class that would later impact the broader Chinese polity. However, given the relatively short time-period since the legalization of private enterprises in the late 1980s, China's new entrepreneurs had no choice but to rely on (and subject themselves to) the party state in order to develop, solidify, and expand their businesses. Hence, the Communist Party steered the wheel in state–business relations from the very beginning, and China scholars researching these relations have thus mostly looked at the many ways by which the party state ensured control over its private entrepreneurs.

Incorporation by Party Membership and Party-Building

Party membership was the most obvious option to create bonds of loyalty between private entrepreneurs and the Communist regime. One group of private entrepreneurs — those who had been high level cadres in state enterprises before these were privatized — had been party members for a long time when they 'jumped into the sea'. Another group had been recruited by local party organizations when it was not yet officially permitted to do so in order to incorporate private entrepreneurs into the implementation of local policies. Moreover, private entrepreneurs were interested in party membership since it brings with it political protection, facilitates the pursuit of economic interests and *guanxi*-making, and thereby provides manifold opportunities for influencing local policy making. According to official data, in 2000, the proportion of party members among private entrepreneurs was already quite high (19.8 percent). According to the bi-annual sample survey on private entrepreneurs conducted by the Chinese Academy of Social Sciences, the percentage of CCP members among private entrepreneurs was 39.8 percent in 2010 and 32.8 percent in 2012, though it should be mentioned that this share was significantly lower than for managers in state-owned enterprises

---

adaptability, see Shen and Tsai (2016); for China's relevance concerning the 'Variety of Capitalism' debate, see McNally (2012, 2013) and ten Brink (2011, 2013).

(96.5 percent) and slightly lower for managers in Chinese-foreign joint venture businesses (41.2 percent) (Zhang and Lü, 2012; He and Ma, 2014: 4).[4] That more than one-third of all entrepreneurs are meanwhile CCP members highlights a steady trend towards closer state-business relations.

For his part, in his often-cited study presenting results of two representative surveys conducted in 1999 and 2005, Dickson estimated that by 2005, some 34 percent of entrepreneurs had held party membership before they started their businesses — an increase from some 25 percent in 1999 (Dickson, 2007: 838). He also reported that, after the promulgation of the 'Three Represents', the pace of private entrepreneurs entering the party increased, as did the willingness of more to join. In total, the 2005 survey showed that '75 percent of the entrepreneurs (…), who represent the economic elites of their communities, were either in the Party or wanted to be (compared to 66.7 percent in the 1999 survey)' (*ibid.*). Interestingly, Dickson also found that party membership paid off for private entrepreneurs, as firms owned by party members had higher sales revenues, hired more workers and enjoyed higher levels of fixed assets than firms headed by non-party members (2007: 841). Entrepreneurs who were already party members or wanted to become a member agreed that joining the party entailed business advantages (almost 50 percent in 2005)[5]; those who had no intention to apply for party membership (some 10 percent of respondents in the 2005 survey) disagreed (by 26.7 percent of the sample) (Dickson, 2007: 840). Besides, some 29 percent of private entrepreneurs reported that they set up party branches in the 2005 survey (up from 18.4 percent in 1999), indicating their willingness to closely

---

[4]Chinese scholars usually refer to the data of the Chinese Enterprise Survey which is conducted biannually as a joint project by the CP United Front Work Department, the All-China Federation of Industry and Commerce, the State Administration for Market Regulation, and the Chinese Academy of Social Sciences (https://cpes.zkey.cc/index.jsp). Unfortunately, access to survey data is strictly regulated for scholars, who are not allowed to obtain the most recent statistics.

[5]One of our respondents even commented that 'wives of party members are more beautiful than those of non-party members' (*dangyuan de laopo bi feidangyuan de piaoliang*) (Interview, Zhengzhou, 13 April 2018).

cooperate with local party authorities and comply with party regulations and ideology.[6]

This trend is also reflected by the official policy of party-building and the increasing number of party branches within private enterprises over the last decade or so. If an enterprise has at least three party members, a party branch has to be set up. According to *Xinhua*, at the end of 2013, party organizations had been established in 1.63 million private firms, 58.4 percent of the national total.[7] In fact, the building of party branches in private enterprises was pushed by a new campaign as early as 2012, even before Xi Jinping became the new General Secretary.[8] Since then, the campaign has gained much momentum. Local party authorities were instructed to encourage a comprehensive party penetration of private companies in their jurisdictions as quickly as possible. In their case study on Anhui province, for instance, Yan and Huang reported that by the end of 2012, 91.6 percent of all private enterprises had established party branches, a 50 percent increase over 2011 (2017: 469).[9] However, it is not so much the mere existence of party branches that counts but what these organizations actually do, and how significant they are for shaping the relationship between the party state and private entrepreneurs. Clearly intended to strengthen the ideological and political supervision of the private sector economy, Yan and Huang found that, interestingly, party-building in private enterprises is actually quite business-oriented and benefits private entrepreneurs a lot. Party branches operate as service-oriented units within a private firm as they help to ensure welfare

---

[6]It is a legal requirement for private enterprises with more than three party members to set up a party branch.

[7]CPC membership reports slower growth, http://www.china.org.cn/china/2014-06/30/content_32814079.htm (accessed 20 September 2016). Yan and Huang report a number of roughly 1.579 million private companies having established party branches by the end of 2014, amounting to 53.1 percent of all Chinese private enterprises (2017: 57).

[8]In March 2012, the Central Organization Department (*Zhongyang zuzhibu*) issued the 'Opinions on Strengthening and Improving Party Building in Nonstate Enterprises', followed by a national conference on party building in private enterprises (Yan and Huang, 2017: 45–46).

[9]As we will discuss later in more detail, party branches had been established in most of the private enterprises we visited.

provision and the safeguarding of labor rights in the workplace, thus reducing the danger of labor-related conflicts. They also run special funds to help workers in need of financial support due to unexpected circumstances. And they often cultivate an 'elite habitus' among their members, inducing them to work harder than non-party member employees for the benefit of the company. Most importantly, however, party-building includes the recruitment of company advisors — so-called 'sent-down' cadres — with the explicit objective of transferring their professional expertise to the enterprise and smoothing state–business interaction. However, as advantageous as this institution may be for private enterprises operating in a market environment as difficult as China's, it also serves the party state's constant efforts to politically co-opt business owners and leading managers.[10]

Incorporation by Membership in PCs and PPCCs

Another co-optation mechanism is to award private entrepreneurs membership in People's Congresses (PCs) and People's Political Consultative Conferences (PPCCs) at the national and local level, a point which will be further elaborated on in Chapter 4. In 2003, Dickson reported that there were 55 entrepreneurs serving as deputies in China's National People's Congress and 65 in the National People's Political Consultative Conference. A year later, more than 9,000 entrepreneurs had been elected to local PCs across China, and another 30,000 to local PPCCs (Dickson,

---

[10]Yan and Huang also point at a number of problems related to party-building in the private sector. Although they found many party branches worked energetically in Anhui, there were as many which seemed to exist on paper only. Moreover, some party branches were 'high-jacked' in the sense that the post of party secretary was often assumed by the company owner and the other leading positions of the party branch assigned to family members employed in the company, transforming these organizations into veritable 'family clubs'. Also, by following the official order to not interfere in a company's business administration and decision-making, the relevance of party branches for management decisions is low, underlining an awkward ambiguity concerning their prescribed role as the 'political core' of a private enterprise — and, more broadly, of China's private economy. As will be shown in the empirical section of this book, our observations concerning party-building in China's private sector widely match what Yan and Huang have observed in Anhui.

2007: 843). In his 2005 survey, 10.5 percent of Dickson's respondents were PC members and 5.3 percent held PPCC positions. Membership in a People's Congress correlated positively with a firm's size, the age of entrepreneurs, and their level of formal education: The bigger the firm, the more senior the entrepreneurs and the higher their formal education the more likely their nomination to a People's Congress. Party membership did also correlate strongly with an entrepreneur's PC mandate. Membership in a People's Consultative Conference, however, did not strongly correlate with party membership, suggesting that non-Communist Party members stood a fair chance of being nominated.[11] Nevertheless, all private entrepreneurs had to register with the state-led All-China Federation of Industry and Commerce (ACFIC/*Gongshanglian*), which is a United Front organization of the Communist Party with local branches down to the county level. Moreover, the scope of a firm's sales volume and the number of years an entrepreneur had been in business were important factors determining PPCC membership, though level of education was not (Dickson, 2007: 843). Put differently, the party state was less strict concerning the formal requirement of party membership of private entrepreneurs when nominating them for a PPCC seat, but 'political oversight' was nevertheless ensured by their membership in the ACFIC. In addition, a business had to be successful, meaning that it contributed substantially to local tax coffers, before its owner could become a PPCC delegate.[12]

---

[11]This is confirmed by a more recent study conducted by Chen (2015) with data from a northern provincial capital's PPCC. It showed that between 2010 and 2013 only 23 of its total members (449) belonged to the Communist Party (5 percent) whereas 74 held membership in a non-Communist ('democratic') party (16.5 percent). Among the 128 private entrepreneurs in the PPCC, none was a Communist Party member and 16 (12.5 percent) belonged to a 'democratic party'. In terms of party affiliation, referring to those private entrepreneurs who had been nominated by different units representing the Communist Party, these made up only 11 percent of the total, while 27.3 percent were affiliated to non-Communist parties and 61 percent to neither of both. That means that at the time, almost 90 percent of all delegates in that PPCC had no Communist Party background whatsoever.

[12]In a similar study, Chen Zhao *et al.* (2008) identified three major factors determining political participation of private entrepreneurs in PCs or PPCCs: (1) the older an entrepreneur or his enterprise is, the more probable that he/she is a delegate; (2) membership in the

Table 1: **Membership of Private Entrepreneurs in PCs and PPCCS in percent (1997–2014)***

	1997	2000	2002	2004	2006	2008	2010	2012	2014	1997–2014
County-level and below	19.26	34.63	31.10	27.86	25.57	28.89	27.33	27.51	19.88	26.58
Prefectural level and above	11.96	19.72	18.39	19.71	16.44	20.00	18.24	14.81	16.77	17.42

Note: *All figures provided by respondents of a representative survey.
Source: Fan and Lü (2018: 70).

According to a recent study (Fan and Lü, 2018) based on a representative survey, membership of private entrepreneurs in PCs and PPCCs at all administrative levels has gradually increased over the years and may have been as high as 44 percent as an annual average during the period 1997–2014 (see Table 1). Official figures, which are hard to come by and often incomplete, might be misleading. Although quotas for private entrepreneurs are numerically fixed for local PCs and PPCCs by official regulations, they are indeed overrepresented by the simple fact that local governments recruit them into other categories than the 'economic sector' as well.[13]

As Chen Minglu has noted, 'nomination of private entrepreneurs to different levels of the PPCC is mainly based on two factors: business success — normally judged by the scale of business activities — and

---

Communist Party or one of the democratic parties makes participation more likely (interestingly, members of parties other than the Communist Party were found to be five times more likely to be appointed and elected to a PC or PPCC); (3) if the parents of a private entrepreneur had once assumed political office, it was more likely that he/she also became a delegate, making family background an important factor in deciding nominations to PC or PPCC positions.

[13]The above-quoted study by Chen analysing data of a local PPCC at provincial level shows that 128 of 449 delegates (28.5 percent) between 2010 and 2013 were private entrepreneurs, but only 16 of them (12.5 percent of all entrepreneur delegates and 44.4 percent of all occupational sector delegates) officially represented the economic sector (Chen, 2015: 618).

social influence and welfare' (2015: 621). Hence, it is generally the rich and reputable who are permitted access to PPCCs, and the richer and more reputable they are, the higher the administrative tier to which they are recruited as CCPP delegates — if they are interested. As a matter of fact, private entrepreneurs are generally very eager to occupy such positions:

> (...) PPCC activities give private entrepreneurs regular and recurring access to officials at different levels and in charge of different sectors and thus provide opportunities to network and lobby (Chen, 2015: 623).

As private sector delegates, who are expected to attend the annual PPCC conferences held at each administrative level, entrepreneurs can submit 'proposals' (*ti'an*) and 'opinions' (*tiyi*), and are in fact expected to do so by party state authorities (see Chapter 4 for more details). As Chen reports in his study, among the 526 proposals submitted to the PPCC in the provincial capital he investigated, 114 came from private entrepreneurs, amounting to some 25 percent of the total (2015: 624). The issues raised in these proposals overwhelmingly pertained to public management and public goods provision, ranging from food security, or the quality of education and medical services to city infrastructure building, garbage collection and environmental protection, just to name a few. A fifth of the measures suggested were concerned with private sector development (*ibid.*), covering, among other issues, access to bank credit and relevant business information, government guidance in technology innovation and the protection of private property rights. They also proposed to set up more communication channels between private entrepreneurs and the government to help the former assert their opinions and to influence the policy process. Interestingly, Chen notes that:

> (...) the private entrepreneurs' proposals do suggest that the PPCC serves as a channel for the economic elite to create climates of opinion and thus influence policy making on various issues so as *to protect their particular interests as a group* (authors' marking) (*ibid.*).

Their proposals, as Chen's suggests, are foremost related to entrepreneurs' dissatisfaction with the state's implementation of private sector policies, and they seem to strategically use their mandate as delegates to make their collective demands known to party and government authorities. In some cases, such action has been successful. One early example was the genesis of the 'Regulation for the Protection of the Rights of Private Entrepreneurs' passed by the government of Guangzhou city in 1999 (see Heberer, 2003a: 355–357), which was first proposed by the Federation of Industry and Commerce of Guangzhou, spearheaded at the time by a group of private entrepreneurs. As we will show in the empirical section of this book, private entrepreneurs do not only act during PPCC sessions by submitting proposals and opinions to be considered by the governments they have to advise, they also conduct surveys and initiate inspection tours between sessions to prepare for policy submissions by gathering empirical data and feedback from stakeholders on specific topics. In fact, intra-group coordination among private entrepreneur delegates in local PPCCs is increasingly noticeable: It would not be illogical to suppose that this further strengthens their collective identity as an influential group, just as Chen has suggested.[14]

In another study on private entrepreneurs' participation in local PCs and PPCCs, Sun Xin and his collaborators introduced the term 'organizational clientelism' to conceptually grasp the costs and benefits of incorporating private entrepreneurs into China's political institutions (Sun *et al.*, 2014). Using data collected during a nationwide survey by the All-China Federation of Industries and Commerce, the Chinese Academy of Social Sciences, the State Administration of Industry and Commerce and the CP

---

[14]The negative impact of increasing representation for private entrepreneurs in China's PC and PPCCs was recently placed in the media spotlight. In September 2016, 45 members of the National People's Congress, many of them executives of private businesses and state-owned companies, were expelled for having been involved in a vote-buying scandal. Already in 2013, 56 provincial lawmakers were convicted for offering more than 110 million RMB (some 16.5 million US-Dollars) to lower-ranking officials to help them get elected to the provincial legislature. The amount of money at stake in becoming a PC or PPCC delegate can also be seen from the annual Hurun Reports which publish a list of China's richest people. In 2015, a record 203 of the 1,271 richest business-people tracked by the report were members of either the National People's Congress or the National People's Political Consultative Conference. See http://www.nytimes.com/2016/09/15/world/asia/china-npc-election-fraud-liaoning.html?_r=0 (accessed 5 April 2018). For the Hurun Reports, see http://www.hurun.net/EN/Home/ (accessed 5 April 2018).

United Front Work Department conducted in 2006, they investigated the extent to which membership in local legislatures (PCs and PPCCs) impacted on private entrepreneurs' access to state-controlled resources — most notably bank loans — and their exposure to 'administrative and policy burdens', i.e. funding local government budgets, assisting failing local SOEs, and providing public goods and services. They found that:

> (...) firms owned by legislative delegates obtain more loans from state-controlled financial institutions, but also carry more administrative and policy burdens from the local government. (...) Local officials channel state resources and other preferential treatments to connected firms in exchange for political and material benefits. In this process, resource allocation is based on clientelistic ties rather than efficiency. Private firms invest heavily in nurturing such ties with local officials through both bribery and contribution to the implementation of various policy tasks. From a comparative perspective, the government-business relationship in today's China resembles the crony capitalism widely witnessed in many East and Southeast Asian countries, such as Japan, South Korea, and the Philippines (Sun *et al.*, 2014: 21).

This clientelistic relationship between private entrepreneurs and party state authorities,[15] as institutionalized in PCs and PPCCs at both the national and local level, may be asymmetric, but it provides each private entrepreneur with an opportunity to hedge against dependency on individual cadres who may defect or lose influence (*ibid.*). This point is

---

[15] 'Clientelism' based on individual *guanxi*-networks can be, and usually is, part of all modes of political incorporation of private entrepreneurs into the party state discussed here, though the degree to which it is relevant does vary. For an explicit application of 'clientelism' in state–business relations — or '*guanxi* capitalism' as a generic mode of entrepreneurs' political incorporation — see e.g. McNally *et al.* (2007); for an introduction to the concept of 'thick embeddedness' as a term to describe the bonds between private capital and the party state, see McNally and Wright (2010). There are also numerous studies, not at least in the economics literature, which measure the effect of close political connections on the business opportunities and success of private entrepreneurs, or which trace the major addressees of these connections in the government (see e.g. Wu *et al.*, 2012; Su and Fung, 2013; Wang, 2016; Xie *et al.*, 2017; Kung and Ma, 2018).

important. Although Sun *et al.* have suggested that private entrepreneurs' position *vis-à-vis* government officials remains precarious, even if they enjoy legislative membership, some of their collective interests, most notably protection of property rights and individual safety, may be better safeguarded from the position of delegate. However, the authors do not derive any hypothesis on collective agency from their findings and do only suggest that private sector delegates may attempt to strategically influence policy-making on an individual basis. From this perspective, private entrepreneurs seem only to be focused on bribing their way into legislative bodies so that they can then reap whatever benefits possible to advance their individual businesses. At the same time, 'legislatures are a helping hand for Chinese leaders to attract reliable co-operators in governance, expand administrative and political resources, and, to some extent, stabilize the authoritarian "rule of the CCP" (2014: 21–22).

In another recent study, Zhang Changdong draws a very pessimistic picture of private entrepreneurs' behavior in local PCs and PPCCs. Upon becoming delegates, private entrepreneurs are foremost interested in 'build[ing] political connections, obtain[ing] political privileges, and mak[ing] policy proposals that may benefit their industries' (2017: 8). Elections have become strongly 'commercialized', such as 'in some regions of Zhejiang Province', where 'they spend hundreds of thousands or even millions of yuan to buy votes' (2017: 11). Party state officials trade delegate positions for local investment and generous donations by private entrepreneurs, which helps them achieve a positive evaluation in annual performance assessment procedures. As Zhang concludes, 'this patron-clientelism may reinforce the co-optation of private entrepreneurs, but conflicts with a credible commitment to economic growth to some degree because the deputy's privileges may lead to rent-seeking that harms productive activities' (2017: 19), invoking the spectre of negative path dependency once genuine legislative reforms are probed. In a similar vein, Zhang Wuchang (Steven Cheung) (2008 and 2009) concludes that local governments compete for private investments and hence strive for close relations with private entrepreneurs. They offer them political positions (such as PC or PPCC membership) and thus foster an exchange of political power and economic advantages to the benefit of both local cadres and the entrepreneurs themselves.

As indicated above, in our interviews, we came across a more nuanced picture of entrepreneurial agency in these legislative bodies. Although we could not trace corruption as an entry card into local PCs and PPCCs, we found that, once private entrepreneurs have become delegates, they actively participate in policy-making and government supervision. They use their mandate to voice complaints and demands, and often do so collectively. Under these conditions, *guanxi* — or 'organizational clientelism' — undoubtedly plays a prominent role, but the asymmetric relationship between private entrepreneurs and the party state within what we have called a regime coalition may gradually change, with private entrepreneurs gaining more political influence. As McNally has noted:

> (…) the persistence of Leninist control creates institutional ambiguities in the governance of China's private sector. To enhance firm success, private entrepreneurs use political *guanxi* networks to embed themselves in party state institutions, carving out over time increasingly powerful positions *vis-à-vis* the state mediated by the application of *guanxi*. *Guanxi* capitalism thus yields idiosyncratic benefits to certain Chinese firms, while also transforming the Chinese political economy in enabling wealth to be translated into power (2011: 3).[16]

'Corporatist Incorporation' via Business Associations[17]

The significance of business associations in post-Mao China and their relationship to the party state has been a thrilling topic for China scholars for a long time. In this context, corporatism has been a prominent — though contested — concept through which to characterize the relationship between private entrepreneurs and the Communist party state. China

---

[16]For a recent study on the relevancy and conceptual evolution of the *guanxi*-concept in the context of 'Greater China', see Wang and Hsung (2016).

[17]We refer to 'business associations' as a generic term that includes trade associations (*shanghui*), industrial branch associations (*hangye xiehui*), private enterprise associations (*qiyejia xiehui*) or entrepreneurial hometown associations (*yidi shanghui*).

scholars are well aware that Schmitter's 'canonical' definition of corporatism[18] does not fully apply here, as the rise of associations, which began in the 1980s, has resulted in a complex re-configuration of state–business relations when compared with the Maoist era. This has triggered a lively scholarly debate on the scope and limits of applying corporatist or civil society theory to the Chinese case, partly informed by ideological stances on the nature of the Chinese state or the potential for civic agency in an authoritarian setting like China's (see below). Whereas some scholars have explicitly rejected the notion 'corporatist state' or 'corporatism' to conceptualize state–business (or state–society) relations in China,[19] others

---

[18] 'Corporatism can be defined as a system of interest representation in which the constituent units are organized into a limited number of singular, compulsory, noncompetitive, hierarchically ordered, and functionally differentiated categories recognized or licensed (if not created) by the state and granted a deliberate representational monopoly within their respective categories in exchange for observing certain controls on their selection of leaders and articulation of demands and supports' (Schmitter, 1974: 93–94).

[19] Jude Howell (2012) is one of those prominent scholars who thinks that 'corporatism' should be avoided when characterizing state–society relations in contemporary China. Her argument is threefold: (1) Although China's regulatory framework may be corporatist, corporatist theory does not take stock of the manifold personalized relations between civil society organizations and the state by which the former can wield influence over the latter; (2) existing societal organizations like the All China-Federation of Trade Unions or the multitude of business associations are not able to aggregate the interests of their member constituencies and only represent the state's interests; and (3) corporatist regulations fail to achieve their goal of social control because of the political resolve of civil society. 'Market logic', Howell argues, undermines the power of corporatist theory in the case of China, with scholars losing sight of the party state's growing dependency on societal cooperation in bringing about capitalist market transformation. Likewise Scott Kennedy, in his study on political lobbying in the steel, consumer electronics and software industries, found that corporatism was insufficient to explain the state–business relationship in China, as authority in the associational system is highly fragmented: 'Associations are primarily voluntary, increasingly financially independent, not ordered hierarchically, and not unchallenged representatives of certain interests' (2005: 44). He also rejected, however, pluralism and clientelism as alternatives to corporatism and argued instead for an analytical perspective foremost pinpointing variation from those ideal types (see also Kennedy, 2008). Others who have critically written on corporatism as an explanatory concept for state–society/business relations in contemporary China are Hurst (2006) and Gilley (2011).

have adhered to the concept because they believed it was a better fit than any alternative proposed — at least as a 'heuristic device' in combination with a wider conceptual understanding of corporatism.[20] For many experts, corporatism remains a useful analytical tool for describing contemporary state–business relations in China, though, as they claim, it must be conceptually refined.

One possibility is to distinguish between the more authoritarian variant of corporatism, 'state-corporatism', and its liberal counterpart, 'societal corporatism', a well-established typology in the corporatist literature. Anita Chan and Jonathan Unger are good examples of China scholars who, with a long-term perspective on societal change in China, have consistently stuck to the concept of corporatism when explaining changing state–society and, more specifically, state–business relations in the post-Mao period (Unger and Chan, 1995, 1996, 2008; Unger, 1996, 2008; Chan, 2008). In a recent paper comparing state–business relations in different East Asian countries, including China, they reiterate their general viewpoint:

> In strict corporatist fashion, only one association is allowed to be recognized as the representative for each constituency. If not literally an appendage of the government (…), associations of all types need to be officially registered, and in order to register must obtain a Party or state-related organization to sponsor it. The sponsor is responsible for the good behavior of the association, and thus needs to be cautious, which often means the sponsor takes on a direct supervisory role. The government agency that serves as sponsor often pre-emptively has done more than this. In fact, all of the major associations in China and a great many minor ones have been established on the initiative of government

---

[20] See, for instance, Hsu and Hasmath who defined corporatism as interest mediation by officially-designated groups which are integrated in the political structure (2013: 141). The authors explicitly acknowledged that corporatism was limited in fully interpreting state–society relations in China, but useful as a 'descriptive term' or 'heuristic device' 'to outline a set of socio-political and institutional arrangements', which 'has received far less criticism than corporatism as an alternative model of national development and state–society relations' (2013: 140). See also Hsu and Hasmath (2014), who defend a local corporatist framework as the most suitable to explain recent developments in state–society (NGO) relations.

agencies, from the national level downwards. This is true of practically all business and trade associations (2015, 184).

Many business associations in China are state-subsidized and their leading personnel selected by the government. They primarily communicate state policies to their members, though in some cases business associations also advise the government on policy-making. 'In all of these respects', as Unger and Chan note, 'these are quintessentially state-corporatist organizations' (*ibid.*). However, state control over business associations diverges substantially between sectors, administrative tiers and localities. Autonomously established business associations have also emerged in post-Mao China, reported early on in Wenzhou, Zhejiang province (Liu, 1992; Yu *et al.*, 2012). Furthermore, Unger and Chan acknowledge that state-corporatist controls in China have decentralized as 'local leaderships have gained greater control over their own economic resources and become less dependent upon higher government levels for financing local government operations' during the reform era (2015: 8). In the same way, state-corporatist controls have been taken over by local jurisdictions, hence constituting 'little corporatist empires' that occasionally work 'against the national state and against the peak level corporatist associations'. Consequently, 'national and local corporatist arrangements uneasily co-exist' (*ibid.*), but they do not compromise the tenets of state-corporatist control *per se* (2015: 9).[21]

Some scholars have used a different, more descriptive, terminology to highlight the changes that have taken place in state–business relations

---

[21] In the remainder of their quoted study, Unger and Chan use the example of the Association of Private Enterprises (*Siying qiye xiehui*) — which was established in the late 1980s by the Bureau of Industry and Commerce (*Gongshangju*) to serve the interests of small- and medium-sized companies, and the Federation of Industry and Commerce (*Gongshanglian*, FIC) which, according to their understanding, represents larger enterprises — to highlight a shift between state and societal corporatism in the 1990s and 2000s. They find increasing maneuvering space for the FIC in the 1990s, followed by a roll-back in the early 2000s when it had been brought again under strict state control. On the contrary, the Private Enterprise Association seemed to flourish under the nominal leadership of the Bureau of Industry and Commerce, suggesting that there was some development of social corporatism here.

over the last three decades. Yang Keming (2013), for instance, introduced 'organizational corporatism' to explain the CCP's strategy of incorporating the private sector by: enforcing the establishment of party branches in private enterprises and business associations; decentralizing party state authority over business associations to local governments in order to ensure against the inevitable demise of a strictly vertically-structured corporatist system; and signaling to private entrepreneurs 'to keep business-to-business' when dealing with the party state and not making political demands, a pre-condition for associational autonomy (as far as it goes in contemporary China). 'Organizational corporatism' thus describes a party state organizational structure that 'is a major institutional mechanism through which corporatism is represented and realized' (Yang, 2013: 79). At the empirical level, the authors found that business associations actually had very little leeway to act politically on their own initiative.[22]

Other scholars, however, have observed rising degrees of autonomy on the part of business associations *vis-à-vis* the party state which, according to them, are not well grasped by corporatist or civil society theory. Therefore, alternative terminologies have been suggested to better address the relationship between the party state and private entrepreneurs. For instance, in an article on the *Wenzhou Business Association* (established in the late 1980s), an often-cited example of China's self-established and relatively 'autonomous' business organizations, Yu Jianxing and Zhou Jun attempted to mediate between the two theory strands by pointing out that 'the separation of society from the state is currently not really possible, and autonomy is not an essential prerequisite for social organizations to participate in the public domain' (Yu and Zhou, 2013: 397). Lacking independent institutional channels, the Wenzhou Business Association rather 'embraces' the local government by establishing a close relationship with

---

[22] However, collective action of Wenzhou's private entrepreneurs was particularly effective during the famous struggle of the Cigarette Utensils Association's (*yanju xiehui*) in an anti-dumping cigarette lighters' lawsuit against the European Union (Huang and Yu, 2005). Chen Yi argued that the collective action of entrepreneurial associations is usually triggered by bigger enterprises, which are then joined by smaller companies. Networks that reduce risks, along with a high level of communication among Wenzhou entrepreneurs, form the foundation of effective collective action there (Chen, 2014).

government departments and officials in order to influence policy-making in the realm of industrial governance:

> Arising as a response to 'market failure' the Wenzhou Business Association has never taken civil society development as its aim, and thus nor has any confrontation been formed with the government. On the contrary, out of realistic needs, it has taken the initiative to function in industry governance as a capable assistant to the government, which rightly serves as a prerequisite for governmental acknowledgement and corresponding empowerment through its remarkable function performance (2013: 406).

The major argument made by the authors is simple: Private entrepreneurs' interests are best represented by business associations which entertain a 'symbiosis relation' (2013: 400) with the government and do not insist on organizational autonomy, which is not available under the current regime. Business associations serve their member constituency best by assuming the role of an 'indispensable helper' (2013: 406) to the government, which is becoming increasingly dependent on business associations in private sector management.[23]

In a later article written by Yu Jianxing and his research team (Yu *et al.*, 2014), the authors introduced 'privileged access' as a concept for questioning the usual correlation between organizational autonomy and lobbying intensity (and success) on the part of societal organizations. The significance of 'autonomy' for successful lobbying, as they have argued, was too easily taken for granted in assessing the existence of a civil society in China, as the term lacked convincing

---

[23]This claim is made on the basis of data on the self-assessment of business officials and the assessment of member enterprises concerning the Wenzhou Business Association's functional effectiveness. However, there is no independent measurement in terms of factual input in policy-making and implementation (which is certainly difficult). The study thus runs the risk of establishing a tautology: The current mode of 'embedded lobbying' of China's business associations is effective because association officials and members claim it is, hence it is effective. The possibility to participate in policy-making does indeed not say much about the scope and outcome of that participation, even if increased participation over time has been observed.

operationalization.[24] In this study, the authors found that self-established, i.e. autonomous, business associations lobbied less than 'official' associations, i.e. those set up by the government. The authors concluded that it was not formal autonomy that counted for lobbying frequency and effectiveness, but the 'privileged access' of 'official' associations to government cadres and policy makers, an insight well established in the literature on Western democratic systems (2014: 318). For the authors, it followed that more nuanced measures of 'privileged access' would be needed to assess the lobbying potential of contemporary Chinese business associations (Yu *et al.*, 2014: 331). However, the theoretical status of 'privileged access' *vis-à-vis* both corporatist and civil society theory remained suggestive and unexplained. As a matter of fact, Yu *et al.* subscribed to the observation made by many China scholars that institutional autonomy for business associations is non-existent in China, hence forcing private entrepreneurs to make use of informal channels, which is what 'privileged access' is all about.

The gap in theoretical explanation has been tackled tentatively in a more recent paper by Shen Yongdong and Yu Jianxing (2017). Once again pinpointing the decreasing corporatist control of business associations in China, they suggest conceptualizing contemporary relations between the state and private entrepreneurs as 'capitalist incorporation'. In the authors' definition, 'capitalist incorporation' denotes a specific arrangement by which the party state simultaneously expands the organizational autonomy of business associations — measured in terms of association officials employed without government interference, financial independence from government funding, relaxed registration of associations due to government deregulation, and the assignment of functional competencies by government decentralization — and indirectly strengthens control over them, allowing for both capitalist development and political stability, and

---

[24]The authors themselves, in their research design, operationalized 'autonomy' as the freedom of a business association to employ its secretary general on the one hand and the number of government officials employed by the association on the other. 'Lobbying frequency' was the dependent variable, measured by asking association officials and members how often they proposed policies in formal and informal ways to government authorities during the year. Data were gathered from business associations in Zhejiang (Wenzhou) and Jiangsu (Wuxi, Ningbo) provinces.

making sure that private entrepreneurs are content with the regime they live under. Like 'privileged access', the theoretical relationship between 'capitalist incorporation' and corporatist or civil society theory is not clear. In any case, the term seems more to suggest corporatist control over business associations than any kind of 'autonomous' agency of the latter.[25]

Obviously, China scholars struggle hard to come to terms with the fact that government–business relations in contemporary China are complex and constantly in flux, and often try as hard to find theoretical alternatives.[26] Corporatism — either understood in analytical or descriptive

---

[25] Interestingly, in a recent case study, Ji Yingying (2018) makes the argument that business associations in China are becoming increasingly autonomous as they gain in organizational cohesion, confront big economic players to the benefit of their membership (made up primarily of smaller entrepreneurs), and strategically make use of government policies and the media to achieve their ends. With this behavior, business associations display a rising potential to bring about confrontational state–society relations in contemporary China.

[26] See, for instance, Hua, Zhang, and Zhou (2012) who addressed the limited compatibility of corporatism, civil society and governance as theoretical approaches to the current relationship between the state and societal organizations (including industry associations), before introducing their own theory of rational choice-based 'interest alignment' under the control of government as an alternative. 'Interest alignment' should 'explain the differences in policy participation by the same type of societal organizations under different circumstances, and on this basis, explore the nature of state and society relations in transition China and test the plausibility of the analytical framework with comparative case studies of policy participation by industry associations' (2012: 92). However, by the way the authors frame their case study on the *Zhejiang Capital Investment Promotion Association*, one must question whether 'interest alignment' is a genuine conceptual, let alone theoretical, alternative to widely defined corporatism. Their major insight is 'that the state makes a strategic choice in deciding whether to support or restrict social organizations, and that the interactions between the state and society organizations are characterized by a low degree of institutionalization. (…) the states decides its degree of control over societal organizations on the basis of risk and yield' (2012: 105). Put differently, as long as the state and industry associations pursue the same policies, the latter can extensively participate in the policy-making process; however, if both sides have diverging policy outlooks, industry associations' participation will be restricted and they can only engage in policy advocacy or lobbying. This theoretical framework thus does not strictly apply Schmitter's analytical definition of corporatism and tolerates different modes of interest representation and aggregation within a corporatist framework. On the variance

terms — is not easily done away with when seeking to understand recent developments which suggest more political leverage for business associations *vis-à-vis* the party state. We believe that, rather than identifying the 'correct' theoretical framework to conceptualize state–business relations, it is more important to show how private entrepreneurs engage in *strategic action* via business associations with the aim of safeguarding their economic interests and how this impacts on state–business relations.

Incorporation via Public Office at the Grassroots

Private entrepreneurs have increasingly been recruited to serve in positions of public office at the grassroots level since the nationwide introduction of direct elections for village committees in 1998.[27] Often, they were encouraged to assume the position of village party secretary by local governments. As An Chen (2015) has shown, peasants have great respect for entrepreneurial village leaders, who help villages by providing better access to markets, gathering market information and increasing villagers' economic capabilities and, in turn, incomes. The party state, for its part, pursues two objectives: (1) help villagers benefit from the management expertise and investment capital of private entrepreneurs, and thus spur economic development; and (2) strengthen local governments' legitimacy by putting capable people (*nengren*) in charge of the village economy. Moreover, putting successful private entrepreneurs into public office allowed the party state to better control this emerging social constituency and let it cultivate views 'increasingly similar to those of local Party and government officials, making them unlikely agents of political change' (Dickson, 2007: 847). Entrepreneurial elites, for their part, felt inclined to run for public office, as doing so promised better access to local officials

---

of formal and informal lobbying by industry associations in contemporary China and its impact on the policy process, see also Kennedy (2009) and Kennedy and Deng (2010).

[27]Direct village elections were first introduced in 1987 on an experimental and voluntary basis. For a systematic overview of this well-researched field, see Schubert (2009) and Schubert and Ahlers (2012). For an early study on the political engagement of private entrepreneurs in rural China, see Gilley (2002).

and the resources they control — most notably land, credit and *guanxi*. Private entrepreneurs becoming village leaders thus appeared to be a win–win situation for all parties concerned — villagers, local governments, and private entrepreneurs (see also Yan Xiaojun, 2012; Yan and Huang, 2017).

Obviously, this arrangement worked out quite well for both the party state and entrepreneurial interests. Arguably, a new entrepreneurial elite has taken over many villages since the introduction of direct village elections, mostly by making promises of transforming and modernizing the village economy. While those promises may have been fulfilled in many villages,[28] a number of case studies have shown that, with private entrepreneurs serving as village heads, vote-buying became ubiquitous, financial and fiscal transparency decreased, the quality of village governance deteriorated, and village revenues disappeared. Consequently, direct village elections, often hailed as a far-reaching democratic reform of the Chinese political system in the early years of their institutionalization, have become discredited in the eyes of villagers in many parts of China, who have sometimes protested against corrupt officials or turned away from grassroots politics altogether (O'Brien and Han, 2009; Yao, 2012, 2013).[29]

Yan Xiaojun, who framed his study on entrepreneurial party secretaries in a county in Northern China as 'rich people taking over' (2012: 339),

---

[28] Although there is yet no study to our knowledge that has compared economic development in villages with private entrepreneurs working as village heads or village party secretaries, we have come across a number of success stories during our fieldwork conducted across China over the last few years. For instance, the renowned head of Lantian Village in Kangmei township of Nan'an city, Fujian province, interviewed by one of the authors in 2011, was a prominent local businessman who had 'digitized' the whole village by connecting each household to the internet, setting up an eBay-like business to sell the villages agricultural products to villagers and external clients, and another business producing commercial video clips. He invested in a huge modern village canteen and pushed township and county officials to further commercialize village operations. At the same time, he displayed allegiance to Mao Zedong, who was his acclaimed paragon!

[29] Interviews, Qingdao Party School, 31 August 2009; Sichuan Provincial Party School, 10 September 2009.

looked specifically at factors behind the recruitment of private entrepreneurs for political roles. Economic clout and political power naturally reach out to one another. For its part, by recruiting private entrepreneurs, the party state strives to strengthen its legitimacy in China's villages, particularly those that face tremendous pressure by economic and social change. As the county party secretary told the author,

> (...) it is crucial for us to continue absorbing capable leaders from the new social stratum to consolidate the Party's grassroots leadership under deepened market reforms. And that remains the top priority for the Party's organizational work (2012: 341).

The social backgrounds of the new entrepreneurial village party secretaries in that county were quite heterogeneous, including owners of large scale outside businesses, owners of local businesses with lineage seniority, large-scale private farm owners, but also local professionals (like village doctors with private practices). The candidates all seemed to enjoy high levels of social prestige among villagers as well as having strong political influence, mostly because of their philanthropic activities, their activism in community services and, not least, their business relations with the local political authorities, all of which they could successfully trade for political appointment. Yan summarizes his findings by predicting that private entrepreneurs would play 'an even more salient role in China's future political development' (2012: 354) in a new power game at the grassroots which privileges those with economic success over anybody else. However, as Xi Jinping's anti-corruption drive has shown, the assumption that private entrepreneurs could easily hijack the party state's grassroots organizations is ungrounded. Once private entrepreneurs (allegedly) switch to political action by themselves or even turn against the hand which nurtures and protects them, they can quickly fall from grace. Even if there exists strong mutual dependency between private entrepreneurs and local governments, driven by the link between economic development and regime legitimacy, there is no indication that entrepreneurial might topples the political supremacy of local cadre bureaucracies. This counts as much for the grassroots as for those administrative levels higher up.

Private Entrepreneurs as an Agent of Political Change?

Against a background of continuous effort on the part of the party state to control and incorporate private entrepreneurs, scholars of Chinese politics have paid much attention to the question of whether, or under which conditions, private entrepreneurs would be willing and able to challenge the party state's political supremacy. Historical experience has provided plenty of evidence which suggests that this segment of a society's 'modern strata' can be an influential political actor in countries experiencing economic and social transformation. They ally with regime elites or side with their opponents, depending on what serves their interests best; either course of action can have significant consequences for regime stability and legitimacy, and for democratization.[30] Private entrepreneurs tend to support authoritarian regimes when their material interests benefit from the regime's policies. They also tend to be conservative when they feel that a new regime's policies, such as demands for higher taxes to pay for new welfare programs or for the nationalization of lucrative industries, would do harm to their businesses.[31] On the contrary, if they come to believe that the regime under which they are governed can no longer defend their interests or if they perceive that the strength of the opposition has reached a tipping point, their support for the *status quo* can evaporate and be replaced by a quest for political change (Chen and Dickson, 2008; see also Huntington, 1991; Merkel, 1999). This certainly requires collective political agency, or coordinated strategic action and, very often, an

---

[30] Often quoted is Barrington Moore's famous dictum 'no bourgeoisie, no democracy', which suggests that the rise of private entrepreneurship is a precondition of democratic change (Moore, 1969).

[31] In Chen An's perspective, it was 'the intensified confrontation between rich and poor in Chinese society that provides all Chinese bourgeois with a common cause in resisting democratization and averting the collapse of the regime' (2002: 413). In the author's definition, the Chinese bourgeoisie comprised largely of private entrepreneurs. Nevertheless, at the time, the later 1990s, private entrepreneurs were deeply suspicious to Marxist fundamentalists within the Communist Party — who accused them 'to have formed a powerful lobby group within the party-state apparatus and have attempted to topple the party from within' (2002: 420)

overarching sense of following a common course. For the most part, however, China scholars have rejected the notion that private entrepreneurs in China act strategically to pursue common goals or that they have developed a *corps d'esprit* of any sort, hence disqualifying them as a force of democratization. For instance, Kellee S. Tsai, drawing on survey data gathered in the 1990s and early 2000s, noted:

> Private entrepreneurs lack a common basis for identity and interaction, challenging the very premise that China's new capitalists might engage in collective action to push for democratic political change. Private entrepreneurs might engage in similar economic activities and appear to share similar interests, but business owners perceive and defend their interests in different ways because of widely varying social and political identities. (…) In short, it is overly simplistic to view business owners as a single class that shares common identities, interests, and behaviors that will have unified political impact (2005: 1132–1133).

In fact, Tsai has found little evidence that China's private entrepreneurs act as a united group in pursuing their interests in her work on class-based collective action, and has rather suggested that they display limited capability to confront state policies, instead relying on informal, individual (rather than group-oriented) and non-confrontational strategies to address their grievances and safeguard their interests (see Tsai, 2007: 145–149).[32] In the conclusion of her 2005 study cited above, she emphasized that

> (…) at present, it would be empirically inaccurate to depict China's business owners as a coherent capitalist class that is likely to act in

---

[32] The social classification of private entrepreneurs is controversial among Chinese scholars. While Huang (2014) argues that they already constitute a specific 'social stratum' (*shehui jieceng*), it remains unclear whether they form a 'social group' or a 'social class' and whether they oppose or challenge the party state or not. For their part, Zhu Guanglei *et al.* contend that entrepreneurs form a social group but not yet a class — without, however, clarifying exactly what kind of group they constituted (Zhu *et al.*, 1999). In fact, Chinese scholars hardly address entrepreneurial political agency beyond corruptive behavior and, as a rule, see private entrepreneurs as politically submissive, much like most Western scholars.

collective defense of its material interests. Rather than growing homogeneity, the private sector has grown increasingly diversified in terms of membership. The illiterate sidewalk vendor, the steelworker-turned cabdriver, and the software designer are all 'private entrepreneurs.' But they have different identities, resources, attitudes, and values and, therefore, as I argue, they also have different behavior patterns. China's capitalists are not equally posed to engage in politics or demand democracy (2005: 1152).

Most China scholars subscribe to Tsai's assertion that private entrepreneurs in contemporary China do not yet constitute a homogeneous social constituency. Even more differences have been found in terms of company size, business significance, and socio-political and geographical background. In fact, due to their greater access to resources, owners of bigger companies act differently from those in smaller and medium-sized ones, those in 'promising' industries and services differ from those in traditional sectors, and those in urban firms from those in rural ones. Differences in gender and geographical location, as well as differences regarding political and economic connections, also have an impact on the variety of perspectives across this new social constituency (see e.g. He *et al.*, 2018; Fan and Lü, 2019). The 'impetus' and reasons for individuals turning to entrepreneurship are also diverse: push entrepreneurs are dissatisfied with their previous living conditions, while pull entrepreneurs are attracted by entrepreneurial gain. Some are driven by opportunity, others by necessity (Williams, 2008).[33] Thus, there is a diversity of preferences among private entrepreneurs.

Tsai in turn distinguishes five sub-groups of entrepreneurs: (1) 'marginalized' entrepreneurs, i.e. petty traders and manufacturers (*getihu*); (2) 'disguised' entrepreneurs, i.e. those operating under the aegis of

---

[33] One of our respondents made an interesting distinction between those entrepreneurs who were born prior to the 1970s being more anxious to fall into official disgrace and eager to secure the protection of cadres; and those who were born after the 1970s being more self-confident. However, what they all had in common was a feeling of uncertainty (*bu anquan gan*), primarily in terms of policies. There was little trust among them in the government's determination to protect and develop the private sector. Interview, private entrepreneur, Fujian, 22 September 2018.

collective or state-owned enterprises (*dai hong maozi*); (3) 'dependent and red' entrepreneurs, i.e. those forced into an asymmetrical relationship with local governments ('symbiotic clientelism'); (4) 'incorporated' entrepreneurs, referring to those who are concurrently working as cadres and thus have strong ties to the state (mostly via various entrepreneurial associations in which they serve); (5) 'rationalizing' entrepreneurs, i.e. those who support the emergence of a 'legal-rational institutional environment' (Tsai, 2005: 1135–1138). While this classification may at first seem to be simplistic because of manifold overlaps between the different categories and the fact that some of them have meanwhile become anachronistic, it nonetheless illustrates the broad variety of origin and social positions among Chinese entrepreneurs. However, as will be shown in Chapter 3 in more detail, private entrepreneurs — according to our definition[34] — nevertheless constitute a coherent group with their own arsenal of strategies, a shared habitus and, arguably, a collective identity.

In most of the literature, private entrepreneurs are regarded as politically conservative and, if not accused of corruption, easily co-opted by the Communist Party. To cite Dickson again:

> In contrast to the popular perception that privatization is leading inexorably to democratization, and by extension that China's capitalists are democrats at heart, the most recent survey data suggests that they are increasingly integrated into the current political system. They are part of the status quo, not challengers on the outside looking in. On a variety of political questions, the views of entrepreneurs are remarkably similar to local Party and government officials (2007: 852).

This has been the assessment of most China scholars over the last 25 years or so. In an early study, Dorothy Solinger pointed to the dominating influence of the party state in the private sector and the ways by which private entrepreneurs strove to cultivate close personal relations with officials in order to access state-controlled resources. She identified 'a bonding and incipient interdependence between the bureaucrat and the merchant' (1992: 136). Margaret Pearson found that state–business

---

[34] See Introduction.

relations were characterized by *clientelism* and *social corporatism* and that private entrepreneurs were using 'safe, well-established, and effective capitalist strategies to maneuver their way *vis-à-vis* the state bureaucracy' (1997: 141). David Wank introduced the notion '*symbiotic clientelism*' to describe pretty much the same phenomenon, but he also noted that the balance within this symbiotic relationship has started to tilt in favor of private entrepreneurs 'as officials and local governments are increasingly dependent on entrepreneurs and their firms for certain resources' (1999: 11). As early as 2003, in his seminal book on 'Red Capitalists in China', Bruce Dickson spoke of 'crony capitalism' in contemporary China and identified *patrimonial ties* between the state and private entrepreneurs, 'in which success in business is due more to personal contacts in the official bureaucracy than to entrepreneurial skill or merit' (2003: 22–23).[35] In another study investigating and statistically measuring level of regime support by private entrepreneurs, Chen and Dickson (2008) called the latter 'allies of the state', while McNally and Wright even asserted that private entrepreneurs are 'thickly embedded' in the party state:

> The interweaving of instrumental and affective ties 'overdetermines' private capital holders' support for the political status quo. Frequent interactions, sentiments of familiarity and trust, and a 'we-group' feeling toward each other have made China's entrepreneurs more positively disposed toward the political establishment than would be the case with solely instrumental ties. (…) Put differently, the interweaving of affective, instrumental and institutional ties that thickly embed private capital holders in the party state, makes support for the political status quo more enduring and 'sticky' than would otherwise be the case (2010: 196).

Junmin Wang takes a slightly different perspective, somewhat challenging the argument that private entrepreneurs are 'supporters' of the

---

[35] David Goodman (2004), who has done extensive research on China's middle classes, highlighted another interesting aspect of state–business relations when his fieldwork revealed that many successful private entrepreneurs had 'blood relations' with political leaders. Coming on top of the existing economic interdependency between the party state and the entrepreneurial middle class, this factor would bind the latter even closer to the regime. See also Goodman (2008).

party state. He comes to three findings: (a) 'The more institutional constraints facing a firm, the less favorable its entrepreneur's opinion of the political regime'; (b) 'The more connected a firm is with the government, the more favorable its entrepreneur's opinion of the political regime', and (c) 'A firm's use of a political connection-building strategy weakens the negative effect that its entrepreneur's assessment of institutional constraints on the firm has on his or her opinion of the political regime' (Wang, 2016: 299). Our own research shows that most entrepreneurs distinguish between the (negatively perceived) local state and the (positively assessed) central state and do not question the political regime *per se*, a point that Wang overlooks. Moreover, he remains rather vague in admitting that his data cannot verify his argument and that, in the end, it is 'impossible to assess private entrepreneurs' political motivations and potential actions' (Wang, 2016: 316).

When it comes to an analysis of political action of private entrepreneurs in post-Mao China, a few studies are, in particular, worth mentioning. In one of them, Kellee S. Tsai (2007) argues that private entrepreneurs have a number of coping strategies to safeguard their economic interests, usually informal in nature and non-confrontational. She distinguished between *avoidant strategies*, *acceptant* and *grudgingly acceptant* behavior, and *assertive political strategies*, the latter of which are used by a small minority of entrepreneurs and comprise of 'participation in formal political institutions, individual lobbying efforts, associational activities, as well as more contentious forms of collective action in collaboration with other entrepreneurs' (2007: 118). In the end, as Tsai wrote, none of these assertive coping strategies 'thus far has entailed overt lobbying for political pluralization or representation' (2007: 139). However, she also noted that 'private entrepreneurs are nonetheless active in pursuing and defending their interests', and their political action — or coping strategies — 'have unintended transformative effects on formal institutions' (2007: 208). This can be seen most notably in terms of institutional subversion and institutional conversion, which bring about 'adaptive informal institutions' (see also Tsai, 2006). Hence, Tsai successfully relativized the tone set in preceding studies to some extent by contemplating the impact of entrepreneurial political agency on the institutional structure of the Chinese political system, which was significant, in her assessment. Even if private entrepreneurs had no intention of proactively changing the existing system, they still did so by asserting their specific interests.

Thomas Heberer (2003a, 2003b), for his part, was the first to apply 'strategic group' theory (see Chapter 3) in his research on the rise of private entrepreneurship in post-Mao China, at the time focusing on the link between the collective action of private entrepreneurs and state capacity. Like Tsai, he identified successful collective lobbying attempts by private entrepreneurs, which, though only loosely organized, aimed to influence local and national economic policy making, potentially resulting in institutional change (by, for instance, changing the legal foundation of the private sector). Scott Kennedy (2005) was the first to look systematically at strategic lobbying by big companies from the industrial and technology sectors of the Chinese economy, making the point that lobbying in China is as common as in any other country. His study confirmed the noticeable influence of large entrepreneurs and business associations on national policy-making though, once again, there was not much coordination between industries or economic sectors.

In a more recent study, Huang and Chen (2016) discovered that entrepreneurs who were previously civil servants and afterwards 'jumped into the sea', i.e. had turned to private entrepreneurship, tend to be less aligned with the party state and more confrontational in their behavior towards state agencies than other entrepreneurs. There is also considerable heterogeneity in terms of their political impact. As Scott Kennedy noted, 'the greater an enterprise's contribution to society, the greater its input into policy' (2008: 170). However, while both large and small or medium-sized entrepreneurs may influence political decision-making in order to protect their interests, the latter's impact is usually more issue-oriented and less continuous. In addition, large entrepreneurs are more inclined to act individually by making use of their personal relationships with local, regional or even central leaders, whereas smaller and medium-sized entrepreneurs, who often lack such networks or patronage protection, rather take the path of collective action via business associations.[36]

---

[36] Interview, Peking, 4 March 2015. Ji (2018) describes the case of a registered non-state business association of smaller entrepreneurs (*getihu*) in a prefectural level city in Anhui province which asserts the interests of its clientele through contentious collective action.

Nee and Opper, for their part, argued that continuous economic decentralization and liberalization have resulted in a decreased impact of party state authorities on economic processes. They stated, however, 'a declining value of political capital' by private entrepreneurs' (2012: 258) and 'markets cumulatively shift the interest of economic actors away from self-enforcing reliance on vertical political connections characteristic of state socialism to self-reinforcing investment in horizontal network ties' (2012: 236). They even predicted that markets would increasingly become non-political spaces. However, this is a blatant overestimation of the power of the market in changing the interaction between the party state and private entrepreneurs, leading to problematic conclusions regarding the nexus between market development and politics in contemporary China. In fact, the steering capacity of the party state in an evolving Chinese market economy has not decreased in recent years but has rather become stronger.[37] Even David Wank's assertion that entrepreneurs offer cadres material benefits while they, in exchange, provide entrepreneurs with access to market advantages (Wank, 1999: 72–81) has changed due to Xi Jinping's anti-corruption drive.

Given the vigorous development of the private sector economy in China since its 'comeback' in the early 1980s, it is important to constantly watch the evolving relationship between private entrepreneurs and the party state in order to understand the future trajectory of the Chinese economy, the dynamics of China's state capacity and the stability of its political system. In this book, we hypothesize that, against a background of continuous market transformation, private entrepreneurs have become a 'strategic group' that increasingly shapes the political system in which they operate. Power relations between the party state and private entrepreneurs, bound together in a regime coalition since the

---

Such cases exist but may be rather exceptional since entrepreneurs, as a rule, prefer to solve conflicts by lobbying or approaching government authorities through informal channels. Ji admits, however, that 'the chance that associations will achieve their goals is higher when the (…) state itself recognizes such associations (…) and provides corresponding opportunities' (2018: 15).

[37] A reason for their overly optimistic assessment of the retreat of the state in China's economy may be related to the fact that Nee and Opper's book is based on research conducted in the Yangzi delta only, one of China's most prosperous regions.

early days of 'reform and opening up', are constantly reconfigured and, as we argue, have become more horizontal. Hence, private entrepreneurs are gaining influence on all administrative levels of the Chinese system, although not (yet) at the expense of party state political supremacy. In general, private entrepreneurs 'play ball' within the institutional structure set up and steered by the party state. In fact, by pushing for economic reforms, private entrepreneurs contribute substantially to system stability and regime legitimacy.[38] At the same time, however, private entrepreneurs' increasing capacity when it comes to negotiating group-specific interests with the regime brings new challenges to the state–business relationship, no matter how much the current leadership under Xi Jinping tries to rein in private entrepreneurs. This book seeks to contribute to this discussion by sharpening our perspective in preparation for an imminent re-alignment of state–business relations. It will do so by looking at the different dimensions of collective strategic action by private entrepreneurs.

References

ACFIC (All-China Federation of Industries and Commerce). (2012). *Blue Book of Non-State-Owned-Economy: Annual Report on Non-State-Owned Economy in China (2011–2012)*. Beijing: Shehui kexue wenxian.

ACFIC (All-China Federation of Industries and Commerce). (2015). *Blue Book of Non-State-Owned-Economy: Annual Report on Non-State-Owned Economy in China (2013–2014)*. Beijing: Shehui kexue wenxian.

ACFIC (All-China Federation of Industries and Commerce). (2017). *Blue Book of Non-State-Owned-Economy: Annual Report on Non-State-Owned Economy in China (2015–2016)*. Beijing: Zhonghua gongshang lianhe.

Chan, Anita. (2008). China's trade unions in corporatist transition. In Jonathan Unger (Ed.), *Associations and the Chinese State: Contested Spaces* (pp. 69–85). New York: East Gate.

Chen, An. (2002). Development, Entrepreneurial Class, and Democratization in China. *Political Science Quarterly* 117(3), 401–422.

---

[38]We therefore question Wank's argument that the strategic behavior of private entrepreneurs 'undermines the infrastructural power of the central state' (1995: 181).

Chen, An. (2015). *The Transformation of Governance in Rural China. Market, Finance, and Political Authority.* Cambridge: Cambridge University Press.

Chen, Jie and Dickson, Bruce J. (2008). Allies of the State: democratic support and regime support among Chinas private entrepreneurs. *The China Quarterly* 196, 780–804.

Chen, Minglu. (2015). From economic elites to political elites: Private entrepreneurs in the people's political consultative conference. *Journal of Contemporary China* 24(94), 613–627.

Chen, Yi. (2014). Jiti xingdong, wangluo yu Wenzhou qiyejia qunti (Collective action, networks and entrepreneurial groups in Wenzhou). *Wenzhou daxue xuebao* (Journal of Wenzhou University) 1, 56–62.

Chen, Zhao, Lu, Ming, and He, Junzhi. (2008). Power and political participation of entrepreneurs: Evidence from Liuzhou, Guangxi, China. *Journal of the Asia-Pacific Economy* 13(3), 298–312.

Deng, Guosheng and Kennedy, Scott. (2010). Big business and industrial association lobbying in China: The Paradox of contrasting styles. *The China Journal* 63, 101–125.

Dickson, Bruce J. (2003). *Red Capitalists in China: The Party, Private Entrepreneurs, and Prospects for Political Change.* Cambridge: Cambridge University Press.

Dickson, Bruce J. (2007). Integrating wealth into power: The Communist Party's embrace of China's private sector. *The China Quarterly* 192, 827–854.

Dickson, Bruce J. (2008). *Wealth into Power: The Communist Party's Embrace of China's Private Sector.* Cambridge: Cambridge University Press.

Fan, Xiaoguang and Lü, Peng. (2018). Zhongguo siying qiyezhu de 'gaizibi beilun' (The 'Gatsby Paradox' of China's private entrepreneurs). *Shehuixue yanjiu* (Sociological Studies) 6, 62–82.

Fan, Xiaoguang and Lü, Peng. (2019). The social composition of China's entrepreneurs: Class and cohort differences. *Social Sciences in China* 40(1), 42–62.

Gilley, Bruce. (2002). The Yu Zuomin Phenomenon: Entrepreneurs and politics in rural China. In Victoria E. Bonnell and Thomas B. Gold (Eds.), *The New Entrepreneurs of Europe and Asia. Patterns of Business Development in Russia, Eastern Europe and China* (pp. 66–82). New York: M.E. Sharpe.

Gold, Thomas B. (2017). Normalizing private business in China. *Journal of Chinese Political Science* 22(3), 461–472.

Goodman, David. (2004). Localism and entrepreneurship: History, identity and solidarity as factors of production. In Barbara Krug (Ed.), *China's Rational Entrepreneurs: The Development of the New Private Sector* (pp. 139–165). New York: Routledge.

Goodman, David. (2008). *The New Rich in China: Future Rulers, Present Lives.* London: Routledge.

He, Canfei, Lu, Jiangyong, and Qian, Haifeng. (2018). Entrepreneurship in China. *Small Business Economics* 52(3), 563–572.

He, Xuan and Ma, Jun. (2016). Zhizhengdang dui siying qiye de tonghe celüe ji qi xiaoying fenxi: dui yu siying qiye diaocha shuju de shizheng yanjiu (The Chinese Communist Party's integration policy towards private enterprises and its effectiveness: An analysis of the Ninth National Survey of Chinese Private Enterprises). *Shehui* (Chinese Journal of Sociology) 36(5), 175–196.

Heberer, Thomas. (1989). *Die Rolle des urbanen Individualsektors für Arbeitsmarkt und Stadtwirtschaft in China* (The Role of the Urban Individual Sector for the Labor Market and the Urban Economy in China). Bremer Beiträge zur Geographie und Raumplanung. Bremen: Universität Bremen.

Heberer, Thomas. (2003a). Strategic groups and state capacity: The case of the private entrepreneurs. *China Perspectives* 46, 4–14.

Heberer, Thomas. (2003b). *Private Entrepreneurs in China and Vietnam. Social and Political Functioning of Strategic Groups.* Leiden: Brill.

Howell, Jude. (2012). Civil society, corporatism and capitalism in China. *Journal of Comparative Asian Development* 11(2), 271–292.

Hsu, Jennifer Y.J. and Hasmath, Reza. (2013). The Chinese Corporatist State: Lessons learned for other jurisdictions. In Jennifer Y.J. Hsu and Reza Hasmath (Eds.), *The Chinese Corporatist State. Adaption, Survival and Resistance* (pp. 136–143). London and New York: Routledge.

Hsu, Jennifer Y.J. and Hasmath, Reza. (2014). The local corporatist state and NGO relations in China. *Journal of Contemporary China* 23(87), 498–515.

Hu, Deping. (2011). *Zhongguo weishenme yao gaige. Siyi fuqin Hu Yaobang* (Why China must reform. Remember father Hu Yaobang). Beijing: Renmin chubanshe.

Hua, Jiang, Zhang, Jianmin, and Zhou, Ying. (2012). Industry associations' participation in public policymaking from the perspective of state-society relations: A conceptual framework and comparative case studies. In Yu Jianxing and Sujian Guo (Eds.), *Civil Society and Governance in China* (pp. 85–109). New York: Palgrave Macmillan.

Huang, Dongya. (2013). *Qiyejia ruhe yingxiang difang zhengce guocheng. Guanyu guojia zhongxin de anli fenxi he leixing jiangou* (How entrepreneurs do impact upon local policy processes. Analysis of the type and structure of our countries crucial cases). *Shehuixue Yanjiu* (Sociological Studies) 5, 172–196.

Huang, Dongya. (2014). *Siying qiyezhu zhengzhi fazhan guanyu shichang zhuanxing zhong siying qiyezhu de jieji xiangfa jiqi fansi* (Private entrepreneurs and political development: Theoretical imagination of private entrepreneurs in the marketization as a class and its reflection. *Shehui* (Chinese Journal of Sociology) 34(4), 138–164.

Huang, Dongya and Chen, Chuanmin. (2016). Revolving out of the Party-State: The Xiahai entrepreneurs and circumscribing government power in China. *Journal of Contemporary China* 25(97), 41–58.

Huntington, Samuel. (1991). *The Third Wave. Democratization in Late Twentieth Century,* Norman: Oklahoma University Press.

Hurst, William. (2006). The city as the focus: The analysis of contemporary Chinese urban politics. *China Information* 20(30), 457–479.

Ji, Yingying. (2018). Emerging state–business contention in China: Collective action of a business association and China's fragmented governance structure. *China Information* 32(3), 463–484.

Kennedy, Scott. (2005). *The Business of Lobbying in China*. Cambridge, MA, and London: Harvard University Press.

Kennedy, Scott. (2008). The price of competition: The failed government effort to use associations to organize China's market economy. In Jonathan Unger (Ed.), *Associations and the Chinese State: Contested Spaces* (pp. 149–175). Armonk: M.E. Sharpe.

Kennedy, Scott. (2009). Comparing formal and informal lobbying practices in China: The capital's ambivalent embrace of capitalists. *China Information* 23(2), 195–222.

Kung, James Kai-sing and Ma, Chicheng. (2018). Friends with benefits: How political connections help to sustain private enterprise growth in China. *Economica* 85(337), 41–74.

Li, Zhiyong. (2017). Minying qiye shi keji chuangxin de zhongyao liliang (Private enterprises are a crucial force for scientific-technical innovation). *Jingji Cankao Bao*, 15 December. http://finance.eastmoney.com/news/1371, 20171215812704910.html (accessed 2 May 2018).

Liang, Chuanyun. (1990). *Zhongguo siren qiye jingying guanli zhinan* (Introduction into the management of Chinese private enterprises). Beijing: Beijing daxue chubanshe.

Lin, Yi-min. (2017). *Dancing with the Devil: The Political Economy of Privatization in China.* Oxford and New York: Oxford University Press.

Liu, Alan P.L. (1992). The "Wenzhou Model" of development and China's modernization. *Asian Survey* 32(8), 696–711.

Liu, Dan. (2017). *Zhongguo minying qiyejia. Chuangxin shengtai xitong de chengshudu pingjia yanjiu* (Research on Maturity Evaluation of Private Entrepreneurs' Innovation Eco-System in China). Beijing: Zhongguo caijing chubanshe.

McNally, Christopher A. (2011). China's changing guanxi capitalism: Private entrepreneurs between Leninist control and relentless accumulation. *Business and Politics* 13(2), 1–29.

McNally, Christopher A. (2012). Sino-Capitalism: China's reemergence and the international political economy. *World Politics* 64(4), 741–776.

McNally, Christopher A. (2013). Refurbishing state capitalism: A policy analysis of efforts to rebalance China's political economy. *Journal of Current Chinese Affairs* 42(4), 45–71.

McNally, Christopher A., Guo, Hong, and Hu, Guangwei. (2007). *Entrepreneurship and Political Guanxi Networks in China's Private Sector* (East West Center Working Papers No. 19). Honolulu: East West Center.

McNally, Christopher A. and Wright, Teresa. (2010). Sources of social support for China's current political order: The 'Thick Embeddedness' of private capital holders. *Communist and Post-Communist Studies* 43(2), 189–198.

Merkel, Wolfgang. (1999). *System Transformation,* Opladen: Leske & Budrich.

Moore, Barrington. (1969). *Social Origins of Dictatorship and Democracy: Lord and Peasant in the Making of the Modern World.* Boston: Beacon Press.

Nee, Victor and Opper, Sonja. (2012). *Capitalism from Below: Markets and Institutional Change in China.* Cambridge, MA: Harvard University Press.

O'Brien, Kevin and Han, Rongbin. (2009). Path to democracy assessing village elections in China. *Journal of Contemporary China* 18(60), 359–378.

Pearson, Margaret M. (1997). *China's New Business Elite: The Political Consequences of Economic Reform.* Berkeley: University of California Press.

Schmitter, Philippe C. (1974). Still the century of corporatism? *The Review of Politics* 36(1), 85–131.

Schubert, Gunter. (2009). Village Elections, Citizenship and Regime Legitimacy in Contemporary Rural China. In Thomas Heberer and Gunter Schubert (Eds.), *Regime Legitimacy in Contemporary China. Institutional Change and Stability* (pp. 55–78). Abingdon and New York: Routledge.

Schubert, Gunter, and Ahlers, Anna L. (2012). *Participation and Empowerment at the Grassroots. Chinese Village Elections in Perspective*. Lanham: Lexington.

Schubert, Gunter, and Heberer, Thomas. (2015). Continuity and change in China's 'Local State Developmentalism'. *Issues & Studies* 51(2), 1–38.

Shen, Xiaoxiao, and Tsai, Kellee S. (2016). Institutional adaptability in China: Local developmental models under changing economic conditions. *World Development* 87, 107–127.

Shen, Yongdong and Yu, Jiangxing (2017). *The Advance of the Party and the Retreat of the Administration. The Politics of State–Society Relations in China*. Unpublished manuscript, presented at Science Po, Paris, 12 January.

Solinger, Dorothy. (1992). Urban entrepreneurs and the state: The merger of state and society. In Arthur Rosenbaum (Ed.), *State and Society in China: The Consequences of Reform* (pp. 121–142). Boulder: Westview.

Su, Zhong-qin and Fung, Hungai. (2013). Political connections and firm performance in Chinese Companies. *Pacific Economic Review* 18(3), 283–317.

Sun, Xin, Zhu, Jiangnan, and Wu, Yiping. (2014). Organizational clientelism: An analysis of private entrepreneurs in Chinese local legislatures. *Journal of East Asian Studies* 14(1), 1–30.

ten Brink, Tobias. (2010). *Strukturmerkmale des Chinesischen Kapitalismus* (Structural Features of Chinese Capitalism). Köln: Max-Planck-Institut für Gesellschaftsforschung.

ten Brink, Tobias. (2011). Institutional Change in Market-Liberal State Capitalism. An Integrative Perspective on the Development of the Private Business Sector in China. *Köln: Max-Planck-Institut für Gesellschaftsforschung*.

Tsai, Kellee S. (2005). Capitalists without class. Political diversity among private entrepreneurs in China. *Comparative Political Studies* 38(9), 1130–1158.

Tsai, Kellee S. (2006). Adaptive informal institutions and endogenous institutional change in China. *World Politics* 59(1), 116–141.

Tsai, Kellee S. (2007). *Capitalism without Democracy. The Private Sector in Contemporary China*. Ithaca/N.Y.: Cornell University Press.

Unger, Jonathan. (1996). "Bridges": Private business, the Chinese government and the rise of new associations. *The China Quarterly* 147, 795–819.

Unger, Jonathan. (2008). The strange marriage between the state and private business in Beijing. In Jonathan Unger (Ed.), *Associations and the Chinese State: Contested Spaces* (pp. 117–148). New York: East Gate.

Unger, Jonathan and Chan, Anita. (1995). China, corporatism, and the East Asian Model. *The Australian Journal of Chinese Affairs* 33, 29–53.

Unger, Jonathan and Chan, Anita. (1996). Corporatism in China: A Developmental State in an East Asian Context. In Barret L. McCormick, and Jonathan Unger (Eds.), *China After Socialism: In the Footsteps of Eastern Europe or East Asia?* (pp. 95–129). Armonk, NY: M. E. Sharpe.

Unger, Jonathan and Chan, Anita. (2008). Associations in a bind: The emergence of political corporatism. In Jonathan Unger (Ed.), *Associations and the Chinese State. Contested Spaces* (pp. 48–68). New York: East Gate.

Unger, Jonathan and Chan, Anita. (2015). State corporatism and business associations in China: Comparison with earlier emerging economies in Asia. *International Journal of Emerging Markets* 10(2), 178–193.

Wang, Junmin. (2016). Taking the 'Red Hat' off Chinese private entrepreneurs. *Sociology of Development* 2(3), 293–321.

Wang, Yuhua. (2016). Beyond local protectionism: China's state–business relations in the last two decades. *The China Quarterly* 226, 319–341.

Wang, Jenn-hwan, and Hsung, Ray-May. (2016). *Rethinking Social Capital and Entrepreneurship in Greater China. Is Guanxi Still Important?* Abingdon and New York: Routledge.

Wank, David L. (1995). Private business, bureaucracy, and political alliance in a Chinese City. *The Australian Journal of Chinese Affairs* 33, 55–71.

Wank, David L. (1999). *Commodifying Communism: Business, Trust, and Politics in a Chinese City.* Cambridge: Cambridge University Press.

Williams, Colin C. (2008). Beyond necessity-driven versus opportunity-driven entrepreneurship. A study of informal entrepreneurs in England, Russia and Ukraine. *The International Journal of Entrepreneurship and Innovation*, 9(3), 157–165.

Witt, Michael A. (2010). *China: What Variety of Capitalism?* Singapore: INSEAD.

Wright, Teresa. (2010). *Accepting Authoritarianism: State–Society Relations in China's Reform Era.* Stanford: Stanford University Press.

Wu, Wenfang, Wu, Chongfeng, Zhou, Chunyang, and Wu, Jun. (2012). Political connections, tax benefits and firm performance: Evidence from China. *Journal of Accounting and Public Policy* 31(3), 277–300.

Xi, Jinping. (2017). *Zhonggong 19da kaimu. Xi Jinping daibiao 18jie Zhongyang weiyuanhui zuo baogao* (Xi Jinpings Report on the Work of the 18th Central Committee). http://www.china.com.cn/cppcc/2017-10/18/content_41752399.htm (accessed 3 April 2018).

Xia, Yuanwang. (2018). Yong '*qin*' '*qing*' shuxie geng duo minying chuanqi (Use 'qin' and 'qing' to write many more private entrepreneur stories). *Henan Ribao* (Henan Daily), 16 April.

Xie, Wenjing, Liu, Keji, Xie, Fei, and Ding, Haoyuan. (2017). Political ties and firm performance in China: evidence from a quantile regression. *Journal of East Asian Studies* 17(3), 331–341.

Xu, Yekun and Li, Weian. (2016). *Zhengji tuidong, zhengzhi guanlian yu minying qiye touzi kuozhang* (Political Performance Drive, Political Connection and Private Enterprises' Investment Expansion). *Jingji Lilun Yu Jingji Guanli* (Economic Theory and Economic Management) 5, 5–21.

Yan, Xiaojun. (2012). 'To get rich is not only glorious': Economic reform and the new entrepreneurial party secretaries. *The China Quarterly* 210, 335–354.

Yan, Xiaojun, and Huang, Jie. (2017). Navigating unknown waters: The Chinese Communist Party's new presence in the private sector. *China Review* 17(2), 37–63.

Yang, Keming. (2013). Keep Business for Business. Associations of Private Enterprises in China. In Jennifer Y.J. Hsu and Reza Hasmath (Eds.), *The Chinese Corporatist State. Adaption, Survival and Resistance* (pp. 66–82). London and New York: Routledge.

Yao, Yusheng. (2012). Village elections and the rise of capitalist entrepreneurs. *Journal of Contemporary China* 21(74), 317–332.

Yao, Yusheng. (2013). Village elections and their impact: An investigative report on a Northern Chinese village. *Modern China* 39(1), 37–68.

Yu, Jianxing, and Zhou, Jun. (2013). Local governance and business associations in Wenzhou: A model for the road to civil society in China? *Journal of Contemporary China* 22(81), 394–408.

Yu, Jianxing, Yashima, Kenichiro, and Shen, Yongdong. (2014). Autonomy or Privilege? Lobbying intensity of local business associations in China. *Journal of Chinese Political Science* 19(3), 315–333.

Yu, Jianxing, Zhou, Jun, and Jiang, Hua. (2012). *A Path for Chinese Civil Society: A Case Study on Industrial Associations in Wenzhou, China*. Lanham: Rowman & Littlefield.

Zhang, Changdong. (2017). Reexamining the electoral connection in authoritarian China: The local people's congress and its private entrepreneur deputies. *China Review* 17(1), 1–27.

Zhang, Houyi, and Lü, Peng. (2012). Siying qiyezhu de jingji fenhua yu zhengzhi mianmao bianhua (Economic differentiation and change of the political status of private entrepreneurs). In Lu, Xueyi, Li, Peilin, and Chen, Guangjin (Eds.). *2013 nian Zhongguo shehui xingshi fenxi yu yuce* (Analysis and prospects of China's social situation) (pp. 301–311). Beijing: Shehuikexue wenxian chubanshe.

Zhang, Wuchang. (2008). *Pingshen mei you jianguo zheme haode zhidu* (In my whole life I have not seen such a good system). *Nanfang Wang.* http://www. jingjixuejiaquan.com/index.php/2018/10/25/28831ca826/ (accessed 14 August 2019).

Zhang, Wuchang. (2009). *Zhongguo de jingji zhidu* (China's economic system). Beijing: Zhongxin chubanshe.

Zhu, Guanglei, Bai, Xuejie, Zhang, Qingxiao and Wang, Gengshen. (1999). *Dangdai Zhongguo siying qiyezhu jieceng shehui shuxing wenti yanjiu* (Research On the Social Class Attributes of Private Entrepreneurs in Contemporary China). *Jiaoxue yu yanjiu* (Teaching and Research) 4, 23–27.

Chapter 3

Conceptual Framework: Private Entrepreneurs as a 'Strategic Group'

Norman Long convincingly argued that 'social action is never an individual ego-centered pursuit. It takes place within networks of relations, (…) is shaped by both routine and explorative organizing practices, and is shaped by certain social conventions, values and power relations' (Long, 2001: 49–50). Correspondingly, all social (and political) action is to be understood as group-related. The conceptualization of social (and political) action in China certainly poses a challenge, given the party state's strict control over Chinese society. However, it is important to continuously sharpen our understanding of group formation and 'strategic agency' in the Chinese polity in order to grasp both power dynamics within the party state and the evolution of state–society relations.

In his seminal book *Political Order in Changing Societies*, Samuel Huntington argued that new social groups must be integrated into a political system in order to guarantee order and stability (Huntington, 1996: 68). Following this, we argue that political order (stability) and political change result from *strategic group formation*, *strategic action*, *strategic alliance-building* (up to the point of *group symbiosis*), and the reconfiguration of power relationships between different *strategic groups* within a given polity over time. In this chapter, we thus suggest applying 'strategic group' analysis to investigate the evolving relationship between the party state and private entrepreneurs in contemporary China. Conceptualizing the latter as a 'strategic group' offers a new analytical perspective on private entrepreneurs, which partly challenges the findings of the above-quoted literature.[1]

So what is a 'strategic group'? Answering this question first requires some reflection on our approach to the concept of 'group' in social science theory. After this, we will turn to the key terms and concepts of the 'strategic group' approach that informs the empirical part of our study.

Departing from Bourdieu

In theoretical terms, 'strategic groups' analysis departs from how Pierre Bourdieu's conceptualizes social groups or classes. Bourdieu's concept sees groups of individuals who dispose of (varying degrees of) *'forms of capital'* and have a group-specific *habitus* within a given *field*, which is an arena of competition where different interests struggle for power and prestige (see Bourdieu, 1986, 1992; Eder, 1989). For instance, private entrepreneurs enjoy *economic* capital from their property rights[2], financial assets, and entrepreneurial activities. They dispose of *cultural capital*, resulting from their entrepreneurial skills and competencies (see also Gümüsay and Bohné, 2018) and from their educational credentials which, in China, are often attained by joining expensive short-term degree programs at renowned business schools or directly buying degrees (though the younger generation of private entrepreneurs increasingly attend Chinese or Western elite universities).

The *social capital* of private entrepreneurs derives foremost from their entrenchment in a multitude of local and trans-local *guanxi* networks

---

[1] 'Strategic group analysis' goes back to the 'Bielefeld School of Developmental Sociology' (see below). We adapted this approach to political science research many years ago and employed it to study democratic transitions in the 1990s (Schubert, Tetzlaff and Vennewald, 1994; Schubert and Tetzlaff, 1998); since the early 2000s, we have used it to study group formation and political agency in China, particularly looking at local cadre bureaucracies and private entrepreneurs (Heberer 2003a, 2003b; Heberer and Schubert 2012; Schubert and Heberer 2017; Schubert, Lin and Tseng 2017).

[2] Although the term 'property rights' is problematic in the Chinese context as all land belongs to the *collective* or the state, land-use rights are treated as analogous to property rights in so far as they are legal entitlements that guarantee exclusive use of the land during the contracted period.

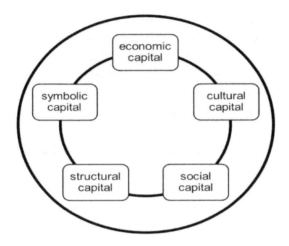

Figure 1:   Total Volume and Distribution of Capital in a Social Field

(including entrepreneurial networks) or personal relationships with party state officials. In addition, private entrepreneurs accumulate *symbolic capital* in the form of reputation, prestige, and privileges (often bestowed on them by party state authorities), i.e. social status. They also enjoy *structural capital, which we would suggest adding to Bourdieu's typology in reference to* specific knowledge of the operational codes and dynamics of the political institutions in the locality where they have set up their companies' headquarters. Structural capital can also be acquired through previous service in government office, as a village head, party secretary, or local People's Congress representative, or as a member of a government committee to advice on issues of policy-making. The different forms of capital can be traded — mutually converted, in Bourdieuan terminology — by all individuals within a social field, including private entrepreneurs, to strengthen their relative position within the field and to achieve their respective objectives (see Figure 1).

Positional closeness due to similar amounts and forms of capital creates not only equal positions of power for private entrepreneurs in social fields but also personal bonds and, arguably, a collective identity. Additionally, common lifestyle patterns, tastes, status symbols, and social practices make them notably different from other social constituencies.

For instance, dining and drinking together in expensive restaurants, buying into and living together in high-end apartment condominiums, active membership in exclusive entrepreneurial clubs and networks or participation and generous donations to social welfare activities not only result in an increase of social capital for private entrepreneurs, but also sharpen awareness of mutual commonalities. Hence, they cultivate what Bourdieu called a distinctive social *habitus*. Positional closeness within a given field of action (*Handlungsfeld*) and a distinctive habitus which private entrepreneurs have adopted, which at the same time confirms their field position, inspires an awareness of shared membership within a social group. At this stage, however, they do not yet engage in coordinated and mobilized *collective action* to safeguard and expand their group-specific interests. This is where 'strategic group' analysis comes in.[3]

The Origin and Theoretical Underpinnings of 'Strategic Group' Analysis

By applying 'strategic group' analysis, we refer to the early work of the 'Bielefeld School of Developmental Sociology', most comprehensively captured, in terms of theory, in 1988 by Hans-Dieter Evers and Tilmann Schiel in their seminal study on 'strategic groups' (see also Evers, 1973, 1997; Evers and Schiel, 1988, 1989). The members of a 'strategic group' are defined by the authors as being 'connected by a common interest in the maintenance or expansion of their shared acquisitive opportunities' (access to 'forms of capital' in Bourdieuan terms). Here, 'acquisitive

---

[3]Bourdieu suggested, by specifically combining 'habitus theory', 'forms of capital theory' and 'field theory', to have provided a 'theory of social action' (*soziale Handlungstheorie*) at the mid-point between Marxist-inspired class theory (structure-focused) and the voluntarism of contemporary rational choice theories (agency-focused). His concept of class — as determined by the distribution of available 'capital' between social groups in a given field and different 'lifestyles' (based on internalized 'habitus') — clearly speaks to both structure and agency. However, in the end, he did not develop a full-fledged 'theory of action' based on his theoretical premises that would explain social change. By applying 'strategic group' analysis, we attempt to proceed where Bourdieu stopped.

opportunities' not only refers to material goods, but also to immaterial resources such as power, prestige, and knowledge.[4] 'Strategic groups' pursue their interests by employing long-term strategies that eventually target the political system which is to be maintained, adjusted, or changed to suit the specific objectives of the 'strategic group'. Moreover, 'strategic groups' maintain an image of themselves as significant societal players or political actors, and build alliances with other 'strategic groups', sometimes resulting in a *symbiosis*, to pursue their respective interests.[5] Group cohesion, solidarity, and social integration stem from a common lifestyle (a shared habitus), increasing self-recruitment,[6] and the foundation of voluntary organizations. One of the core notions of this concept, alongside 'common interest' and 'collective agency', is 'strategic action'. As Evers and Schiel noted in a later theoretical shift, intending to place more analytical emphasis on 'strategic action':

> [S]trategic groups are defined just by the fact that they act strategically. Our theoretical framework tries to make plausible why and with which goals in mind, strategies are pursued, and which successes and failures of the bundled strategies can be considered possible outcomes (1989: 567).

---

[4] In their 1988 study, Evers and Schiel established a link between specific 'modes of appropriation' and 'strategic groups', whose intention it is to protect and expand their 'mode of appropriation', resulting in corresponding political orientations or ideologies concerning the way a political system should be structured. Their later shift to 'strategic action' as the major criterion to define 'strategic groups' was due to the fact that a materialist analysis was not very fruitful and caused a whole plethora of theoretical problems.

[5] For the Chinese case, it has often been argued that party bureaucrats and private entrepreneurs have co-existed in symbiosis since the early years of 'reform and opening' (*gaige kaifang*), with many party cadres 'jumping into the (capitalist) sea' (*xiahai*) and many private entrepreneurs seeking to establish close clientelist relations with the party state to nurture their economic undertakings. Symbiosis is also characteristic for the relationship between entrepreneurs and the military in Indonesia and Thailand, even today.

[6] In the original theory, self-recruitment alluded to the observation, as captured in the famous 'Law of the Bureaucracy', that strategic groups do systematically expand the number of their group-members in order to increase political influence and facilitate access to important resources.

From this perspective, 'strategic groups' are categorically different from 'interest groups' or 'power elites', as delimited and observable objects, but also from 'classes' which are categories stemming from social aggregation and theoretical abstraction. In fact, 'strategic groups' come close to what Bourdieu meant when he conceptualized strategic action in social fields (and what Giddens meant by 'structured agency' in his revision of class theory). 'Strategic groups' occupy a medium-range position between collective actors (agency) and classes (structure), hence have a 'dual nature' in that they embody the structural segmentation of a given society on the one hand and the actor-centered dimension of that segmentation on the other. Put differently, 'strategic groups' are both an analytical category and empirical object. Hence, 'strategic groups', like private entrepreneurs, bureaucrats, landlords, public servants, professionals or workers, are analytical categories (or a theoretical construct) in so far as they help us to understand the 'deep structure' of a given society by abstracting from observable objects like political elites or interest groups (and their manifold alliances crisscrossing class divisions). At the same time, however, they do figure as the empirical manifestations of 'strategic groups' 'at the surface of society' and thus are observable objects.[7]

The theoretical tension between a 'strategic group' understood as an analytical category and an empirical object at the same time also determines our adaption of the original concept which links the rise and decline of 'strategic groups' to the process of class formation within a given society. From our point of view as political scientists, strategic groups are not only the result of social segmentation but also of the similar exposure of individuals to the structural and institutional constraints of a given political system which binds them together and urges them into action within

---

[7]This was also the original understanding of Evers and Schiel of 'strategic groups': 'In our approach, we try to mediate between the theoretical system of classes as a deep structure and the empirical data of the surface' (1988: 13). In that sense, 'strategic groups', as a theoretical construct, bridge the Weberian distinction between ideal type (*Idealtyp*) and real type (*Realtyp*). Analytically, the term 'strategic group' is also a heuristic device to deal with the fact that, as Mancur Olson (1971) has convincingly shown, all social action is goal-oriented; empirically, it draws on the fact that the actors in pursuit of these goals are observable, though they are not necessarily acquainted with all the others who are following the same courses of action in different places at the same time.

contested social fields. The term 'strategic groups' thus denotes a specific power configuration within a political system and, at the same time, highlights the strategic agency of collective actors to maintain or expand their privileged position within a social field or the polity.

Core Group and Clientele

Essential to the concept is further the distinction within 'strategic groups' between a *core group* and a clientele. It is the core group — or 'leadership group', in Gidden's terminology — that, at least heuristically, represents the wider group, or clientele, and engages in 'strategic action' to protect the collective interests of all group members. As in our case, large and influential entrepreneurs with high levels of social standing among the populace and the cadre bureaucracies constitute the core group, whereas small- and medium-sized entrepreneurs figure as their clientele. The former have privileged access to high-level party-state officials, are often nominated to People's Congresses, People's Consultative Conferences or Party Congresses at higher administrative levels, serve in leading positions in China's 'Democratic Parties' (*minzhu dangpai*), often figure as presidents or prominent members of big business associations and entrepreneurial clubs, and are in possession of influential *guanxi*-networks connecting them informally with other members of the economic and political elite. Large entrepreneurs dispose of substantial economic and social resources which can be mobilized for political purposes. Obviously, party state officials at all administrative levels pay more attention to larger and more significant entrepreneurs than to the owners of small- and medium-sized companies. Large entrepreneurs, for their part, may support or represent the latter when talking to government authorities. For example, the owner of a large company in Kunming producing health care products told us that he would regularly arrange meetings in his company inviting entrepreneurs as well as experts and leading officials from relevant government bureaus to discuss the development of the health care sector, other policy demands or business problems concerning companies of varying scale.[8] A leading figure of the China Chamber of Private Economy International

---

[8] Interview, Kunming, 10 March 2017.

Cooperation (*Zhongguo minying jingji guoji hezuo shanghui*) under the All-China Federation of Industry and Commerce (*Gongshanglian*)[9] pointed out:

> Larger entrepreneurs are more self-confident than owners of small and medium-sized enterprises. As a rule they approach the government directly. If necessary they establish contacts to governments in support of small and medium-sized enterprises.[10]

They engage in systematic and high-level lobbying and push for policy change that primarily serves their own businesses and industries, but may eventually help other entrepreneurs as well. The (social) capital of small- and medium-sized business entrepreneurs is more limited (though they may be quite important in localities with an underdeveloped private sector). Therefore, they frequently rely on large entrepreneurs, who are willing to spend part of their social capital to the benefit of the whole 'strategic group'.[11] Ideally, the core group is the catalyst of the thinking and strategic action of all other group members in their common struggle for an advantageous field position, i.e. access to critical resources and power which guarantee the group's survival and further development. Due to its social status and high-level political connectedness, the core group arguably enjoys the clientele's support and trust to serve all group member's interests. This becomes most obvious, as we show later in more detail, when core group members are voted into leading positions in business associations and, consequently, then expected to trade their social capital for solving problems of individual members or the wider constituency of private entrepreneurs.[12]

---

[9]The Federation of Industries and Commerce is a-party affiliated organization under the CCP's United Front Department.

[10]Interview, Beijing, 3 March 2017.

[11]Small and medium-sized business entrepreneurs help large business entrepreneurs to build up even more social capital by voting them into their positions as leaders of business associations or, by corporate vote, recommending them for political office to government and party authorities.

[12]Larger entrepreneurs are also sought after by their smaller peers on a private level and asked for help related to issues the latter cannot handle themselves.

Collective 'strategic action'

The term 'strategic action' refers to goal-oriented action to preserve and extend access to resources deemed important for strengthening the position of a 'strategic group' in social fields. 'Strategic action' is usually coordinated and carried out by specific interest organizations or networks which can be understood as action platforms of strategic groups. Berner speaks of *organized networks of collective strategic actors*, making the point that business associations, clubs, professional organizations, and parties serve 'strategic groups' as *nodal points* or *nerve centers* where strategic action is devised, planned, and communicated to all members of the network (2005: 6). Put differently, these nodal points enable strategic groups to bundle their overarching interests and turn them into strategic action without speaking to all members of the group:

> People only need to get in contact with one member of an association to be able, in principle, to communicate with all. The flow of information is easier, more reliable, and less dependent on coincidence than in pure personal relations. At the same time, the chance to actually influence political decisions is vastly improved by organizations as collective lobbying and bargaining are more momentous than individual efforts (*ibid*).

This theoretical conceptualization has important implications for our understanding of *collective action* by 'strategic groups', which figures prominently when we analyze the political significance of private entrepreneurs and state–business relations in contemporary China.

In China, resources for collective action are controlled by the party state, and the costs of participating in such action can be high. However, party state authorities — by controlling access to land, capital, market information, and *guanxi* — can at any time intervene in private enterprises, forcing companies into compliance with state policies. As such, private entrepreneurs have no choice but to attempt to influence political decision-making and thus create a more favorable environment for their business operations. This is particularly true of companies which rely on public resources or depend heavily on government procurement. Hence, they make use of and cultivate different official and unofficial communication channels to officials and, as we argue, engage in manifold patterns of (collective) *strategic* action to safeguard their interests (see Chapter 4). In fact, many of our respondents confirmed a self-awareness of private entrepreneurs as 'strategic actors'. For instance, one leading cadre of the 'Strategic Federation of the Shandong Chamber of Commerce in Guangdong Province' (*Guangdong sheng Shandong shanghui zhanlüe lianmeng*) commented:

> We call ourselves 'strategic' since we intend to act strategically. We want to collaborate in the long run and act with determination and a clear objective and vision. (…) We have to unite closely and to look for partners who can help us to increase our influence. We have to exchange information, meet, discuss and coordinate our action and we have to lobby.[13]

Acting strategically as a group means acting goal-oriented and planned: However, it does not necessarily mean acting in a coordinated fashion across space, i.e. translocally; neither does it mean openly challenging state power. But how can we understand and conceptualize unco-ordinated collective strategic action? James C. Scott argues that

> (t)here is a vast realm of political action (…) that is almost habitually overlooked. It is ignored for at least two reasons. First, it is not openly declared in the usually understood sense of 'politics.' Second, neither is it group action in the usually understood sense of collective action. The argument to be developed here is that much of the politics of subordinate groups falls into the category of 'everyday forms of resistance,' that these activities should most definitely be considered political, that they do constitute a form of collective action, and that any account which ignores them is often ignoring the most vital means by which lower classes manifest their political interests (Scott, 1989: 33).

Hence, Scott defines these 'hidden forms' of protest[14] as manifesta-tions of collective action by which subordinated groups are responding to

---

[13] Interview, Guangzhou, 7 March 2017.

[14] 'Hidden forms' of peasant collective action according to Scott are providing false infor-mation about yields, land under cultivation and income, the delivery of low-quality pro-duce to the state, non-compliance with official regulations, tax evasion, slacking, theft, or

the hegemony and domination of the state apparatus. These responses are characterized by a widespread absence of coordinated and planned activities, and tend to avoid open confrontation with state power. Such collective action takes place in a low-key and small-scale manner; the actors are not necessarily aware of the fact that they are challenging state authorities. However, as 'unpolitical' as it seems, such uncoordinated collective action is still of considerable political significance (Hollander and Einwohner, 2004).[15] We hold that Scott's 'hidden forms' of protest pertain to those everyday forms of strategic behavior in a given society, which exist in different places at the same time, but without coordination of any sort. Although not belonging to the 'subordinated groups' in Chinese society, private entrepreneurs employ their own 'hidden' means and instruments to safeguard or assert their (political and economic) interests across China. While this happens without much coordination, the behavior of private entrepreneurs often challenges party state authorities, though they usually do not intend to openly question the CCP's legitimacy.

In a similar vein, Diana Fu has recently shown that individual actions create an 'accumulated effect' triggering social and institutional change, even if these activities are not coordinated and organized to accomplish shared goals. 'The power of individual contention', she writes, 'derives from the aggregation of atomized acts over time'. She referred to Hungarian historian István Rév who had shown how Hungarian peasants developed a sense of identity and belonging despite an absence of formal organization: 'They were atomized, but not completely lonely' (2018: 15–16).[16]

For his part, Mancur Olson has convincingly shown that even if single members of a group are acting in a way that benefits all members of that group we can speak of collective action (Olson, 1971: 22–25). In other words, even if, as Searle argues, private entrepreneurs act individually,

---

the destruction of public property. Even such 'low-key' forms of peasant resistance can in time entail political change because of the high social and economic costs it exacts. As Scott emphasized, peasant resistance will take such forms in any society where other ways of expressing discontent are unavailable. See Scott (1985, 1989).

[15]Economist John R. Commons (1934: 72) has already distinguished between organized and unorganized collective action and pointed to the 'purposeful' character of the latter.

[16]Fu quotes Rev (1987).

they often pursue a 'we-intention' (Searle, 1990; see also Sellars, 2000) or engage in 'collective intentional behavior', i.e. a 'shared intention of potential cooperation' (Schweikard and Schmid, 2013). Problems involving private sector development are rarely confined to individual enterprises and in most cases trigger demands for policy arrangements which impact many private entrepreneurs or business sectors. Hence, what individual entrepreneurs do for the benefit of their individual businesses is often part of a larger endeavor of private sector interests. As such, even when acting individually with a primary focus on their own business operations, individual entrepreneurs often defend or pursue interests relevant to the wider group of private entrepreneurs in China. If large numbers of them do so, and thus 'converge in the same direction' (Zhou, 2004: 321), they engage in (uncoordinated) collective action. If such action entails visible policy change that satisfies all group members then, arguably, the willingness to participate in further collective (and coordinated) action is strengthened — thus facilitating the formation and consolidation of an overarching entrepreneurial identity.[17]

Due to their 'positional closeness', private entrepreneurs pursue similar strategies to protect group-specific interests all over China, underpinned by a shared awareness of belonging to the same social constituency. In fact, direct communication and coordination are not necessary conditions to make them act as a 'strategic group'. While engaging in political action, members of 'strategic groups' do not need to know or even be in contact with other members of the same group in order to be influential and effective. This means that they do not need direct coordination, provided that a large number of them act in a coordinated fashion

---

[17]Along the same lines, Greenstein has made the argument of 'action dispensability' in connection with the question 'whether an individual's actions were necessary for a particular outcome to have taken place' (Greenstein, 1992: 123). In fact, individual action can be regarded as a constitutive element or part of collective action: If, as in our case, private entrepreneurs pursue similar demands and objectives and communicate them to party state officials through their personal networks, these individual concerns can add up to a meaningful impact on subsequent policy-making which then benefits all entrepreneurs. Becoming aware of the net-result of fragmented individual strategic action, the group awareness of private entrepreneurs and their inclination to collective action will be strengthened.

or at least in similar ways.[18] This is what we call the core of a 'strategic group' — influential entrepreneurs who set the agenda for all other members of the group (see above). This is an important point, which has been raised, albeit in a different context, by Zhou Xueguang many years ago, when he noted that

> (the) institutional structure of state socialism reduces the barriers to collective action by producing 'large numbers' of individuals with similar behavioral patterns and demands that cut across the boundaries of organizations and social groups. The creation and reproduction of these 'large numbers' of individuals provide the basis for social mobilization on a broad scale (1993: 58).

Since the position of private entrepreneurs in Chinese society — their field position in Bourdieuan terms — is structurally the same, entrepreneurial demands, their behavioral patterns (strategic action), and ways of thinking are indeed similar all over China. For instance, we found in our fieldwork that no matter the level of development in a specific location, private entrepreneurs everywhere complained about the difficulty of accessing land, labor, and credit, or about the privileged market position of state-owned enterprises, which enjoy favorable treatment of party state authorities and have ample opportunity to get hold of these production factors. All over China, private entrepreneurs are eager to be nominated to local PCs and PCCs or become honorary chairpersons of business associations, though only the most prestigious stand a chance to success in this regard. All over China, they work hard to open up or widen communication channels with local governments to solve company-related problems or influence local policy-making. To do so, they work through different

---

[18]The idea of uncoordinated, even 'anarchic' strategic action is also captured, at least to some extent, by the 'garbage can model' introduced by Cohen, March and Olsen (1972), who analysed decision-making processes in complex organizations like a university. Particularly, the aspect of 'fluid participation' in organizational decision-making has some resemblance to the idea of similar yet uncoordinated strategic action across space and time, though the 'garbage can model' wants to explain policy choices and not the observation that these outcomes may be the same in different places due to similar conditions for choice-making.

kinds of business associations and a multitude of informal circles. Although the strategies that large numbers of private entrepreneurs across China pursue are usually not coordinated beyond the local level, as this is strictly sanctioned by the regime, their 'dispersed' political agency produces arguably the same net results in terms of policy outcomes and institutional change as would be in the case of more coordinated action across the country. Once a social group or class, in the sense of Bourdieu, has crossed over the threshold of coordinated, collective strategic action in one or more social fields, a 'strategic group' becomes a major force that makes a strong impact on the political system. But even if that threshold has not yet been crossed and collective strategic action is still mostly uncoordinated, a 'strategic group' can bring about substantial change within that system.

Identity

Eckstein and Gurr have shown that, despite all their diversity, 'social units' such as social groups and entrepreneurial organizations constitute 'units of analysis'. Even when they 'vary enormously in size, function, and primacy for their members' they 'are collective individuals, having an identity (…) independent of their individual members' identities' (1975: 239). Private entrepreneurs in contemporary China, as we argue, do also share such an identity: They are well aware of belonging to a specific social constituency that differs from other constituencies in significant ways. However, different categories of private entrepreneurs display different levels of identity *cohesiveness* so that it is in fact more appropriate to speak of the common *identities* of entrepreneurs. Currently, we observe the development of collective entrepreneurial identities based on membership in business associations and entrepreneurial networks ('clubs' and chat groups), on joint action in formal political institutions (PCs and PCCs), on common political views coming to the fore during social interaction between private entrepreneurs, and on similar lifestyles stemming from a crystallizing entrepreneurial 'habitus'.[19] Online action

---

[19]The link between similar life-style patterns and collective identity among China's private entrepreneurs is increasingly discussed both within and outside China. See e.g. Thurman

in WeChat-Chat groups (*Weixin qunzu*), which has become increasingly popular in China over recent years, contribute to strengthening the sense of group identity among private entrepreneurs.

Charles Tilly (2002: 49–50) distinguishes between different identities in the political domain and examines the functionality of identities. Some identities have a mobilizing effect and induce collective action, some do not. Moreover, we have to differentiate between *mechanisms* of identity mobilization such as networks, business associations, etc. on the one hand, and *forms* of identity mobilization (formal, informal) on the other. In China, as our interviews showed, large entrepreneurs in particular — as delegates to local PCs and PCCs or as leading members in business associations and entrepreneurial clubs — display a rather strong group identity, as they see themselves as the forerunners of economic development in China. Most of our respondents displayed at least the existence of a number of group commonalities, which came to the fore in the way they reported on their respective experiences of private entrepreneurship in a difficult Chinese business environment, in how they depicted their lifestyles, expressed ideas concerning their understanding of the contemporary world and uttered sentiments unveiling a 'need of belonging' to overcome the vicissitudes of life in China's turbulent economy (see also Shepherd and Haynie, 2009; Shepherd, 2015; Gümüsay, 2017).

Tying in with Bourdieu's group concept, 'strategic group' analysis also departs from the claim that members of 'strategic groups' share a *collective identity*, with which they distinguish themselves from other social groups. As mentioned above, a collective identity among private entrepreneurs results from their joint belonging to online and offline networks and organizations spurring collective action and self-organization. It also stems from their shared life experiences, lifestyle patterns, value orientations, and strategic goals, which stand separate from their mutual exposure to the constraints and pressure stemming from the political system,

---

(2016), Pham (2015) and Di Zhu (2018), and the report on the lifestyle of China's richest people in *Hurun Baifu* (Hurun Report) 2015 or 2017. http://www.hurun.net/CN/Article/Details?num=5602F6026D18 (accessed 2 January 2018).

including their discrimination due to the party state's protection of state-owned enterprises.[20] As Xue *et al.* noted

> 'new technology prompts the discussion and interaction among dispersed people, shaping group boundaries and fostering collective identities based on common interest, beliefs, and ideas (2016: 5; see also Garret, 2006).'

Moreover, private entrepreneurs sometimes even appeal explicitly to an *esprit de corps* in order to unite and to defend their interests. Sometimes they do this to encourage entrepreneurs to act as role models within Chinese society, through philanthropic activities such as generous donations and a solid commitment to corporate social responsibility (Vermander, 2014; Quan, 2014), or by promoting and 'instilling' Confucian ethics within their companies and in the wider society.[21] As an entrepreneur in Xuzhou (*Jiangsu*) told us:

> Welfare and social responsibility should become part of an entrepreneurs' identity. For instance, if entrepreneurs take care of their workers, their welfare, their continued training and spare time, this could create a specific identity among entrepreneurs. And this would at the same time guarantee the success of entrepreneurs as a social group. If entrepreneurs are merely merchants (*shangren*) who sell or buy something then they cannot be called entrepreneurs. Taking care of one's workers and of societal issues, welfare and social responsibility: this creates a transition from merchants to entrepreneurs. And we have to steadily go down this path.'[22]

---

[20] As Liu (2017) has recently pointed out, these constraints mostly relate to the state's monopoly of land; over-bureaucratic regulation leading to additional costs; pressure by state-owned enterprises; difficulties gaining credit from state-owned banks or prohibitive high interest rates for private credit; and the heavy tax burden. The short durability of 3.7 years in average of private enterprises (2.5 years for small and medium ones) further highlights the difficult business environment for private enterprises in China (Liu 2016).

[21] In fact, 'Confucian entrepreneurship' has been a 'hot issue' in China for some years now, as a new brand of private entrepreneurs has embarked on the endeavour to develop a specific style of Chinese management — or management with 'Chinese characteristics' (Niedenführ, 2018).

[22] Interview, entrepreneur, Xuzhou, 8 September 2018. This statement points at the possible future of Chinese entrepreneurial identity characterized by citizen awareness and an identification with their responsibility for corporate social responsibility.

The awareness of being members of the same group and sharing a group identity based on the factors just mentioned feeds into the willingness of private entrepreneurs (and 'strategic groups' *per se*) to engage in (widely uncoordinated) collective strategic action. Hence, there is a link of mutual self-strengthening between strategic action and identity.

Summary

To sum up the key concepts and terms of our theoretical framework (see also Figures 2 and 3), we define a 'strategic group' as a social group, whose members:

- have common interests which they pursue strategically through long-term, goal-oriented collective action within a social field (a field of action) in order to influence policy-making, create institutional change and shape the political system in a way that their group-specific interests are protected long-term;[23]
- constitute a *core group* and a *clientele* within the whole 'strategic group';
- have an awareness of being members of the same group, draw boundaries between themselves and other social constituencies, displaying a distinctive *habitus* and *esprit de corps*, and hence share a *collective identity*;
- operate within a multitude of formal and informal organizations (interest groups and networks), by which they accumulate knowledge and capacity to plan and carry out strategies for safeguarding the overarching interests of all members of the group (see Heberer, 2003b: 6).

Moreover, members of 'strategic groups' do not need to communicate directly across the whole polity in order to coordinate collective strategic

---

[23]Take note that only under conditions of a 'revolutionary situation' would 'strategic groups' try to change the political system or replace the ruling regime with another one that suits their interests better. Particularly those groups that are part of a regime coalition (like private entrepreneurs in contemporary China, according to our conceptualization) are more prone to incrementally change the system from within as long as they feel sufficiently privileged or protected by it.

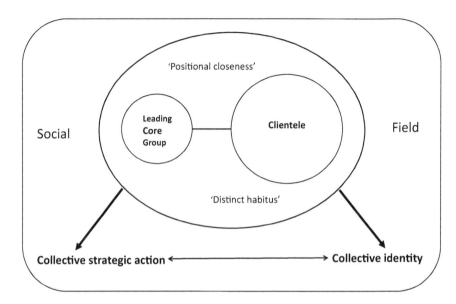

Figure 2: Key Terms of 'Strategic Group' Analysis

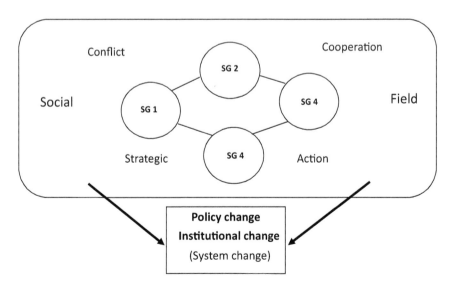

Figure 3: 'Strategic Groups' and Political Change

action, as the combination of 'positional closeness', a common 'habitus' and group-specific interests is a sufficient condition to initiate action which makes their impact felt everywhere.

In the ensuing chapters, we will assess the empirical evidence gathered during our extensive fieldwork on the different dimensions of collective strategic action by private entrepreneurs in contemporary China. We will also explore the formation of an overarching collective identity of private entrepreneurs which is, at this point, still hard to substantiate with the available data. At the same time, we highlight the impact of private entrepreneurs on policy-making and institutional change, though this does not stand at the center of our analysis. Finally, we will reflect on the evolving relationship between private entrepreneurs and the party state within the current regime coalition over the last decade, pinpointing changing power configurations which may re-define the significance of China's entrepreneurs for the future stability and legitimacy of the current regime in China.

References

Berner, Erhard. (2005). *Networks, Strategies and Resistance*: *The Concept of Strategic Groups Revisited* (Working Paper No. 218). Bielefeld: University of Bielefeld. https://www.ssoar.info/ssoar/bitstream/handle/document/42351/ ssoar-1995-berner-Power_resources_and_dominance_.pdf?sequence=1&is Allowed=y&lnkname=ssoar-1995-berner-Power_resources_and_ dominance_.pdf.

Bourdieu, Pierre. (1986). The forms of capital. In John G. Richardson (Ed.), *Handbook of Theory and Research for the Sociology of Education*. Westport: Greenwood, 241–258.

Bourdieu, Pierre. (1992). *Rede und Antwort* (Speech and Response), Frankfurt/M.: Suhrkamp.

Cohen, Michael D., March, James C., and Olson, Johan P. (1972). A garbage can model of organizational choice. *Administrative Science Quarterly* 17(1), 1–25.

Commons, John R. (1934). *Institutional Economics. Its Place in Political Economy*. Madison: University of Wisconsin Press.

Eckstein, Harry and Gurr, Ted R. (1975). *Patterns of Authority: A Structural Basis for Political Inquiry*. New York: John Wiley & Sons.

Eder, Klaus. (1989). *Klassenlage, Lebensstil und kulturelle Praxis*. Frankfurt/M.: Suhrkamp.

Evers, Hans-Dieter. (1973). Group conflict and class formation in South-East Asia. In Hans-Dieter Evers (Ed.), *Modernization in South-East Asia*. Oxford and Kuala Lumpur: Oxford University Press, 108–131.

Evers, Hans-Dieter. (1997). Macht und Einfluß in der Entwicklungspolitik. Neue Ansätze zur Theorie Strategischer Gruppen (Power and influence in development politics. New approaches to the theory of strategic groups). *Entwicklung und Zusammenarbeit* 38(1), 15–17.

Evers, Hans-Dieter and Schiel, Tilmann (Eds.). (1988). *Strategische Gruppen. Vergleichende Studien zu Staat, Bürokratie und Klassenbildung in der Dritten Welt* (Strategic groups. Comparative studies on state, bureaucracy and class formation in the third world). Berlin: Dietrich Reimer.

Evers, Hans-Dieter and Schiel, Tilmann. (1989). Strategische Gruppen und bürgerlicher Staat. Eine Antikritik aus Bielefeld (Strategic Groups and Civic State. An Anti-Critique from Bielefeld). *Kölner Zeitschrift für Soziologie und Sozialpsychologie* 41(3), 563–568.

Fu, Diana. (2018). *Mobilizing without the Masses. Control and Contention in China*. Cambridge and New York: Cambridge University Press.

Garrett, R. Kelly. (2006). Protest in an information society: A review of literature on social movements and new ICTs. *Information, Communication & Society* 9(2), 202–224.

Greenstein, Fred I. (1992). Can personality and politics be studied systematically? *Political Psychology* 13(1), 105–128.

Gümüsay, Ali A. (2018). Unpacking entrepreneurial opportunities: An institutional logics perspective. *Innovation, Organization and Management* 20(3), 209–222.

Gümüsay, Ali A. and Bohné, Thomas M. (2018). Individual and organizational inhibitors to the development of entrepreneurial competencies in universities. *Research Policy* 47, 363–378.

Heberer, Thomas. (2003a). *Private Entrepreneurs in China and Vietnam. Social and Political Functioning of Strategic Groups*. Leiden: Brill.

Heberer, Thomas. (2003b). Strategic groups and state capacity: The case of the private entrepreneurs. *China Perspectives* (46), 4–14.

Heberer, Thomas and Schubert, Gunter. (2012). County and township cadres as a strategic group. A new approach to political agency in China's local state. *Journal of Chinese Political Science* 17(3), 221–249.

Hollander, Jocelyn A. and Einwohner, Rachel L. (2004). Conceptualizing resistance. *Sociological Forum* 19(4), 533–554.

Huntington, Samuel. (1996). *Political Order in Changing Societies* (2nd edn.). New Haven: Yale University Press.

Liu, Xingguo. (2016). Zhongguo qiye pingjun shouming weishenme duan? Minying qiye jin 3.7 nian (Why is the durability of Chinese enterprises so short? For Private enterprises merely 3.7 years). *Jingji Ribao* (Economic Daily), 1 June 2016. https://finance.qq.com/a/20160601/007943.htm (accessed 1 May 2018).

Liu, Zhongliang. (2017). *Minying jingji daole zuiweixian de shihou? Zhongguo minying qiyejia zhen ku, zhen lei, zhen weixian* (Did the private economy arrive at the most dangerous point? Chinese private entrepreneurs: really painful, really tiresome, really dangerous). http://www.yangqiu.cn/waihui-gendan/1471842.html (accessed 3 May 2018).

Long, Norman. (2001). *Development Sociology. Actor Perspectives*, London: Routledge.

Olson, Mancur. (1971). *The Logic of Collective Action. Public Goods and the Theory of Groups*. Cambridge: Harvard University Press.

Niedenführ, Matthias. (2018). Managementinnovation aus China? Der Emerging Trend des 'Confucian Entrepreneur' (Management Innovation from China? The Emerging Trend of the 'Confucian Entrepreneur'). In Deutsch-Chinesische Wirtschaftsvereinigung (German-Chinese Economic Association) (Ed.), *DCW Yearbook 2018*. Cologne: DCW, 67–76.

Pham, Minh-Ha T. (2015). *Asians Wear Clothes on the Internet*. Durham-London: Duke University Press.

Quan, Zhezhu. (2014). (Ed.). *Zhongguo minying qiye shehui zeren* (Social Responsibility of Chinese Private Entrepreneurs). Beijing: Gonshang lianhe chubanshe.

Rév, István. (1987). The advantages of being atomized: How Hungarian peasants coped with collectivization. *Dissent*, Summer, 335–350.

Schubert, Gunter and Heberer, Thomas. (2017). Private entrepreneurs as a 'strategic group' in the Chinese polity. *The China Review* 17(2), 95–122.

Schubert, Gunter, Lin, Ruihua and Tseng, Jean Yu-chen. (2017). Are Taiwanese entrepreneurs a strategic group? Reassessing Taishang political agency across the Taiwan Strait. *Asian Survey* 57(5), 856–884.

Schubert, Gunter, Tetzlaff, Rainer and Vennewald, Werner (Eds.). (1994). *Demokratisierung und Politischer Wandel. Theorie und Anwendung des Konzeptes der strategischen und konfliktfähigen Gruppen* (Democratization and Political Change. Theory and Application of the Concept of Strategic and Conflict-capable Groups). Münster-Hamburg: Lit-Verlag.

Schubert, Gunter and Tetzlaff, Rainer (Eds.). (1998). *Blockierte Demokratien in der Dritten Welt* (Blocked Democracies in the Third World). Opladen: Leske&Budrich.

Schweikard, David P. and Schmid, Hans Bernhard. (2013). Collective intentionality. In Edward N. Zalta (Ed.). *Stanford Encyclopedia of Philosophy* (Summer 2013 Edition). Stanford: Stanford University Press. https://plato. stanford.edu/archives/sum2013/entries/collective-intentionality/ (accessed 30 March 2018).

Scott, James C. (1985). *Weapons of the Weak*: *Everyday Forms of Peasant Resistance*. New Haven and London: Yale University Press.

Scott, James C. (1989). Everyday forms of resistance. *Copenhagen Journal of Asian Studies* 4, 33–62.

Scott, James C. (1990). *Domination and the Arts of Resistance*. New Haven and London: Yale University Press.

Searle, John. (1990). Collective intentions and actions. In Philip R. Cohen, Jerry Morgan, and Martha E. Pollack (Eds.), *Intentions in Communication* (pp. 401–415). Cambridge, MA: MIT Press.

Sellars, Wilfrid. (2000). On reasoning about values. *American Philosophy Quarterly* 17(2), 81–101.

Shepherd, Dean A. (2015). Party On! A call for entrepreneurship research that is more interactive, activity based, cognitively hot, compassionate, and prosocial. *Journal of Business Venturing* 30(4), 489–507.

Shepherd, Dean A. and Haynie, J. Michael. (2009). Birds of a feather don't always flock together: Identity management in entrepreneurship. *Journal of Business Venturing* 24(4), 316–337.

Shepsle, Kenneth A. (2010). *Analyzing Politics. Rationality, Behavior, and Institutions*. New York and London: W.W. Norton and Company.

Thurman, Judith. (2016). The empire's new clothes: China's rich have their first homegrown haute couturier. *The New Yorker*, 21 March. https://www.newyorker.com/magazine/2016/03/21/guo-pei-chinas-homegrown-high-fashion-designer (accessed 22 May 2019).

Tilly, Charles. (2002). *Stories, Identities, and Political Change*. Lanham: Rowman & Littlefield Publishers.

Tilly, Charles. (2006). *Identities, Boundaries, and Social Ties*. Abingdon, New York: Routledge.

Vermander, Benoit. (2014). *Corporate Social Responsibility in China*: *A vision, an Assessment and a Blueprint*. Singapore: World Scientific.

Xing, Jianhua. (2013). *Fujian siying qiyezhu jieceng de zhengzhi canyu* (Political Participation of the Class of Private Entrepreneurs in Fujian). Beijing: Shehui kexue wenxian chubanshe.

Xue, Ting, Stekelenburg, Jacquelien van, and Klandermans, Bert. (2016). Online collective action in China: A new integrated framework. *Sociopedia.isa.* http://www.sagepub.net/isa/resources/pdf/China%20Collective.pdf (accessed 2 September 2018).

Zhou, Xueguang. (1993). Unorganised interest and collective action in Communist China. *American Sociological Review* 58(1), 54–73.

Zhou, Xueguang. (2004). *The State and Life Chances in Urban China: Redistribution and Stratification.* Cambridge: Cambridge University Press.

Zhu, Di. (2018). *Consumption Patterns of the Middle Class in Contemporary China.* Singapore: World Scientific.

Chapter 4

Investigating Strategic Action via Formal Channels

The future of 'Socialism with Chinese characteristics', economic and technical innovation and the accomplishment of the Party's paramount goal to make China become an 'overall and fully developed country by 2050', as prominently emphasized during the 19th National Party Congress of the CCP in October 2017, certainly depends on the sound development of the private economy and on private entrepreneurship. In fact, in today's China, local governments depend more than ever on private sector success, the subsequent tax revenues stemming therefrom, and the provision of employment.[1] It can thus be expected that

---

[1] For instance, in Xuchang, Henan Province, private sector entities accounted for 97 percent of all enterprises, 85 percent of all jobs, and more than 80 percent of the local GDP and tax income in 2018. See *Minying jingji shuxie 'Xuchang xianxiang' — Xuchang shi fazhan minying jingji cujin minjian touzi jishi zhi* (Documentary 1: Private economy writes the 'Xuchang phenomenon' — Xuchang city develops private economy and private investment). *Henan Ribao (Henan Daily)*, 10 April 2018. https://news.dahe.cn/2018/04-10/294818.html (accessed 7 February 2019). Employment pressure is particularly high across China, inspiring new ideas for job-generation. The government declared May the '2018 private enterprise job market month' in which networking services in institutions of higher learning, neighborhood communities, urban sub-districts (*jiedao*) and rural townships were set up in order to facilitate job seeking by juveniles. See *Beijing Wanbao*, 18 April 2018: 7.

entrepreneurial influence in the regime coalition will rise, however, the question as to how this will impact on regime legitimacy and stability remains open.

This chapter focuses on the strategic action of private entrepreneurs via formal channels while Chapter 5 focuses on informal channels and on so-called 'connective collective action'. Both chapters aim to show how entrepreneurs pursue their interests, exert their influence and extend their bargaining scope *vis-à-vis* the party state — and within the regime coalition which connects them to party state elites. We argue that by looking closely at the different 'weapons' of entrepreneurial agency through the conceptual lens of the 'strategic group' approach, a new and more comprehensive picture of the political dynamics of state–business relations in contemporary China emerges. In fact, private entrepreneurs are increasingly shaping this relationship, although much of the scholarly literature suggests otherwise.

Private entrepreneurs as a 'strategic group' make use of a diverse arsenal of efficient 'weapons', or strategies, to successfully safeguard and expand their group-specific interests *vis-à-vis* the party state. These interests can be roughly divided into (1) *economic interests*, i.e. an advantageous business environment with secure property rights, low taxation and reasonable access to land and credit, profit maximization and value creation as well as profitable business opportunities; (2) *political interests*, i.e. protection by the government(s) and meaningful influence on public policy-making; and (3) *social interests*, i.e. contributing to social welfare and problem-solving (social entrepreneurship) as well as public and official attribution of social status or *face*.

Generally speaking, we identified a broad diversity of strategic preferences among different types of entrepreneurs. For instance, the owners of large enterprises who assume public functions and play the role of what has been called an 'intelligent key player' in the management literature (Jahn, 1999), are more frequently members of People's Congresses and People's Political Consultative Conferences at the higher administrative levels. They are also prominent voices in industrial and trade associations. In fact, this entrepreneurial segment is more self-confident than smaller entrepreneurs and also more likely to initiate strategic action, and thus has greater political clout.[2] Its members constitute a core elite within the social constituency of private entrepreneurs and makes them the recognized spokespersons and representatives of the latter. As one entrepreneur put it:

> The government is only listening to big businessmen. Ma Yun [*the founder of the Alibaba Group, the authors*] is a prominent example. He has direct access to the Chinese leadership since his business is one of the largest in China and also enjoys a strong international reputation. The government listens to him and to his advice. He is also the president of the Zhejiang Chamber of Commerce and thus well connected in the business community. He can speak for us entrepreneurs and for our interests. Whether the government listens to an entrepreneur or not depends on the size and significance of an enterprise and the innovative character of its entrepreneur.[3]

Large entrepreneurs are, consciously or subconsciously, pushing the political agenda of private entrepreneurship in contemporary China. At the same time, business leaders with greater economic and financial resources are more prone to engage in individual-based political activities than the owners of small and medium-sized firms with fewer resources. This makes them a core group of 'opinion-leading activists' among private entrepreneurs (Dolata and Schrape, 2014), and sometimes even *political* entrepreneurs who mobilize support from within their wider constituency for a common cause. However, smaller entrepreneurs can achieve a 'large number effect', as one of our respondents pointed out:

> If you bring a larger amount of small entrepreneurs together and make them act in concert, they also can become an influential 'large group'.[4]

The leverage held by private entrepreneurs, with which they bargain with the party state bureaucracies, depends, however, not only on their

---

[2] Clifford Geertz emphasized early on that small entrepreneurs 'lack the capacity to form efficient economic institutions' (Geertz, 1963: 40).
[3] Interview, entrepreneur, Beijing, 2 March 2017.
[4] Interview, entrepreneur, Jiangyin, 25 August 2012.

size but also on a number of important factors: the significance of their respective business in a specific jurisdiction in terms of local economic development (compared to state-owned enterprises) and cadre performance evaluations, their financial resources, and their social capital. As Huang (2013) has shown, the more a local government depends on private enterprises in terms of tax generation, the lower its political control over them and the stronger the bargaining capacity of these enterprises in terms of influencing local policy implementation. Moreover, entrepreneurial leverage depends on the economic activity of a business. For instance, enterprises in the new energy sector are able to cash in on political opportunities and the attention paid to them by party state authorities so that, in some locations, they have meaningful power to bargain for land, tax reductions, and other policies beneficial to them (see also Huang and Zhang, 2018).

Overall, we can distinguish between three different dimensions of strategic collective action pursued by private entrepreneurs in contemporary China: (1) *formal* collective action; (2) *informal* collective action; and (3) *'connective'* collective action, which we treat as a special variant of strategic collective action in contemporary China. Formal collective action refers to the activities, most notably political lobbying, of private entrepreneurs in People's Congresses, People's Political Consultative Conferences,[5] Party Congresses, and in business (trade and industry) associations. In the following sections, we deal with collective action of private entrepreneurs via formal channels as observed during our fieldwork.

People's Congresses (PCs) and People's Political Consultative Conferences (PPCCs)

Entrepreneurs as PCs and PPCC deputies

The party state exerted itself at the beginning of the reform process to include private entrepreneurs in the decision-making processes of PCs and

---

[5]For private entrepreneurs the PCs are of greater significance than the PPCCs since many leading officials and, as a rule, the party secretaries and government heads of the respective locality attend the former's sessions.

PPCCs. A fixed number of seats in both organizations are reserved for business-people. Entrepreneurs are mostly nominated by the All-China Federation of Industry and Commerce (ACFIC), by the CCP or by non-Communist parties. According to a study conducted by the ACFIC and other organizations as early as 2009, 51.1 percent of all private entrepreneurs surveyed were members of a PC or a PPCC. In recent years, the number of entrepreneurial deputies in PCs, PPCCs or even Party Congresses at all levels has continuously risen.[6] It was also found that PC or PPCC members have increasingly taken over political positions such as that of a vice-chairperson of a provincial or prefectural city's PPCC, or a vice-party secretary of a municipality. In some places, entrepreneurs have become leading government or party cadres at the county or township level (e.g. a vice bureau head, *fukeji*) if their annual tax payment exceeded a certain amount.[7]

Private entrepreneurs have also entered Communist Party Congresses in increasing numbers over the years. According to another source, 7 private entrepreneurs were deputies at the 16th National Party Congress (2002), 17 at the 17th Party Congress (2007), and 34 and 27 at the 18th (2012) and 19th (2017) Party Congresses, respectively.[8] However, their

---

[6]Only in 2018 there has been a decrease, according to official figures. This might have been due to the anti-corruption campaign as many private entrepreneurs were accused of vote buying to get access to PCs and PPCCs in recent years. Within the newly established social credit system, all entrepreneurs running for a PC or PPCC position shall now be reviewed with respect to their tax payments, law-abidance, corrupt practices, environmental and ecological behavior, social responsibility, and so on. This may have led to more restraint on their part when it comes to running for public office. In addition, we were told that the Chinese leadership is trying to recruit more managers, technicians and lower-level staff from the private sector. Interview with Guangzhou Federation of Industry and Commerce, Guangzhou, 6 March 2017.

[7]See *Di baci quanguo siying qiye chouxiang diaocha shuju fenxi zonghe baogao* (Report on the data analysis of the 8th national sample survey on private entrepreneurs). http://www.china.com.cn/economic/txt/2009-03/26/content_17504790.htm (accessed 20 March 2016).

[8]For figures up to the 12th Congress see Sun Rongfei (2014); for the 2012 figures see *Shiba da minying qiyejia daibiao gong 34 wei bi shangjie 17wei duo yibei* (34 deputies attend the 18th Party Congress, twice as much as the 17 deputies attending the last congress). *Xinkuaibao* (Express News), 9 November 2012. http://news.163.com/12/1109/03/8FRC7DSU0001124J. html (accessed 25 July 2018). For the 2017 figures, see *Shenme yangde qiyejia cai neng*

impact is less obvious in the Party Congresses than in PCs and PPCCs and can hardly be researched systematically.

Lang Peijuan (2015) has shown that private entrepreneurs at the 12th National People's Congress (2013–2017) constituted the second largest group of deputies (23 percent), following the category of party cadres (64 percent). Private entrepreneurs also constituted more than 30 percent of the deputies from the provinces of Shandong, Hebei, Hunan, Liaoning, and Henan. At the local level, private entrepreneurs have been found to be the second largest group among all deputies in many regions in China (Zhang, 2017: 17). A leading figure of the Zhejiang People's Congress stated accordingly that, in the PC, 'the voice of entrepreneurs is strong and one of the common people weak'.[9] In fact, private entrepreneurs are very eager to secure nominations to PCs and PPCCs. Once a PC or PPCC deputy, they also qualify for leading positions in business associations (see below). For example, one private entrepreneur interviewed in Jimo (Qingdao) was not only a member of the Qingdao Political PPCC but concurrently chairman of the 'Committee for Promoting Small- and Medium-Sized Enterprises' of an urban district in Qingdao city. He noted:

> Being a member of the Political Consultative Conference of Qingdao opens the door for further influential positions. We can use these positions for supporting private sector development which is crucial to China's further progress.[10]

Another entrepreneur told us that he was also chairman of Qingdao's 'Weifang Chamber of Commerce'.[11] Both emphasized that membership

---

dangxuan shijiuda daibiao? (Which kind of entrepreneurs can be elected deputies to the 19th Party Congress?). *Jingji Zhoukan* (*Economic Weekly*) 40, 16 October. http://money.163. com/17/1016/23/D0TH8RRH002580S6.html#from=keyscan (accessed 25 July 2018). In the latter report, private sector deputies are called 'red entrepreneurs' (*hongse qiyejia*). The report also contains a name list of these deputies. It is further argued here that 99.9 percent of all private enterprises have party organizations.
[9] Interview, Hangzhou, 3 April 2018.
[10] Interview, entrepreneur, Jimo, 1 March 2016.
[11] Weifang is a prefectural city in Eastern Shandong Province.

in PCs or PPCCs strengthened their connections to local governments and other entrepreneurs and were also helpful to push through new business deals.[12] Therefore, a seat in a PC or PPCC is an important component of an entrepreneur's social capital that facilitates access to influential entrepreneurial networks, though it also works the other way round: Having secured a fair amount of social capital by becoming a leading official or chairman of a renowned business association, the probability that a private entrepreneur will be nominated as a deputy to a PC or PPCC rises considerably. Thus, seeking PC or PPCC membership is one of the core strategic interests of private entrepreneurs in contemporary China, no matter how restricted their impact on formal policy-making in these bodies may be.

Becoming a politically active entrepreneur also correlates with great individual wealth. In 2014, 52 entrepreneurs serving in PCs and 42 entrepreneurial PPCC members were listed in the 2013 annual Forbes China Rich List and had total assets of more than one trillion RMB.[13] According to a report by the All-China Federation of Industry and Commerce published in 2009, one-third of China's wealthiest entrepreneurs, with assets totaling 548.7 billion RMB, had become CCP members and 28.3 percent had become deputies to party congresses at various levels (Gongshanglian, 2009).[14] Interestingly, the private assets of the entrepreneurial deputies to the 2018 National PC and PPCC increased from 3.1795 trillion to 4.1162 trillion RMB, even though the total number of deputies fell to 152 in 2018, down from 209 the year before.[15]

---

[12] Interviews, Qingdao, 1–4 March 2016, and Hangzhou, 27, 29 February 2016.

[13] See 2013 annual Forbes China Rich List, https://www.forbes.com/sites/russellflannery/2013/10/13/here-comes-the-2013-forbes-china-rich-list/#59c98f39b9ac (accessed 25 July 2018). For the 2018 annual Forbes China Rich List see https://www.forbes.com/china-billionaires/list/ (accessed 25 July 2018).

[14] For an overview of the wealthiest Chinese entrepreneurs and its composition in 2016 see also *2016 nian Hurun quanqiu fuhao bang* (2016 Hurun list of the world's wealthiest persons), http://www.hurun.net/CN/ArticleShow.aspx?nid=15702 (accessed 4 July 2016).

[15] Luqiu and Liu have pointed out that according to a Bloomberg report in 2012 'the wealth of the richest 70 legislators in China's National People's Congress (…) was 12 times that of the total wealth of all the members of the US Congress, Supreme Court, and the US President' (2018: 389).

The majority came from business sectors such as pharmaceutics and health, internet technology, and the chemical industry (Zhu, 2018). In general, the composition of the group of entrepreneurs in PCs and PPCCs reflects the party state's policy to promote economic reform through industrial upgrading and technological innovation, and its determination to make progress in key industries such as artificial intelligence, robotics, and e-services. In the 2018 National PPCC, many entrepreneurial deputies are real-estate tycoons and owners and managers of high-tech firms such as e-commerce platforms, mobile game developers, cybersecurity firms, social network providers, and market intelligence companies. The intention seems to be to incorporate leading and promising private *technopreneurs* into the political system.[16] In addition, 'social entrepreneurs', meaning those committed to poverty alleviation and social welfare provision, are a further group of private entrepreneurs who have recently been awarded seats in the National PC or PPCC (Yu and Leng, 2018).[17]

All this points to the fact that it is the most promising and wealthy entrepreneurs who are selected to become deputies to the national parliamentary bodies and national Party Congresses. As we show below, these entrepreneurs do not only represent their individual firms and parochial interests but rather, in most cases, speak out for the private sector *per se*, addressing its problems and demanding action from the state to facilitate and push its development. In this sense, large entrepreneurs act on behalf

---

[16]See e.g. *Zhonggong Zhongyang Guowuyuan yingzao qiyejia jiankang chengzhang huanjing, hongyang youxiu qiyejia jingshen geng hao fazhan qiyejia zuoyong de yijian* (Central Committee of the CCP and State Council on creating an environment for the healthy growth of entrepreneurs, promoting a spirit of outstanding entrepreneurship and even better developing the role of entrepreneurs), 8 September 2017. http://www.gov.cn/zhengce/2017-09/25/content_5227473.htm (accessed 26 September 2017). See also Ma and He (2018).

[17]A Chinese report lists criteria for being selected as a deputy: being a role model ('model worker', *laomo*); displaying excellent and innovative entrepreneurship; abiding by the law; enjoying a favorable reputation with the local authorities and holding party membership for a reasonable time period. See *Minqi weihe yao jian dang zhibu? Zhongzubu geile zhengmian huiying* (Why must private enterprises establish party branches? A positive response by the Central Organization Department). http://www.guancha.cn/politics/2017_10_23_431863.shtml (accessed 1 May 2018).

of the whole group of entrepreneurs and display a 'we-intention' that is strategically employed to safeguard collective interests.

Strategic action in PCs and PPCCs

Overall, PCs and PPCCs at all administrative levels have become important platforms for private entrepreneurs to engage in strategic action. As official PC deputies, entrepreneurs are entitled to submit — individually or collectively — proposals (*jianyi*), motions (*yi'an*), written criticisms, and suggestions (*shumian yijian*) via the Standing Committee of their respective PC (Zhonghua Renmin Zhengzhi Xieshang Huiyi, 2011).[18] Motions are first submitted to the motion committee (*ti'an weiyuanhui*). The committee examines if a motion fulfills the respective criteria for being sent to the government. If so, it is passed to the government bureau concerned. In the PPCCs, less-binding 'proposals' (*ti'an*) can be submitted by the deputies, which are then passed either to the respective PC or directly to the responsible government bodies by the Standing Committee of the PPCC. Some motions are discussed during a PC or PPCC session, others are simply passed on to the authorities.[19] Government bureaus must by law respond to submissions of PC or PPCC deputies within three months.[20] So the critical question is: How do private entrepreneurs exactly make use of their mandates in the two national legislative bodies?

The case of the Wenzhou People's Congress is illustrative in this context. Entrepreneurial deputies are selected through three channels: The Federation of Industry and Commerce, non-Communist parties (*minzhu dangpai*), and representatives of the districts and counties. Each of these channels has been assigned a certain number of deputies. As a rule,

---

[18] See also *Renda yi'an yu zhengxie ti'an you he qubie* (What is the difference between motions to the PC and proposals to the PPCC). http://www.china.com.cn/chinese/zhuanti/274015.htm (accessed 04 July 2016).

[19] Interview, Research Office of the General Office of the Political Consultative Conference of Guangdong Province, Guangzhou, 5 March 2017.

[20] According to officials at the local People's Congress in Shenzhen, government offices are punished by point deductions in the annual cadres' evaluation process, if PC or PPCC deputies are not satisfied with their responses. Interviews, Shenzhen, 7 and 9 March 2016.

selected entrepreneurial deputies are large entrepreneurs with a major economic and social impact in Wenzhou. Of the 550 deputies, 110 (20 percent) were entrepreneurs in 2013. One of their major activities in the Wenzhou PC was to participate in inspection tours to private enterprises in the municipality in order to learn more about the problems the private sector had been facing and to come up with policy suggestions to solve them. These suggestions have either been submitted to the government through the normal PC procedure or directly to the mayor or party secretary of Wenzhou. If the party secretary reads and comments on such a report, its political significance and likelihood of implementation are particularly heightened and local authorities will pay more attention to it.[21] Therefore, these reports have to be worked out carefully and are an important component of strategic acting and lobbying on the part of private entrepreneurs.[22]

A leading member of the Wenzhou People's Congress told us that a significant change had occurred among entrepreneurial deputies over the previous two decades: a transition from a pure interest in improving the situation of an entrepreneur's individual enterprise to a stronger focus on private sector policies, and eventually to an interest in more general social issues. At the same time, as our respondent pointed out, collective action on the part of those deputies had become much more salient. Entrepreneurial deputies organize expert groups to investigate problems in specific industries and draft policy proposals for administrative reforms, local credit policies, etc. The success of such motions and suggestions depends on the urgency of the issue at stake, as perceived by the local authorities, but the fact that they are pushed forward by groups of entrepreneurs helps influence that perception, as does the framing of these policy measures as responding to the public interest. Moreover, PC motions become more pressing if they are coordinated with entrepreneurial deputies in the local PPCC and the local chapter of the All-China Federation of Industry and Commerce. This coordination has become an

---

[21] Interview, People's Congress Wenzhou, 25 September 2013.
[22] Interview, People's Congress Wenzhou, member of the Standing Committee, 25 September 2013.

important aspect of strategic action by private entrepreneurs in Wenzhou and, arguably, elsewhere in China.[23]

According to a report written by Chinese journalist Wang Zhongxin (2014) entrepreneurial deputies, mostly heading larger companies such as the founder of the Taizi Milk Corporation in Hunan Province, have repeatedly demanded specific training courses for private entrepreneurs at the Central Party School and a stronger participation of entrepreneurs in economic policy-making, among other issues. Obviously, this helped them to link up with the top echelon of the party state elite. They also requested that a top deputy position in each county government and even a vice-premier position in the State Council be filled by an entrepreneur, who would be responsible for designing economic policies. The report noted further that entrepreneurs openly demanded more political influence, membership in business associations, and local branches of the Federation of Industry and Commerce all the way up to positions as deputies in PCs and PPCCs, and as deputies at Party Congresses (Wang Zhongxin, 2014). Another report explicitly states that entrepreneurs are increasingly participating in both legislative bodies to pursue the interests of their enterprises and their industries, often emphasizing that this serves China's economic development.[24]

Many of their proposals target the party-state's control of the economy and demand better access to land, credit, public sector investment, tax reductions, incentives for industrial innovation, more autonomy for business organizations, and establishing vocational training programs so as to overcome a lack of skilled labor, just to name a few. In fact, there are many instances of individual initiative, particularly by prominent, large entrepreneurs, that target 'collective entrepreneurial goods'. An interesting example is Ding Shizhong, the chief executive and son of the founder of the prominent *Anta* sports products company in Jinjiang, Fujian province. As a deputy to the National PC, he submitted suggestions during the

---

[23] *Ibid.*

[24] *Qiyejia ti, yian jingji fenxi: 'xin yi lun gaige yuannian' de zhengce qidai* (Political expectations of the '1ˢᵗ year of new reforms": analysis of suggestions and motions of entrepreneurs), finance.ce.cn./rolling/201403/10/t20140310_2447847.shtml (accessed 28 January 2016).

plenary sessions of 2011 and 2012 calling for stricter action against the infringement of intellectual property rights, tax relief for private enterprises, easier access to credit, and so on.[25] Nan Cunhui, Chairman of the Board of the *Zhengtai Group* and a member of the Standing Committee of the National PPCC, submitted 11 proposals during the 2013 session concerning issues such as private investment in sensitive areas like finance and energy, private credit schemes, and tax reductions for promising enterprises.[26] Yuan Yafei, Chairman of the Board of the *Sanbao Group* and a member of the national PPCC, submitted four proposals in 2016. One of these concerned the import of sophisticated medical equipment by private hospitals, which had hitherto been denied access to such imports in favor of state-owned hospitals. Another deputy called for the equal treatment of private enterprises and state-owned enterprises, something legally mandated but rarely implemented, and another asked for stronger protection and support from the Chinese government for investments by private enterprises in foreign countries.[27]

Although these examples have all involved large entrepreneurs who spoke out at the national level, their demands are relevant for a broad constituency of private entrepreneurs across the country. In fact, similar issues are raised in different localities and at different administrative tiers all the time without much coordination, reflecting what we classified as *uncoordinated collective and strategic action* in Chapter 3.

Entrepreneurs often do not want to dominate PC or PPCC sessions by pushing their business interests too hard, as this can easily backfire, especially in recent years when private entrepreneurs have come under more

[25] Interview, 6 September 2012.
[26] See 'Lüzhi jinze gongyuan Zhongguo meng – fang quanguo zhengxie changwei, Zhengtai jituan dongshizhang Nan Cunhui (Diligently do one's duty to realize the Chinese dream – Interviewing the chairman of the board of Zhengtai Company and member of the Standing Committee of the PPCC), http://www.chintelc.com/news-view.asp?id=126 (accessed 26 February 2016).
[27] See *Minqi 'zouchuqu", shi gonggei ze gaige luodi de jihao jihui. Zhuan fang quanguo zhengxie weiyuan, Sanbao jituan dongshizhang Yuan Yafei* ('Going out' of private enterprises is a big opportunity of reform. Special interview with the Chairman of the Board of Sanbao Company Yuan Yafei). *Zhongguo Xinwen Zhoukan* (China Newsweek), 14 March 2016: 46–47.

Table 1: Motions Related to Private Sector Development, Hainan Province PPCC (2013–2016)

Year	Motions (total)	Motions related to private sector	Percentage
2013	557	15	2.69
2014	615	14	2.28
2015	552	19	3.44
2016	416	21	5.05

Source: Data provided by PPCC of Hainan Province, Haikou, 14 March 2016.

scrutiny by the party state due to the anti-corruption campaign. They have had to prove, as we were often told, that they act as responsible citizens concerned with overall public interest. Therefore, they tend to select only a few issues related to private sector development for submitted motions, opinions or suggestions during a PC or PPCC session.[28] In the case of PPCC of Hainan Province, for instance, entrepreneurs submitted between 2.7 and 5 percent of all motions between 2013 and 2016 directly related to private sector development in that province (see Table 1).

Most of the motions submitted concerned issues related to the provision of public services in urban and rural infrastructure, education, science and technology, culture, sports, and so on. As private entrepreneurs represent only one segment of the deputies in PCs or PPCCs, they have to bundle their individual interests into collective motions if they want to make an impact on local policy-making, as we were told by our Hainan respondents. Most of them had been pre-selected by the local Federation of Industry and Commerce which sends its own deputies to the PPCC. However, the Hainan case differs substantially from Guangdong Province where PPCC members submitted 177 motions (27.8 percent of all motions submitted) related to economic issues including private sector development in 2017. The respective report of the PPCC's Standing Committee

---

[28] Interviews with entrepreneurial members of the Guangzhou People's Congress, 6 March 2017; the Guangzhou Chamber of Industry and Commerce, 6 March 2017; the Qingdao Chamber of Industry and Commerce, 27 March 2017; the PPCC Chenyang District Qingdao, 28 March 2017; and the Qingdao PPCC, 26 March 2017.

specifically mentions that as a result of such motions a number of policies related to the development of private enterprises in Guangdong had been enacted and implemented by the provincial leadership, as spelled out by the 'Opinion on the Innovative Improvement of Refinancing Mechanisms for Small and Medium-Sized Enterprises', the 'Policy Measures for Stabilizing and Developing Small Enterprises in Guangdong Province' or the 'Policy Measures for Promoting Economic Strong Development of the Private Economy'. The report further specified that the provincial government supports the development of small- and medium-sized enterprises with less than 250 million RMB. Furthermore, in October 2016, the fees for administrative services for these enterprises had been abolished and tax rates been reduced.[29]

Our own research confirms these observations and also illuminates the thought-processes of private entrepreneurs in regards to their own policy impact in PCs and PPCCs. As an entrepreneur in Qingdao told us:

At times, membership in a PC or PPCC is crucial for influencing policies. If you are a member of an official organization this creates trust. I mean the government will trust you more. Among the entrepreneurial members of the PC or PPCC those from the same industry are most important since they can more easily align in their efforts and put forward motions as a group. Motions do not necessarily lead to a policy change. This is something we are certainly aware of. They rather attract attention to a problem that the authorities should tackle. Let me give you one example: If private enterprises obtain credit from a bank, they have to pay an annual interest of 10 percent. For state-owned enterprises this rate is 6 to 6.5 percent less. Recently we have complained about this in the local PC. Of course, this problem cannot be solved at the local level.

---

[29] *Chen Weiwen, Zhengxie di shiyi jie Guangdong sheng weiyuanhui changwu weiyuanhui guanyu shiyi jie sici huiyi yilai ti'an gongzuo qingkuang de baogao* (Report on the work of the Standing Committee of the 11th Political Consultative Conference of Guangdong Province) (17 January 2017): document received during fieldwork in Guangdong in March 2017. In a different study, Huang and Chen (2017) found that 25.6 percent of the proposals transmitted by the All-China Federation of Industry and Commerce to the National PC were proposals concerned with the private sector economy in general, 55.4 percent with issues of specific private sector industries and 9.6 percent with issues of individual business associations or individual private enterprises, a clear evidence of interest representation by the ACFIC in the National PC in the period 2012–2017.

But the outcome was that the city government helped us to obtain credit via the local branch of the People's Bank (*Renmin yinhang*). Normally, such loans are very difficult to get. Though we had still to accept to pay an interest rate of 10 percent, it is a success since first we were granted fresh loans, and second, to pay an interest of 10 percent is far better than to take a usury loan from private creditors with an interest rate up to 60 percent.[30]

Another respondent stated:

Entrepreneurs can influence policies. People's Congresses are an important organization for this. Though the government decides which suggestions can be put forward, it is not only money and *guanxi* which count. The government listens to constructive suggestions, particularly from larger entrepreneurs. Ma Yun [a business magnate, and co-founder and executive chairman of Alibaba Group, the authors] is an obvious example for this. Whether the state listens [to proposals] depends on the size of an enterprise. (…) There are, of course, further channels for exerting influence such as lobbying or bargaining via trade associations.[31]

Therefore, it is not always the 'big' policy impact which counts, but the many small steps taken by these bodies to promote the interests of the private sector. A female entrepreneur operating a medium-sized company in Qingdao who is a member of a non-Communist party told us that membership in the PC or PPCC does not have a major impact on her own enterprise. That would only be the case if entrepreneurs were dependent on public tenders or financial support by the government. Nevertheless, as she said, non-Communist party member deputies often meet to discuss proposals and motions to be collectively submitted during PC and PPCC sessions to enhance their possible impact. A significant segment of her party, the China National Democratic Construction Association (*Zhongguo minzu jianguo dang*), consists of entrepreneurs. The proposals or motions they presented to the PC's plenary session were, like those of entrepreneurial deputies nominated by the Communist Party,

---

[30] Interview, middle-level entrepreneur, Qingdao, 26 March 2017.
[31] Interview, entrepreneur, Beijing, 2 March 2017.

related to government policies pertaining to private sector development. The idea behind these suggestions, she emphasized, was more to help solve local problems than to criticize the government.[32]

Individual motions by entrepreneurs, though permitted, are not always welcomed. In fact, PC Standing Committees encourage entrepreneurial deputies to submit motions or suggestions in the interest of a larger group, for example, a specific industry sector or small- and medium-sized private enterprises.[33] We have found that proposals submitted by entrepreneurial deputies to a PC or PPCC on the county, city, provincial, and central levels refer to similar issues. Their recommendations are pretty much the same in most locations and often refer to issues like access to land and loans, tax reduction, industrial upgrading (premiums and awards for innovation, support for improved management and the education of professional staff), fairness in market access (investment by private enterprises in businesses still monopolized by state-owned firms), greater leeway for business organizations, assistance for the development of middle and smaller enterprises, protection of property rights, workshops on issues related to private sector development to be attended by entrepreneurial deputies and party and government leaders during the annual meetings of the two legislative bodies, better implementation of central policies helping private entrepreneurs, or schemes to ensure the continued education of entrepreneurs at institutions of higher learning.[34]

The local branches of the All-China Federation of Industry and Commerce often organize preparatory meetings for PC deputies or PPCC members to coordinate their submission of motions or suggestions concerning private sector development.[35] For instance, in the PPCC of Guangdong Province, there have been 36 issue groups (*jiebie*) for this purpose, and each PPCC deputy is assigned to such a group. Private

---

[32] Interview, Qingdao, 19 February 2015.

[33] Interview, People's Congress Wenzhou, member of the Standing Committee, 25 September 2013.

[34] Interviews with deputies to PCs and PPCCs in Fujian, Jiangsu, Hubei, Zhejiang. See also the case of Fujian province: Xing Jianhua 2013: 182–183.

[35] Interviews with entrepreneurs who were PC deputies or PPCC members: Beijing 2 March 2017; Guangzhou 6 March 2017; Lincang 17 March 2017; Hangzhou 21 March 2017; Qingdao 26 March 2017.

entrepreneurs can be members in different groups. Most of them join the economic group, but — depending on their respective business sectors — also concurrently join groups focusing on agriculture (as agricultural entrepreneurs), science and technology (as experts or owners of private research institutes), health (as operators of private hospitals), or education (as investors in private educational entities). Joining those groups and acting collectively in PCs and PPCCs also fosters group awareness among private entrepreneurs and encourages them to cultivate long-term strategic approaches to private sector development which transcend their immediate business interests.[36]

'Strategic corruption' in PCs and PPCCs

Quite often, it seems, private entrepreneurs engage in illegal activities to ensure their nomination to positions of political influence (Pei, 2016). In recent years, two major methods for acquiring deputy positions have been applied strategically: (a) bribing leading cadres who give final approval for entrepreneurs to become deputies or obtain leading positions in these bodies and (b) bribing PC or PPCC electors to support the respective appointments of entrepreneurs. In September 2016, it was officially announced that 523 out of the total number of 619 deputies of the 12th People's Congress of Liaoning Province had been dismissed due to election fraud, next to another 45 Liaoning deputies to the National People's Congress.[37]

---

[36] Interview, People's Congress Wenzhou, member of the Standing Committee, 25 September 2013.

[37] See *523 ming Liaoning sheng Renda daibiao sheji huixuan an ji cizhi huo bei bamian* (523 People's Congress deputies of Liaoning Province involved in vote buying cases already resigned or were dismissed), https://mp.weixin.qq.com/s?__biz=MzIwMTY1M TQ3Mw==&mid=2653311936&idx=1&sn=8d97cf501988b6aab4df23e19530ab76&sce ne=2&srcid=0914yLSverIzWg4ZMYcQRfE1&from=timeline&isappinstalled=0&key= 7b81aac53bd2393d944ccffd4b4a0536e9877a1aa87f4ebbb189d9127c4f0de8abbcc9788 e93c40f718536edf35368d6&ascene=2&uin=OTcwMDk4MTUz&devicetype=android-22&version=26031741&nettype=WIFI&pass_ticket=t07clFZl5dpercent2FFDZY1lcAo 2Xx7HpAUWS0jiCyFpercent2B0419JNokbQtk08xNPqBRfWz4hdpercent2B (accessed 16 September 2016).

Many of them were renowned private entrepreneurs.[38] In 2014, the CCP's Central Discipline Inspection Commission found that 518 of 527 deputies and 68 staff members of the PC in Hunan's Hengyang city had received bribes totaling 110 million RMB in 2012 and 2013. While the money primarily came from private entrepreneurs (56 percent), local cadres and managers of state-owned enterprises also paid for their election to the provincial PC. Shortly after this was uncovered, Xi Jinping himself stated that 44 of the 93 candidates for new deputy positions in Hunan's provincial PC were private entrepreneurs. He also pointed out that corrupt practices by private entrepreneurs were a widespread phenomenon in many provinces.[39] His statement resulted in the nationwide examination of the composition of local People's Congresses regarding deputies with a private entrepreneurial background.[40]

The Liaoning and Hengyang cases were certainly not the only ones in recent years. The official 'Reports on Crimes of Chinese Private Entrepreneurs' in the years 2012–2014, written by political scientist Lang Peijuan (2015: 25–26) showed, for example, that the number of illegal activities ascribed to this group was on the rise. Other reports have revealed that more than 100 influential entrepreneurs (including 15 PC and PPCC deputies) were detained and sentenced between 2004 and 2013 (Huang Ye, 2013), and described numerous criminal cases in which private entrepreneurs were involved (Li Junjie, 2010).[41] The hoped-for benefits of such corrupt behavior, which has been observed throughout the

---

[38] See e.g. Sheji huixuan an ji cizhi huo bei bamian (Deputies involved in vote buying cases already resigned or were dismissed), http://www.360doc.com/content/16/0914/12/195201_590722024.shtml (accessed 16 September 2016).

[39] Hengyang huixuan yin gaoceng zhennu. Xi Jinping zhuiwen '*Gongchandangyuan nar qule*' (Vote buying in Hengyang makes high levels furious. Xi Jinping asks 'Where have the CCP party members gone?'). *Yunnan Xinxi Bao*, 25 February 2014, http://news.ifeng.com/mainland/detail_2014_02/25/34146829_0.shtml (accessed 26 February 2016). Similar cases were found in Shanxi in 2000 and in Yunnan in 2003, see Li Yuejun (2014).

[40] Interview, Guangzhou People's Congress, member of the Standing Committee, Guangzhou 5 March 2017.

[41] However, against the background of China's current anti-corruption campaign, it is hard to judge from the outside to what extent these cases brought forward against private entrepreneurs are based on sound legal grounds.

country (Li Kecheng, 2013), include enhanced social status, better political connections, immunity from rent-seeking by local cadres, company protection, and improved business opportunities.

Also, in order to obfuscate their rising presence in local PCs and PPCCs, private entrepreneurs often register as workers, peasants, or technicians to veil their actual social background. All 15 candidates named in the Hengyang PC as 'workers' were in fact entrepreneurs, as were 10 of the so-called 13 'peasants'. Informal price-lists existed for these positions: 15 million RMB to be a deputy of the national PPCC and 25 million to be one of the national PC.[42] As such, fake registrations could only have taken place with the consent of the relevant party authorities. Again, this example illustrates the above-mentioned 'symbiotic alliance' between private entrepreneurs and leading local cadres all over China, which collateralizes the corrupt behavior of many entrepreneurs in PCs and PPCCs.

This kind of 'strategic corruption' to secure nominations as deputies to China's legislative bodies displays another form of uncoordinated collective action by private entrepreneurs, though one that does not immediately help private sector reform and may even be detrimental to it.[43] 'Strategic corruption', which is certainly not restricted to buying access to PCs and PPCCs (Pei, 2016), is a powerful weapon in the hands of private entrepreneurs, which threatens China's economic system, allowing it to potentially degenerate into 'crony capitalism'. Put differently, it can strengthen the collective impact of private entrepreneurs on policy-making and change power relations within the regime coalition to their advantage. It is no surprise, therefore, that the Xi Jinping government has increasingly targeted private entrepreneurs in its anti-corruption campaign in recent years.[44]

---

[42] Wang (2014). See also *Hengyang huixuan yin gaoceng zhennu* (2014).

[43] For his part, political scientist Li Yujun (2014) has classified this behavior as a 'survival strategy' in the rough-and-tumble of China's evolving market economy, which keeps private entrepreneurship in a state of political and legal uncertainty.

[44] The Report on Corruptive Behavior of Entrepreneurs (2014–2017) revealed that the percentage of private entrepreneurs involved in corruption added up to 84.1 percent of all listed cases, while the rest (15.1 percent) was traced back to state-owned entrepreneurs. See Lin Ping (2018).

At the same time, the reports on illegal behavior show that private entrepreneurs must be careful not to appear 'too political' or become involved in the 'wrong' networks, since criminalization or corruption charges may follow suit. The above-mentioned 'Report on Crimes of Chinese Private Entrepreneurs' also highlighted the political vulnerability of private entrepreneurs who, in many instances, are dependent on the goodwill of the authorities. As one interviewee frankly admitted:

> The destiny of entrepreneurs lies in the hand of the government, since the latter controls everything such as business licenses and permits, and all kinds of business operations.[45]

This dependence means that entrepreneurs have to turn to *guanxi* relationships with leading officials or to practices classified as 'corrupt' (bribery, etc.) in order to protect their businesses. The case of China's former security chief and Politburo Standing Committee member, Zhou Yongkang, who was put on trial for corruption and other charges and sentenced to life in prison in 2015, is an illuminating example of the close relationship between leading officials and private entrepreneurs. In the course of the investigation, almost 300 business-people came under investigation, and it were mostly prominent entrepreneurs who has been involved in such cases (Beijing Guofayuan, 2016). However, the anti-corruption drive under Xi Jinping, which began in 2013, rendered contacts between entrepreneurs and officials much more difficult. Currently, many cadres are reluctant or even refuse to meet entrepreneurs individually or, as it was common practice for many years, attend banquets or other activities arranged by entrepreneurs. Therefore, problem solving by leveraging good *guanxi* with government officials has become more complicated. As one real estate entrepreneur in Yushu County, Jilin Province complained:

> Prior to the anti-corruption campaign, officials gained profit from some large projects. But now, without any personal gain from such projects they are more concerned with their protection and safety. The political

---

[45] Interview, Qingdao, 19 February 2015.

situation is constrained now… nothing happens or it goes very slow, and we find ourselves in a complete deadlock.[46]

Non-communist parties and strategic action

Special attention also needs to be given to entrepreneurial strategic action occurring within China's non-communist parties, which are also represented in PCs and PPCCs. Officially, China is a multi-party state 'under the leadership of the Communist Party'. Since the early days of the People's Republic, eight 'democratic parties' were allowed to exist next to the CCP.[47] We interviewed entrepreneurial members of three of them: the 'China National Democratic Construction Association' (*Zhongguo Minzhu Jianguohui*), the 'China Association for Promoting Democracy' (*Zhongguo Minzhu Cujinhui*), and the '9·3 Society' (*Jiusan Xueshe*). Of these, the first consists mostly of entrepreneurs, while the second and third have a broader membership of intellectuals and professionals from various fields. All these parties, with a total membership of less than a 100,000, hold seats in PCs and PPCCs at all administrative levels. In fact, most of our respondents who were deputies of one of these three 'democratic parties' emphasized that they had joined them because doing so made it much easier to obtain a seat in these legislative bodies and thus gain access to high-level party leaders. Interestingly, they preferred a PPCC deputy position over a PC one, since PPCC deputies are simply nominated and do not need to be elected like PC members, a more complicated procedure. Moreover, our interviewees argued that the role of the PPCC has become more important in recent years and that the voices of their parties are more acknowledged and prominent.[48] Non-Communist

---

[46]Yushu, entrepreneur, 12 September 2015.

[47]There is another official category called 'no-party faction' (*feidangpai*). It does not denote a party, but an officially recognized group of socially respected or influential individuals who are assigned 'no-party faction' status after a thorough check on their personal integrity and political reliability. This check is conducted by the CCP Organization Department (*zuzhibu*). *Feidangpai*-status is another United Front mechanism to assert party support for those who may not want to apply for membership but are deemed important enough to the party for being particularly labeled notwithstanding.

[48]Interviews, Jinuo, 1 March 2016; Qingdao, 4 March 2016.

Party entrepreneurial deputies have also become more visible by acting collectively. For example, in Qingdao municipality two-thirds of the city's PPCC motions were submitted by entrepreneurial members from non-Communist parties between 2012 and 2017. Most of them were members of the PPCC 'Economic Group' or the 'Democratic Parties' Group'.[49]

Business Associations

Business associations[50] are an important organizational resource for strategic action by private entrepreneurs. They are generally defined as 'business interest organizations that represent their members' political and economic preferences, although at times they also figure as 'vehicles for governments to implement public policies' (Aldrich and Staber, 1988). Zhang and Zhu (2018) have shown that 'business actors generally develop more collaborative relations through extensive intra- or inter-sector alliances and through the comparatively strong coordinating roles of collective interest-representing organizations.' In addition, they are vehicles for organizing collective and strategic action and can serve as a long-term 'bridge' between enterprises, entrepreneurs, and industry sectors on the one hand and state agencies on the other.

From the outside, these organizations negotiate agreements with local governments based on issues considered important by their member enterprises.[51] Internally, they aggregate the demands and preferences of their members, foster compliance and, arguably, push for the formation of a *shared identity* among private entrepreneurs by 'unifying' their thinking and opposing 'bad competition to the benefit of mutual cooperation', thus increasing their willingness to engage in strategic collective action.[52]

---

[49] Interview, Qingdao PPCC member, entrepreneur, 26 March 2017.

[50] We use 'business association' as a generic term for the variety of Chinese trade associations, industrial branch associations and entrepreneurial associations.

[51] For example, members of Shenzhen's Furniture Industry Association are bargaining with the local government on issues such as tax reduction, environmental protection, special allowances, land acquisition, etc. Interview, Shenzhen, 21 September 2015.

[52] Interview, Haikou, 13 March 2016.

Associational diversity

Nowadays, Chinese business associations are part of a multitude of *entre-preneurial organizations*. Of these, many organizations, like the Association of Individual Households (*Getihu xiehui*) or the Association for Private Enterprises (*Siying qiye xiehui*) which were established in the late 1970s and early 1980s, are official or state-led (*guanban*) and have been established by the party state as a means of registering, organizing, monitoring, and controlling private enterprises.[53] The China Enterprise Federation (*Zhongguo Qiye Lianhehui*; CEF), sometimes referred to as the China Entrepreneurs' Association (*Zhongguo Qiyejia Xiehui*), is particularly influential. This organization, which also functions as an employers' association, not only protects the rights of entrepreneurs and represents enterprises in all respects, but also represents them in collective bargaining or mediating with trade unions and workers.[54] Though the Chinese Enterprise Federation is closely linked to local governments, it claims to be 'independent'. The president of its Guangdong branch even contended to be more powerful than the 'All-China Federation of Industry and Commerce', which is a United Front organization of the Communist Party (see below).[55] A leading official of its Shenzhen branch told us that the Chinese Enterprise Association's most prominent function is to solve entrepreneurial problems 'with the help of the government', highlighting the close relationship between this organization and the party state.[56] The China Association for Small- and Medium-Sized Commercial Enterprises (*Zhongguo Xiaoshang Qiye Xiehui*), for its part, represents the interests of

---

[53] Recently these organizations are undergoing reform. In Shenzhen they are already decoupled from the 'Bureau of the Administration of Industry and Commerce' (*Gongshangju*) and have become more autonomous. Membership is now voluntary and no longer compulsory. The purpose of these organizations is to represent the interests of small-scale self-employed firms. Interview with the Chairman of the Shenzhen Association of Private Enterprises, 8 March 2016.

[54] For more details, see the official homepage of this organization: http://www.cec-ceda.org.cn/ (accessed 3 August 2018).

[55] Interview, Guangdong Provincial Entrepreneurs' Association (Guangdong sheng Qiyejia Xiehui), Guangzhou, 7 March 2017.

[56] Interview, Shenzhen Entrepreneurs' Association (Shenzhen Qiyejia Xiehui), Shenzhen, 9 March 2016.

smaller private enterprises,[57] whereas the China Association for Private Entrepreneurs (*Zhongguo Minying Qiyejia Xiehui*), which operates under the auspices of the All-China Federation of Industry and Commerce, represents private entrepreneurs of all sorts.[58] There are many more business associations across the country, creating a system of highly fragmented entrepreneurial interest representation. That this might be a deliberate policy of the CCP to prevent horizontal and vertical integration of private entrepreneurs' associations is usually contested by government officials who argue that associational diversity is the result of the market which has created many opportunities for entrepreneurial organizations and that, in the end, 'competition is good for business'.[59]

Besides entrepreneurial associations,[60] one can distinguish between trade associations, or chambers of commerce (*shangye xiehui*), and industry-sector associations (*hangye xiehui*), of which there existed almost 100,000 at the end of 2016 (Xu, 2017). These often claim to be genuine interest organizations that effectively communicate business and trade issues to governments at all levels. However, their links to local governments are as strong as those of entrepreneurial associations, and party state officials usually consider them transmission belts through which to communicate government policies to the private sector and to help implement them.[61]

---

[57] For more details see the associations' website: http://www.zxsx.org/ (accessed 3 August 2018).

[58] See http://www.shzzpt.org/index.php?m=content&c=index&a=show&catid=140&id=6 (accessed 3 August, 2018).

[59] Interview, PPCC Qingdao, member of the Standing Committee, 28 March 2017.

[60] A number of organizations like the Association of Chinese Enterprises (*Zhongguo qiye xiehui*), the Association of Young Chinese Entrepreneurs (*Zhongguo qingnian qiyejia xiehui, AYCE*), or the China Youth Federation (*Zhonghua qingnian lianhehui*) specifically target younger entrepreneurs.

[61] See, for example, the implementation of local government environmental policies which are often steered by industrial associations: Hangye xiehui shishi ziyuanxing huanjing zhili: Wenzhou anli yanjiu (Industry associations voluntarily implement environmental governance: Studying the case of Wenzhou). 2015. *Zhongguo Xingzheng Guanli* (Chinese Public Administration), 10 March, http://www.cpaj.com.cn/news/2015310/n24933603.shtml (accessed 2 February 2016).

Business associations can be further divided into those directly established by local governments and those 'autonomous' chambers of commerce (*minjian shanghui*) set up by entrepreneurs themselves. The former are established by government authorities and are mostly funded by the government, including their leading administrative staff. They act under the auspices of the official All-China Federation of Industry and Commerce (ACFIC) on each government level. The latter do not receive government funding and mostly rely on fees and donations of their members. They do elect their leading officials on their own but still maintain a close relationship with their local government (Zhang and Ma, 2008). Therefore, many 'autonomous' chambers of commerce (or entrepreneurs' associations) still register with the local ACFIC chapter (see below).[62] As one entrepreneur explained to us, 'collaboration with the government is the most effective way of promoting our interests'.[63]

The All-China Federation of Industry and Commerce

The ACFIC (*Gongshanglian*) is a national organization under the umbrella of the United Front Department (*tongzhanbu*) of the Central Committee of the CCP. It has branch organizations across the country which operate under the government at each respective administrative level. It was originally founded in 1953 and was revived after the Cultural Revolution in 1979. In 2016, the ACFIC had 3,407 branch offices at the county level and above. Its total membership at the end of 2015 stood at 4.38568 million, of which 2.3146 million were corporate members (enterprises), 2.0154 million individual entrepreneurs, and 55,689 were 'group members', i.e. chambers of commerce (*shanghui*).[64] In addition, 41,670 chambers of

---

[62] Chambers of commerce are 'encouraged' to join the All-China Federation of Industry and Commerce as associated organizations but are not currently obliged to do so.

[63] Interview, Hangzhou, 21 January 2018. Kung and Ma (2018) have recently shown that good connections to local officials are helpful to alleviate the negative effects of weak property rights. This makes it reasonable for many enterprises or business associations to register with the ACFIC branch office in the jurisdiction in which they operate.

[64] An entrepreneur told us that the minimum criteria for becoming a member of ACFIC is enterprise assets of at least 30 million Rmb and an annual tax payment of more than 5 million RMB. Interview, Beijing, 8 September 2015.

industry and commerce were associated with various branch levels of the federation.[65] Each local ACFIC branch acts autonomously from higher organizational levels but maintains close links with party state authorities at the same administrative level.

Officially, the principal task of the ACFIC is to assist the state in managing the private sector. Moreover, it acts as a 'bridge' between the party state and private entrepreneurs. A document issued by China's political leadership in 2010 specifically demanded that the ACFIC represent the interests and demands of private entrepreneurs, thus strengthening its role in representing entrepreneurial interests.[66] Huang and Chen (2017) showed that the ACFIC's function shifted from that of an instrument of pure control for the party state to an organization increasingly speaking out for private entrepreneurs in recent years. The organization has been participating in the Conferences on Economic Development of the State Council and the National Development and Reform Commission (*Fagaiwei*) and has thus been directly involved in policy-making. In addition, it has been assigned 61 out of the 2,200 seats in the National PPCC, and similar numbers in local PPCCs.[67] Therefore, it can be concluded that entrepreneurs have a variety of channels through which to take advantage of the ACFIC for interest representation, transmitting entrepreneurial demands to higher authorities, strategic action, and lobbying activities.

The 'Regulations on the Registration of Social Associations' (*Shehui tuanti guanli tiaoli*) promulgated by the central government in 2016

---

[65]Official data provided by the English website of the All-China Federation of Industry and Commerce, http://www.acfic.org.cn/web/c_0000000200020001/ (accessed 25 July 2018). The Chinese website provides less and somewhat different data http://www.acfic.org.cn/gslgk_303/jianjie/ (accessed 4 May 2018). Both private and state-owned enterprises can join ACFIC and its local branches. At the time of writing no more recent data were available.

[66]See *Zhonggong Zhongyang, Guowuyuan guanyu jiaqiang he gaijin xin xingshixia gong-shanglian gongzuode yijian* (Statement of the CCP's Central Committee and the State Council on strengthening and improving the work of the Federation of Industry and Commerce under the new conditions), https://wenku.baidu.com/view/eda8cc593b3567ec-102d8ae2.html (accessed 6 April 2018).

[67]This number does not include the large number of private entrepreneurs dispatched by other organizations or not registered as entrepreneurs but as members of other social groups.

stipulates that business organizations are allowed to directly register with the Bureau of Civil Affairs without having to secure prior affiliation with a government agency, thus giving entrepreneurs more leeway to establish their own associations than other social groups. This doesn't change the fact, however, that ACFIC is eager to incorporate business associations into its organizational structure wherever they come to the fore, and that most of them actually register. At the same time, the ACFIC, whose leading officials were often high-level cadres in the party state apparatus before, positions itself between the local authorities and private entrepreneurs, which seems to contribute significantly to problem-solving in the private sector economy of the relevant jurisdiction — at least at the declaratory level.[68] For instance, ACFIC officials in Shenzhen contended that the chapter's close relations to party and government bodies where decisive for its successful push of recent regulations to protect the interests of local private enterprises.[69] However, whether the branch organizations of the federation are genuinely useful as platforms of entrepreneurial strategic action depends on the attitude and agency of its local leadership and can vary substantially across China.

In fact, we came across many regional differences concerning ACFIC activities. In Guangzhou, for instance, we were told that, with the support of the local party committee, the ACFIC would periodically organize meetings attended by representatives of all government departments related to private sector administration. In these meetings, representatives of industry associations could express concerns and make suggestions for how to improve the environment for private sector development. Moreover, critical opinions raised were put online in order to increase pressure on various offices to help in problem-solving. In addition, regular

---

[68] Interview, Shenzhen, 9 March 2016. The 2016 Spring Festival event of the federation, for instance, was attended by a member of the Standing Committee of Shenzhen's party committee who was concurrently acting as executive vice-mayor, and also by two vice-chairmen of the city's PC and the PPCC as well as other high-ranking local officials. See *Shenzhen Qiye* (Shenzhen Enterprises), 20 January 2016.

[69] Interview, Shenzhen, 8 March 2016. See also the volume *Cujin minying jingji fazhan xiangguan zhengce fagui xuanbian* (Selection of policies and legal regulations related to promoting the development of the private economy), 2014, Shenzhen: Shenzhen Federation of Industry and Commerce/Shenzhen General Chamber of Commerce.

meetings between the mayor of Guangzhou, the president of the city's PC and private sector representatives have been established, where the latter speak out and suggest practical solutions for pressing problems.[70] Our respondents among private entrepreneurs confirmed the existence of such channels but were somewhat suspicious with regard to their effectiveness. Nonetheless, they agreed that the ACFIC had been able to open and arrange new channels for strategic action *vis-à-vis* local governments.[71]

We found that in Northern and Southwestern China local ACFIC chapters are foremost concerned with implementing policies prescribed by local party organizations.[72] In the more developed coastal areas of Eastern and Southern China, however, they actively strive to improve the institutional environment for private sector development. At the same time, they tend to be more influential in larger cities compared to smaller ones. In less developed areas, ACFIC's significance for private sector development is rather limited. As e.g. the chairman of the ACFIC in Enshi city, Hubei province, told us:

> The Federation can only solve relatively small problems such as schooling of the children of private entrepreneurs. Sometimes I can help myself through personal channels. To be honest, currently, the chance to solve problems via our federation is relatively small.[73]

As seen across China, larger entrepreneurs usually do not need the support of ACFIC — or any business association, for that matter. The above-quoted chairman told us that larger entrepreneurs are indeed reluctant to attend meetings of the ACFIC. And the owner of the Hualong Trust

---

[70] Interview at the Guangzhou Federation of Industry and Commerce, 6 March 2017.

[71] Interview, entrepreneur, Guangzhou, 7 March 2017.

[72] In Lincang, a prefectural city close to the Myanmar border in Yunnan province, we were told that the leadership of the local chamber of commerce (affiliated to the local ACFIC chapter) was nominated by the United Front Department of the local Party Committee and appointed by the Organization Department of that Committee after upper level approval. Strongly controlled by the local authorities itself, the Lincang Chamber of Commerce strictly monitored and guided private enterprises (Interview, Vice chairman of the chamber, Lincang, 17 March 2017). During our fieldwork in Jilin province (Changchun, Yushu city) we made pretty much the same observations.

[73] Interview, Enshi, 10 September 2013.

Company, one of the largest private enterprises in Enshi, noted that he would not count on any business organization for support in business-related matters. His three sons were deputies to the prefectural PC and PPCC, and he himself used to be a member of the provincial PC. He was the largest developer and investor in the prefecture of Enshi, and thus was in a strong bargaining position *vis-à-vis* local government authorities: 'If it does not work here, I can always leave'.[74] However, such threats are hardly necessary. The close relationship between this entrepreneur and local officials was highlighted by the director of Hualong's public relations department, a retired former vice-president of the prefectural PPCC who, at the time of our visit, also served as vice-party secretary of the company. He was responsible for party construction (*dangjian*) and enterprise culture (*qiye wenhua*), i.e. as he explained to us, being in-charge of disciplining the company's workers and staff.[75] Large entrepreneurs like our respondent in Enshi often hire former high-ranking officials to ensure smooth business operation by making use of the latter's networks within the local government.

Regional difference and functional effectiveness

There are considerable regional differences in terms of the functioning and effectiveness of business associations across China (Liu and Zhang, 2018; Zhu and Wu, 2018). In South China, they seem to have much greater influence over local policy implementation than their counterparts in Northeastern, Northwestern or Central China, and also seem more willing to engage in collective action. This phenomenon is well known in China and very much stems from different levels of economic development and diverging historical trajectories in terms of private sector

---

[74]Leaving a locality in case of dissatisfaction with economic conditions is not uncommon for private entrepreneurs, as our fieldwork in Jinjiang suggests (interviews at the Jinjiang government's Development Research Centre, 5 September 2012, and with the party secretary of Chendai township in Jinjiang, 6 September 2012). However, many of our respondents stated that they would not change the location of their enterprise's headquarters so easily, as moving to another locality means the loss of precious *guanxi* and, therefore, more entrepreneurial risk.

[75]Interview, entrepreneur, Enshi, 16 September 2013.

development (ten Brink, 2013). As one private entrepreneur commented, 'in Northern China business associations are a mere formality; in South China, in contrast, they are imbued with more concrete content.'[76] Another stated: 'A major reason for the rapid development of entrepreneurs in southern China is that they act in concert (*baotuan*). In Northeastern China, they are considered to be 'lone wolves' (*dan da du dou*)'.[77] In Northern and Central China, entrepreneurs in many locations — particularly those owning small- and medium-sized companies — feel that business organizations are not of much use, and many of our respondents simply equated them with the government.[78] An entrepreneur in the county-level city of Yushu in Jilin Province complained:

> The functional efficiency of business organizations, particularly on the county level, is very low. (…) The government rarely cares about smaller enterprises. Big enterprises can easily obtain subsidies from the government. For small ones this is impossible. Local governments primarily bear in mind their own development reports and short-term achievements. They don't care for smaller enterprises as they don't care for a locality's well-being and future.[79]

This is not only the case in North China's 'rust belt', even in more developed areas, business associations are often conceived of as a 'second government' by private entrepreneurs:

> Certainly, the situation of business associations in Jiangsu is much better than in North and Northeast China. But it counts nothing compared with those in Zhejiang and Guangdong. In Jiangsu, for instance, government bodies were turned into business associations in a top-down fashion. Thus, they were operating like government bodies. Industry associations should actually be independent organizations of an industry sector and

---

[76] Interview, Qingdao, 3 March 2016.
[77] Interview, entrepreneur, Changchun, 10 September 2015.
[78] Some would even call these associations 'second governments'. Interview, Beijing, 3 March 2015.
[79] Interview, Yushu, 12 September 2015.

not government bodies. The government has not yet fully understood this.[80]

As this statement indicates, government guidance of business associations is particularly salient in North and Northeastern China, as in Jilin province. The secretary-general of the Jilin Chamber of Commerce claimed that his chamber, an organization affiliated to the Federation of Industry and Commerce of Jilin Province which operates under direct government control, would facilitate contacts to government authorities and leading officials. However, many interviewed entrepreneurs and officials of business organizations in Jilin complained that local cadres in this province were very 'conservative' (*baoshou*), which would hinder healthy private sector development. Again, such approaches differ hugely from those seen in the coastal areas in South China.[81] As a general rule, the less developed an area and the smaller the number and size of local private enterprises, the more rigid the control by local authorities. This often results in more individual activities on the part of private entrepreneurs seeking to safeguard their economic interests and little, if any, joint strategic action.

Even in more developed areas, business associations are facing many challenges. An investigative report by the Federation of Industry and Commerce of Guangzhou, an experimental city where reforms are tested to strengthen the development and autonomy of business associations, reveals that, even here, associations are facing daunting challenges such as: excessive administrative controls and overregulation by the government, an excess of association leaders, low levels of service and information provision for members, lack of funding, few members and professional staff, and also limited contact with local authorities (Guangzhou FIC, 2016).[82] Although there are significant differences between business

---

[80] Interview, Wuxi, director of a research institute focusing on private sector development, 26 August 2012.

[81] Interview, Changchun, representative of the Federation of Industry and Commerce, Jilin Province, 10 September 2015.

[82] An older survey among private entrepreneurs on their assessment of the work of business associations by the Qingdao Federation of Industry and Commerce in 2012 discovered similar problems such as insufficient membership services (30.0 percent); short-sightedness

associations in terms of effectiveness even within a single city, such as Guangzhou, the problems discussed above apply — in varying degrees — to all of them and negatively impact their reputation and standing among the community of private entrepreneurs. Hence, the role of business associations as a platform for entrepreneurial strategic action is often hampered.

The significance of associational leadership

Obviously, the impact of business associations on public policy depends on the quality of their *guanxi* with party state authorities (see also Wang and Zhang, 2014). Hence, it varies between business sectors and localities. As a matter of fact, leading members with strong *guanxi* with local officials are of utmost importance for an association's overall performance and success. For instance, one entrepreneur in Zhongshan City in Guangdong Province told us that the chairman of the Aerosol Industry Association was a highly prestigious expert called 'the father of Chinese Aerosol' and a close friend of his. The chairman frequently visited the enterprise of our interviewee, helping him and other entrepreneurs to solve practical issues through his excellent connections with leading cadres at all echelons.[83] In addition, as one female entrepreneur told us, 'not the trade association itself but the leading figures of an association are decisive, particularly if the latter have close relations with local officials.' This is, as she continued to explain, the most important social capital of

in their activities (29.3 percent); activities incompatible with an association's statute (24.5 percent); the arbitrary charging of fees (15.4 percent), etc. Qingdaoshi Gongshang Lianhehui 2012: 21–22. Replies to questions regarding the autonomy of industry associations and chambers of commerce were answered as follows: totally independent (37.7 percent); relatively independent (35.5 percent), not independent (23.8 percent) (2012: 16). In addition, entrepreneurs mentioned the following problems with respect to business associations: lack of funding (41 percent); lack of professional staff (38 percent); low quality of the association's work (32 percent); lack of government support (31 percent); low levels of acceptance and support by society (20 percent), and massive government interference (6.0 percent) (2012: 18). Many interviewees told us, however, that the effectiveness of business associations has in principle improved over recent years.

[83] Interview, Zhongshan, 16 September 2014.

an association. Hence, it is the business elite, i.e. those entrepreneurs heading large and successful firms, who have the final say in all important matters a business organization pursues.[84]

Usually, the leaders of industrial and trade organizations are renowned and wealthy entrepreneurs selected from those in possession of the organization's membership. Those elected must not only pay significant sums of money to an association but they must also be large, influential entrepreneurs with a broad range of contacts to party and government officials. At the same time, leading positions in business associations enable private entrepreneurs to expand their *guanxi* to local party state officials, reel in new business opportunities for themselves and earn seats in the local legislative bodies, which again helps improve their social capital and political connections. Once in these positions, they are then the preferred contact-point for local governments to help carry out specific projects in a jurisdiction. It is often senior local government officials and the leading entrepreneurs of business associations who negotiate on the implementation of upper-level policies for which entrepreneurial commitment is critical. As a matter of fact, local governments expect business associations to help them with local policy implementation. Along the same lines, they expect business associations to mediate in case of friction between government authorities and individual entrepreneurs. For instance, when an entrepreneur submits a petition to higher authorities, the chairman of a local business association may be asked to convince this entrepreneur to withdraw it.[85]

Sure enough, the leaders of business associations do not always act in the interest of the association's overall membership but at times use their position for pursuing their parochial business interests in the name of the association, something that can be highly detrimental to collective strategic action of private entrepreneurs.[86] However, this is the deal: Large and influential entrepreneurs help a business association by sharing part of their social capital to safeguard the collective interest of all

---

[84]Interview, Beijing, 13 September 2014.
[85]Interviews, entrepreneurs and representatives of entrepreneurial organizations, Shenzhen 21 September 2015; Qingdao 2 March 2016; Haikou, 9 March 2016 and 11 March 2016.
[86]Interview at the Wenzhou Chamber of Commerce, 24 September 2013.

members, but in return they expect, and are granted, some surplus value from this 'generosity' for their own political networks and business interests.

Cutting ties between governments and business associations (tuogou)

Business associations tend to recruit their leading personnel among influential party and government officials in order to get better access to the local authorities and to better facilitate communication. However, in May 2015, the CCP's Central Committee and the State Council issued a 'Comprehensive Pan for Separating Industry Associations and Chambers of Commerce from Government Bodies' (*Hangye xiehui shanghui yu xingzheng jiguan tuogou zongti fang'an*). This was followed by the adoption of the 'Administrative Measure for Leading Personnel of National Trade and Business Associations' (*Quanguoxing hangye xiehui shanghui fuzeren renzhi guanli banfa*) in September of the same year, which prohibits active leading party or government officials (*lingdao ganbu*) from taking over leading positions in such associations, as presidents (*huizhang*) or general secretaries (*mishuzhang*), for instance.[87] The idea was to create a distance between the business sector and local authorities so as to prevent the formation of an overly tight relationship and to make business associations more autonomous. This decision was by no means welcomed by the associations. In fact, as many of our respondents stated, close links to local cadres are indispensable for the work of business associations as they are the gatekeepers of critical resources and information upon which private entrepreneurs depend.

---

[87] However, implementation is sluggish, as the central government stated in 2017. See e.g. Minzhengbu guanyu qingli guifan yi tuogou quanguoxing hangye xiehui shanghui bu qi shoufei de tongzhi (Ministry of Civil Affairs on clearing up and standardizing the decoupling of national industry associations and chambers of commerce from government administration and from imposing charges on enterprises). (2017). http://www.gov.cn/xinwen/2017-06/18/content_5203355.htm (accessed 7 February 2019). Shen Yongdong and Song Xiaoqing (2016) have discussed the problems of the separation between governments and business associations in great detail.

As a leading figure of the Yacht Industry Association (*Youting hanghui*) in Guangzhou told us:

> Previously, the organization we were affiliated to [*the Maritime Safety Agency, the authors*] was responsible for our industry. The vice-director of the respective bureau was concurrently appointed head of our association. This facilitated our business operations and helped us to provide funding, advice and other support for our members. Now we are separated from this office and are left on our own. Everything is more difficult now. We face staff difficulties and a lack of financial resources. In fact, for everything we need such as imports, money transfer, industry and market surveys, service provision for members and official documents we are dependent on party state authorities. Now, nobody helps us to solve administrative and financial problems or problems with government bureaus.[88]

Another respondent told us:

> By prohibiting that local cadres become key figures in our associations we feel just like children without mothers. We are now lacking important links and communication channels to the local authorities.[89]

Recruiting leading local officials into a business association for reasons of *guanxi*-building with the party state authorities is one objective; another is the acquisition of public funds for running specific activities, which is easier for an association if it can work through an active cadre on board.[90] Due to the stricter separation of associations from governments, this has become much more difficult in recent years, to the extent that it causes financial stress. Many associations have tried to compensate their funding shortfalls by arbitrarily imposing special fees on private enterprises (often in the name of the local government). However, this practice undermines their members' trust in business associations which, in the end, is not in the interest of the party state. A document issued by the

---

[88] Interview with an official of the Yacht Industry Association, Guangzhou, 5 March 2017.
[89] Interview, entrepreneur, Hangzhou, 3 April 2018.
[90] Interview, entrepreneur, Beijing, 2 March 2017.

'Development and Reform Commission' (*Fagaiwei*) of the State Council in 2017 thus explicitly prohibited the charging of such fees and demanded stricter scrutiny of association expenditures (Development and Reform Commission, 2017). In order to counterbalance the loss of public funding, the central government suggested that local governments should instead pay for the delivery of public services by these associations. However, local governments often do not pay. A leading figure of an association in Hangzhou told us that until the time of our interview they had been waiting for government payment for services such as the introduction of standardization parameters, the organization of training courses, or policy suggestions with regard to industry sector development.[91] To circumvent the official requirement that they distance themselves from the party state and to ensure that the government continues to support business associations, many of them now frequently recruit retired senior officials as advisors. Having served many years in government, these cadres still entertain close contacts with party state authorities and thus are important figures for maintaining and stabilizing crucial connections between business associations and local governments.

Nevertheless, there have been some important changes in the relationship between the party state and business associations in recent years, especially after the launch of the anti-corruption campaign in 2013. Individual contacts between local officials and private entrepreneurs has become a sensitive issue that nowadays runs the risk of being labeled 'corrupt behavior'. Therefore, local cadres have become reluctant to meet entrepreneurs in private. A major entrepreneur in Mile County (Yunnan Province) investing in a large ecological forest park who, at the time of our visit, was vice-president of the provincial Sapling Industry Association (*shumiao hanghui*) told us that he does not dare to approach local officials individually anymore, but only in an official capacity through his business association. Only in this way, he managed to get a huge mortgage loan from the provincial department of forestry (*linyeting*). However, as a rule, entrepreneurs with less developed contacts to higher officials ask the respective association to guarantee for a loan.[92] This

---

[91] Interview, Hangzhou, 23 March 2017.
[92] Interview, Mile County, entrepreneur, 15 March 2017.

shows that business associations now assume a more institutionalized role in contemporary state–business relations, and even figure as a protective shield against charges of corruption caused by the illegal granting of an undue advantage. As the secretary-general of the Jilin Provincial Chamber confirmed:

> Because of ongoing anti-corruption activities, individual contacts to officials have become problematic. Contacting a cadre is very difficult now. Our association, however, can establish such contacts and arrange meetings in the name of our organization. This reinforced our function as a platform for the exchange between entrepreneurs and the government.[93]

Business associations and collective action

In contrast to North China, in southern cities like Wenzhou, Zhejiang province (see also Chen Yi, 2014), or Zhongshan, Guangdong province, we have found that collective action initiated by entrepreneurial associations is very common. Here, tightly-knit networks between association officials and government cadres, along with a high level of communication among member entrepreneurs, are conducive to proactively approaching the government in case of any urgent matters that associations may have identified. Thus, as has already been indicated above, in South China, business associations seem to have much greater impact on local policy implementation than their counterparts in Central, Northeastern or Northwestern China, and are also more willing to engage in collective action, though entrepreneurial interests and objectives are broadly similar across the whole country.

We have found many examples of collective action initiated by business associations. One entrepreneur in Hangzhou told us that the signatures of 600 renowned entrepreneurs were collected in the city in 2012 and sent to both the provincial government and Zhejiang's Bureau of Finance in a demand for stronger support in getting access to loans.[94] The entrepreneurs had two demands: (a) that the government should

---

[93] Interview, Changchun, 10 September 2015.
[94] Interview, entrepreneur, Hangzhou, 1 March 2015.

establish a special task force to find solutions to the credit issue, and (b) that the government should urge banks to repeal the decision to give no further loans to private enterprises. The background to this petition was that private individuals were offering short-term loans at exorbitant interest rates (up to 80 percent). The banks, for their part, had demanded that each loan was firstly repaid entirely after its expiration, prior to a possible renewal of the loan. This forced enterprises to find bridging loans which could only be obtained by paying usurious interest. As a rule, it is the banks which arrange bridging loans and receive high commissions for doing so. This placed a tremendous burden on private businesses, and finally resulted in the collective mobilization of Hangzhou's private entrepreneurs.[95]

Similarly, the Hangzhou Furniture Association protested by sending a report to both the party secretary and the mayor of Hangzhou, in which they complained that banks needed the approval of their superiors in the 'bank system' (*yinhang xitong*) before lending, hence making it more difficult for private enterprises to get access to bank loans. They asked the authorities to intervene in their interest. This was followed by government-organized talks attended by representatives of both the banks and the entrepreneurs. However, it turned out that the problem

---

[95] Interview, Hangzhou, 1 March 2015. During two rounds of intensive interviews with the president of a number of industrial sector associations in Wenzhou in September 2017, numerous demands were made to the Wenzhou city government supporting the private sector as it weathered the enduring economic crisis in this former stronghold of 'capitalism with Chinese characteristics', most notably by attracting high-skilled labor, providing financial services, initiating preference policies for private enterprises, and setting up a platform for Chambers of Commerce, including those in other countries, to facilitate access to business information and spawn mutual help. Interestingly, the president of the Wenzhou E-Commerce Association insisted that the city government should send cadres to serve as association presidents. He claimed that, if these important positions are taken by renowned local businessmen, other entrepreneurs would rather not cooperate with this association. Generally speaking, the de-linking of leadership positions in business associations from party state personnel (often retired cadres), as this respondent pointed out, was running contrary to the best interests of the members of a business association, as important ties with the local bureaucracy were cut and, hence, an important communication channel to solve business-related problems closed (interview, Wenzhou, 23 September 2017).

could not be solved by the local government.[96] In both cases, the issue was eventually solved by the entrepreneurs themselves in that larger and more prosperous enterprises assisted smaller enterprises by establishing privately funded credit associations.[97] This kind of self-help contributes to institutional change: It reduces entrepreneurs' dependence on the state, and creates new institutions beyond the state-controlled banking system, thus fueling an ongoing discussion in China over the privatization of the banking and credit sector.[98]

When Shenzhen hosted the Summer Universiade in 2011, the city government decided that heavily polluting industries, such as furniture production, should be closed down. The reason given was that this sector would emit excessive toxic gas emissions. Shenzhen's furniture industry sector association (*Shenzhen jiaju hangye xiehui*) immediately reacted and started to bargain with the local government. It promised that the 200 targeted enterprises would upgrade by using more environmentally-friendly technologies, suggested that the government should close the enterprises for two months only, and demanded corresponding compensation of 500,000 RMB to be paid to each firm. On this basis, a compromise was eventually achieved.[99]

In another case reported by Ji Yingying, a business association in the prefecture-level city of Bengbu (Anhui Province) successfully defended the interests of smaller enterprises supplying local supermarket chains. The suppliers complained that the supermarkets would urge them to sign unfair contracts, charge unreasonable fees, and delay payments. Since the supermarket company refused to negotiate with the suppliers' association

---

[96] Interview, entrepreneur, Hangzhou, 21 March 2017.

[97] Interview, entrepreneur, Hangzhou, 1 March 2015.

[98] Interview, entrepreneur, Hangzhou, 1 March 2015. For their part, members of the 'Hainan Tourist Hotel Association' collectively protested against the price charged for electricity, which was, in their view, not only too high but also discriminatory, since industrial enterprises were charged much less than the service sector. Some even refused to pay at all, and the entire association demanded equal treatment as compared with industrial enterprises. In negotiations with the government a compromise was finally reached, by which pricing would vary according to the hour of the day. Interview, Haikou, 11 March 2016.

[99] Interview at the association, Shenzhen, 21 September 2015.

and the government was not willing to assist in solving the problem, the suppliers turned to collective action and organized public protests. Their strategy was to point to documents of the central government that were in favor of their demands and to announce that they were prepared to petition to higher authorities if the problem could not be solved in Bengbu. This alarmed the local government, since petitions to higher levels can have a negative impact on the careers of local officials. It stepped in on the side of the suppliers so that the conflict with the supermarket chain was finally solved (see Ji, 2015; 2018).

These few cases illustrate a more general observation: Collective action by private entrepreneurs (or their business associations) is primarily related to economic or administrative problems and does not question the political regime. Such action is possible as long as practical solutions for the problems at stake are proposed and no connection is made with more fundamental problems related to China's political system. As such, it is important to look at how collective action is framed by private entrepreneurs and their business associations. In the context of the recent China–US trade war some industry sectors come under tremendous pressure and many factories have had to close down, at least temporarily. A dramatic rise in the cost of raw materials, a decline of the RMB exchange rate and of exports to the US have forced many private enterprises to halt production. Business associations, for example those in the knitting and textile industry in regions particularly affected (Zhejiang, Jiangsu), have published many reports and urgently demanded that the government takes measures to protect and support these industries. Closing down many of them factories, according to this argument, would be detrimental to employment and the 'people's livelihood' (*minsheng*), hence endangering social stability (*wending*) (Ye, 2018). Interestingly, these statements copied the wording of a document issued after a meeting of the Politburo of the CCP Central Committee on 1 August 2018, on the importance of safeguarding the 'people's livelihood' and preserving 'social stability' in times of economic crisis (see Zhonggong Zhongyang Zhengzhiju, 2018). By strategically using official terminology, many business associations try to undergird their efforts to safeguard private sector interests with political correctness. These reports and appeals are often posted by business associations or other members of WeChat user groups uniting private

Table 2: Preferred Strategies of Private Entrepreneurs for Dispute-Solution, Qingdao City (in percent)

Legal action	64.6
Guanxi	18.0
Petitions	7.0
Through social forces*	5.2
Through money	5.2
Total	100.0

Note: *'Social forces' relates to business organizations.
Source: Qingdaoshi Gongshang Lianhehui (2015: 6).

entrepreneurs throughout China. This arguably strengthens the prestige of business associations and also reinforces a feeling of solidarity within the business community, which may later be helpful in spurring further collective action, both online and offline (see Chapter 5).[100]

Private entrepreneurs can choose between different forms of collective action to protect their interests. A report by the Qingdao Federation of Industry and Commerce published in 2015 details the preferred strategies of private entrepreneurs for solving disputes they might face, and found that taking legal action was by far the most prominent choice, topping the activation of *guanxi* (see Table 2).

Interestingly, the survey did not offer the options 'collective action' (*jiti xindong*) or 'lobbying' (*youshui*). That makes the results of this survey highly questionable. In our interviews, most entrepreneurs indicated reservation toward turning to legal action, which they called ineffective and even dangerous, as they would have to make a stand against local officials who might become resentful and thus endanger their business operations.[101] The overwhelming majority of our respondents reiterated

---

[100]This connection was made by a Chinese entrepreneur in a talk in Duisburg on 7 August 2018.
[101]In fact, in the same survey, only 30.1 percent of all respondents were convinced that there was major progress regarding the development of the Chinese legal system (Qingdaoshi Gongshang Lianhehui, 2015: 10).

time and again that individual *guanxi* was the most important resource for safeguarding one's own business interests, while only a small minority would turn to a business association — which, for its part, is well reflected by the figure given in Table 2 ('social forces').

In fact, the trust of private entrepreneurs in terms of the conflict-solving effectiveness of business associations is rather limited, as is their willingness to actively work through business associations to safeguard any possible collective interest. Strikingly, entrepreneurs often state that the practical significance of these organizations for enterprise development is rather negligible. Larger companies solve problems by activating their private networks and by directly approaching the authorities on an individual level. Smaller companies often find that local governments are not helpful in solving their problems at all. They prefer to communicate informally with relevant government bureaus or local officials, with whom they have a personal relationship, to solve their problems and hardly rely on business associations to assist them. Since business associations are strongly dependent on the local state to serve their members they must closely cooperate with local governments, as many of our respondents stated. After more than three decades of market reform and transformation, trade and business associations in China have thus widely remained functional vehicles of the party state. Formal autonomy, it seems, is neither possible nor desirable since major resources such as land, export permits, bank loans, tax reduction, and so on, are closely administered and monitored by the state. It is thus not surprising that most entrepreneurs we interviewed noted that it is a 'must' for them to cultivate individual relationships with government agencies. If at all, our respondents acknowledged that business associations are helpful in obtaining policy advice and market information, providing vocational training (*peixun*), setting up contacts with government bureaus and officials, and organizing trips to learn about business practices and market conditions elsewhere.

Generally speaking, our findings confirm Deng and Kennedy (2010) as well as Yu *et al.* (2013, 2014) in the sense that business associations with close relations to local governments display a stronger bargaining capacity *vis-à-vis* the state than associations with weaker connections. However, regional differences and differences between industry sectors make for important intervening variables. An entrepreneur in Zhongshan told us:

> The chamber of commerce cannot solve the 'big' problems' [i.e. problems related to the political environment, the authors] but they are able to bargain issues such as labor conflicts and tax reductions, and they come up with problem solutions in specific industry sectors.[102]

Still, trade and industry associations, much like chambers of commerce, in many instances are simply not powerful enough to truly benefit their members. Wu Jinglian, one of China's most prominent economists, has repeatedly pointed out that the function of these associations is not yet clearly defined as they are torn between the interests of local governments and those of their entrepreneurial constituency. Internal conflicts are frequent and, in many cases, large entrepreneurs, who usually figure as presidents of business associations, pursue foremost their own agenda and not those of the other members (Wu, 2017). As explained above, we argue that the interest of large entrepreneurs, the core elite within the strategic group of private entrepreneurs, in most of the cases cannot be detached from those of the wider group, and when it comes to policy initiatives, large entrepreneurs often address concerns relevant to most private entrepreneurs. However, business associations can certainly do much better in many parts of China to articulate these concerns and strengthen the connection between large and smaller entrepreneurs among their membership, which explains the widely shared skepticism we found among many of our respondents when they were asked to assess the performance of those business associations which they had joined. In most cases, they argued that business associations are the 'second-best choice' outside of their individual networks. For those larger entrepreneurs who are willing to serve as the chairpersons or leading officials of business associations, they foremost figure as amplifiers of their social standing and political influence.[103]

---

[102] Interview, Zhongshan, 19 September 2014.
[103] Interview, professor, Party School Quanzhou, 9 September 2012.

Strategic action by extraterritorial chambers of commerce (yidi shanghui)

This specific type of business association describes modern entrepreneurial hometown associations representing private entrepreneurs outside their native place, their *laojia,* uniting business-people originating from the same province. Extraterritorial Chambers of Commerce not only work for the interests of their fellow 'townspeople' in an unfamiliar environment and provide support for them, but also organize business delegations to other cities and help their members get in touch with leading officials there. This promotes close connections between local governments and business communities outside the city (or province) where the chamber is located, hence extending the networks of these communities further afield.

An interesting example is the Chaoshan Chamber of Commerce (*Chaoshan shanghui*) in Shenzhen which in 2016 had some 3,000 members. It supports social and charity projects in Chaoshan (comprising the four cities of Shantou, Chaozhou, Shanwei, and Jieyang in Guangdong province) and provides assistance to its members in terms of information, loans, investments and business contacts. It also undertakes lobbying activities with the help of a network of 410 Chaoshan chambers of commerce across China and around the world. Since the Chaoshan people differ linguistically from other population groups in Guangdong and possess a strong identity of their own, they prefer doing business with other Chaoshan businesspeople.[104]

Another example is the Zhejiang Chamber of Commerce (*Zhejiang shanghui*) in Hainan Province. Its chairman in 2016 was formerly a leading military figure in Hainan and turned to private entrepreneurship after his retirement, making use of his excellent connections in Hainan Province. At the time of our fieldwork in Hainan (March 2016), the chamber was negotiating with local banks, trying to get them to accept rural land near an entrepreneur's hometown in Zhejiang as collateral for bank credits in Hainan. Banks are normally reluctant to accept such collateral, which makes maintaining excellent contacts with local banks (particularly

---

[104] Interview at the Chaoshan Chamber of Commerce, Shenzhen, 23 September 2015.

with bank managers who originate from Zhejiang Province, as we were told) essential for obtaining such loans. At other times, members of the chamber with strong financial resources may act as guarantors for banking facilities, confirming the 'patrimonial' role that large entrepreneurs often assume *vis-á-vis* their smaller peers.[105] The Zhejiang provincial government is particularly eager to secure investment by the Zhejiang *shanghui* members in their home province. It also supports Zhejiang enterprises across China by placing orders and through preferential policies for returnees. Consequently, Zhejiang business-people maintain close contacts to their home province. They are proud of Zhejiang's economic development and, as in the case of the members of the Zhejiang *yidi shanghui* in Hainan, emphasize that their culture, beliefs, and values as different from those of local populations, like Hainan natives. These values constitute an overarching sense of belonging among Zhejiang entrepreneurs in Hainan, grounded in both a pronounced geographical and cultural identity and a deep pride in their success 'far afield'. However, this collective identity does not only apply to Zhejiang entrepreneurs in Hainan, but rather reflects a general sentiment among them, no matter where they are located:

> Concerning all our Zhejiang people, and particularly concerning we Zhejiang entrepreneurs, we say that whether an external environment is good or bad, it does not matter. We Zhejiang entrepreneurs have developed under very bad conditions. Wherever there are Zhejiang entrepreneurs, Zhejiang will flourish and the entire country will flourish. If Zhejiang fares poorly, the country will fare poorly, too. No matter whether the economic situation is good or bad, whatever kinds of difficulties we face, nothing can stop us Zhejiang entrepreneurs![106]

---

[105] Interview, Zhejiang Chamber of Commerce, Haikou, 11 March 2016.

[106] See *Zheshang Quyu Jingji* (Zhejiang Entrepreneurs and Regional Economy), published by the 'Association for Promoting the Regional Economy of Zhejiang Province' (*Zhejiangsheng quyu jingji cujinhui*) No. 3, 2016, 27. This organization represents entrepreneurs who have been trained at Zhejiang University, hence is an alumni network concerned with network building and improving the economic environment for private enterprises in Zhejiang province.

There are, of course, significant differences among extraterritorial chambers of commerce concerning their internal structure, membership services, strategies and business environment which may impact significantly on their relationships with local government authorities. The Shandong Chamber of Commerce in Guangzhou,[107] for instance, claims to operate very strategically, and even calls itself the 'Shandong Strategic Federation'.[108] By 'strategic', as we were explained in rather abstract terms, it means the 'careful selection of collaboration partners, designing and pursuing long-term goals, harnessing new and beneficial opportunities, and being decisive in accomplishing the association's goals'. One respondent pointed out that even though active party state cadres had to leave the association because of new government regulations, 'the *guanxi* are still there', highlighting that purposefully making use of contacts to former officials does also belong to the Shandong Chamber of Commerce's strategic arsenal.[109] In a written piece for the Shandong Chamber of Commerce in Guangdong, one of its members defined strategic action on the part of this association as follows: (1) To comprehensively examine policies and examine how to make them beneficial to entrepreneurs; (2) to carefully analyze, read and understand policies in order to take advantage of them; and (3) to create conditions and construct an environment which makes policies suit entrepreneurial interests (Li Jianguo, 2013: 75). The Shandong Chamber of Commerce, the author added, should pursue a 'three-wants-policy' (*sanyao zhengce*): policies for us, from us, and suitable to us. Finally, he pointed out that it is necessary to actively approach local authorities and to maintain close relations with them, even if they 'look down on our chamber or have prejudices' (*ibid*: 75).

---

[107]This association is part of a nationwide network of extraterritorial Shandong chambers of commerce with excellent relations with both the Shandong and Guangdong provincial leaders. Lobbying via these channels is a declared part of the chamber's strategic behavior, resulting not only in the winning of government-assigned projects via public tenders for member companies or assignments for the services of this chamber (training courses, etc.) but also in more leeway for the chamber's activities.

[108]As one of our respondents, working for the Shandong Chamber of Commerce in Guangdong noted in a tautological fashion, 'we call ourselves 'strategic' since we want to progress in a very strategic way'. Interview, Guangzhou, 7 March 2017.

[109]Interview, Guangzhou, 7 March 2017.

For its part, the above-mentioned Shenzhen Chaoshan Chamber of Commerce has a 'Strategic Decision-Making Committee' (*zhanlüe juece weiyuanhui*) which is responsible for designing long-term strategies of the organization. These do not only comprise of lobbying activities directed at local governments, but also a financial commitment by the association to improve infrastructure and assist in welfare and charity projects in the Chamber's hometowns.[110] Part of their strategic thinking was targeted at Shenzhen proper in order to build up influence there as well. It was proudly explained to us that already 70 of the association's members were deputies to PCs and PPCCs on different administrative levels in Shenzhen, and that this number would likely increase.[111]

The Luojiang Chamber of Commerce in Kunming, Yunnan province, represented 12,000 entrepreneurs from Luojiang (now a district of Quanzhou City) and Jinjiang (a county-level city under Quanzhou prefectural city, one of our field sites) in Fujian Province, who primarily do business in furniture production, real estate, natural and mineral resources, and construction. Its chairman is in the garment industry and a member of the Standing Committee of the Fujian Chamber of Commerce in Yunnan. This chamber was originally a hometown association founded to protect members who felt economically discriminated against in Yunnan. The Luojiang Chamber of Commerce also runs its own businesses, such as an investment firm, a real estate firm, a credit guarantor firm (*danbao gongsi*), and so on. Only its leading members (chairman and vice-chairmen) can purchase shares of those companies, though they claim to operate in the interest of all members. According to the association's president, the reason for this arrangement is to guarantee that only entrepreneurs with sufficient financial resources, who are trusted by their peers, should become shareholders, since they would be expected to compensate for losses in case of company failure. Financial prowess and the trust of fellow members resides with the president, which means that these are critical requirements for any leadership position in the association. The number of shareholders in any company under the association should

---

[110] Specifically mentioned were the construction of an express train station and an international airport in their home area.

[111] Interview, Chaoshan Chamber of Commerce, Shenzhen, 9 March 2016.

be less than 30 so that its administration remains manageable. According to the president, the function of these companies was to generate income for the chamber of commerce, though the bulk of the profit was certainly skimmed by the shareholders themselves. He called this a 'strategic decision' to strengthen the chamber of commerce in order to improve its services for all members.[112] Besides, a major function of the Luoyang Chamber of Commerce is to bargain with the local government to protect the interests of the Luojiang entrepreneurs in Kunming.[113] The association also takes care of members who face problems with the local police, tax authorities, environmental protection office, and other government bureaus. As the association's chairman commented:

> We are very strong, particularly in comparison to local chambers. People from Fujian are relatively united and show much solidarity (*tuanjie*) with each other ... As entrepreneurs, we constitute a social group (*shehui qunti*).[114]

While the Chaoshan and Luoyang Chambers of Commerce are two examples of very active extraterritorial business associations in a very lively economic environment, things are much different in the case of the Shuangqiu Chamber of Commerce in Guangdong, an organization for entrepreneurs originating from this prefecture-level city in Henan Province, which was only established in 2016. At the time of our fieldwork in Guangzhou (2017), it had 200 members. The chairman of the association told us that chambers of commerce usually collapse if they are unsuccessful in providing effective services to their members. Often enough, failure is also related to differences in regional or local 'economic cultures':

> Here in Guangdong both society and the government are relatively open-minded. This is very beneficial to the development of private enterprises.

---

[112] Interview, 10 March 2017.
[113] The association's president had been elected after paying 800,000 RMB to become eligible to run for the position. He pointed out that the most needed requirements to qualify for the election are economic power (*jingji shili*), management capability (*jingying nengli*), previous experience in leading a chamber, and ability in mediation (*tiaojie nengli*).
[114] Interview, Kunming, 10 March 2017.

We Henan people are relatively conservative. In our province, if we want to negotiate a business deal we invite people and are very polite in bargaining prices. Here, it is different. People are not so polite. They don't invite you to discuss a price. They just let you know the price without any room for bargaining.[115]

On a more positive note, the vice-chairman of the Shuangqiu Chamber of Commerce added:

The business environment here is very different from the one in our hometown. In Henan you need somebody in the government supporting you, here you don't. In contrast to Henan there are not so many problems with the local authorities such as the tax office or the Bureau of Industry and Commerce. Here, the administrative principle is to foster the private sector whereas in Henan it is to administer it. We feel much more free here than we do in Henan. I do not have to constantly think about how to influence the authorities. In Henan you need *guanxi* for everything, here it is not necessary.[116]

As a matter of fact, there are different regional narratives of self-ascription and ascription that separate extraterritorial chambers of commerce from their local environment. This invokes a collective identity among association members that helps when engaging in strategic action. A female entrepreneur in Qingdao argued:

Yes, Shandong people are conservative, and businesspeople in South China are more open-minded. But, in Shandong, local people will help you if you are in need. Not because money or profit is involved. It is emotion, affection that counts here. In the South people will help you only if cash flows. I don't want to go to the South, because the concept of human relations is different there. Yes, it is much easier to do business in South China, whereas here the human factor (*renwen*) has priority. I have empathy with people who express human feelings, and thus find it difficult to accommodate the thinking in the South where you name a price to pay to help somebody. Here, cash is not so important, and

---

[115]Interview, Guangzhou, 7 March 2017.
[116]Interview, Guangzhou, 7 March 2017.

people are not necessarily willing to help even if you offer money for that.[117]

An entrepreneur from Quanzhou city in Fujian province noted:

> Take, for instance, people from Guizhou Province. They are lazy, uneducated and ignorant (*suzhi cha*). All day long they play Majiang. Everything is difficult in Guizhou, and the working attitude of the authorities is bad. Compared to other Chinese we Fujian people are special. Take, for instance, people from Guangdong. Only after discussing a business deal, and only if this discussion was successful, they will invite you for dinner. People from Wenzhou say 'let's talk *and* eat'. But we Quanzhou people prefer to eat first and afterwards talk about business. Even if the business negotiations fail, we are still both humans. The meaning is that we Fujian people are fairly relaxed and easy-going. Quanzhou people sell you a cup for 1,05 Yuan, i.e. the lowest price, because they are happy with a minimal profit.'[118]

We found that members of extraterritorial chambers of commerce foremost displayed a strong local identity which, arguably, weighed heavier for them than their belonging to the social constituency of private entrepreneurs or shared interests stemming from their business operations in the same industry sector. In other words, locality — a feeling of belonging grounded on place of origin, language, and (self-ascribed) cultural tradition — reinforces mutual trust between private entrepreneurs. It adds momentum to the determination of private entrepreneurs to engage in strategic action resulting from positional closeness in social action fields and a common social habitus (see Chapter 3). Extraterritorial business associations differ from other business organizations because they are grounded in shared commonalities beyond mere economic interest. In addition, as hometown associations, they protect and assist their members in a more difficult, if not hostile, alien environment where they usually lack widespread individual *guanxi* to put them on a par with their local competitors. Therefore, the ties and trust between members in such

---

[117]Interview, Qingdao, 26 March 2017.
[118]Interview, Luojiang Chamber of Commerce, Kunming, 10 March 2017.

associations are particularly strong and make them one of the most important platforms for entrepreneurial strategic action in contemporary China.[119]

Political lobbying in formal institutions

Lobbying is a strategy for promoting private interests in politics and society by making use of formal and informal channels. Lobbying targets not only government and party bodies but also public opinion. Chinese scholars differentiate between legitimate (*youshui*) and illegitimate (*guanshuo*) lobbying. Governments and the public often regard lobbying as illegitimate because success is supposed to result from corruptive behavior by those who engage in it. In fact, it is hard to tell the difference. Be that as it may, lobbying as a strategic tool has become increasingly accepted in Chinese politics and the need for legitimate channels through which to lobby has been a driving force behind private entrepreneurs seeking membership in PCs or PPCCs, leading positions in business associations or access to entrepreneurial clubs. For the same reason, lobbying has come under serious scrutiny since the early days of the Xi Jinping era.[120]

Whereas large and influential entrepreneurs often lobby on their own, using informal channels, business associations are particularly crucial for lobbying on behalf of small- and medium-sized entrepreneurs, though these, as our interviews have consistently shown, also prefer to work through their individual networks. As a general rule, a private entrepreneur would only look for the support of an association if his or her individual *guanxi* cannot do the trick. On the other hand, as was explained earlier, larger entrepreneurs are eager to become deputies of (national or provincial) PCs or PPCCs and leaders in business associations, as these positions help them accumulate even more social capital, which can be traded for economic gain and political influence. In the following, we highlight political lobbying in formal institutions as a more visible strategy through which entrepreneurs defend their group-specific interests.

---

[119] Interviews, entrepreneurs, Qingdao, 26 March 2017 and Kunming, 10 March 2017.
[120] Scott Kennedy (2008) was one of the first to systematically examine lobbying in China and showed that it had become a widespread phenomenon since the 1990s.

Lobbying in PCs and PPCCs

Collective political lobbying in China's legislative bodies and business organizations has, arguably, become increasingly effective over the years.[121] One well-known case goes back to 2004, when entrepreneurial deputies at the annual PC and PPCC sessions lobbied other deputies to support 18 proposals for a revision of the Company Law (*gongsifa*). At these sessions, 601 PC and 13 PPCC deputies at the national level jointly submitted the suggestions with the support of 544 further PC deputies. In the initial stage, the entrepreneurs hired lawyers who sent modified drafts directly to the Standing Committee of the National PC. At the same time, they attempted to underscore the arguments for modification by sending out expert academic assessments to deputies and journalists and posting these assessments online. Entrepreneurs, lawyers, and leading company staff directly approached members of the two legislative bodies by letter or phone in order to persuade them to support these drafts. The drafts were also discussed at conferences organized by entrepreneurs to which both relevant government officials and influential members of the National PC and PPCC were invited, along with members of the relevant PPCC issue working groups (*jiebie lianzu*). The Legal Office of the State Council alone received more than 1,000 motions in total and finally decided to revise the law in August 2004 (Pang, 2016).

Sometimes larger enterprises or conglomerates jointly engage in lobbying. In 2013, for example, ten of the roughly three million private express delivery firms turned to the Law Commission of the National PC concerning the regulation that private firms were not permitted to deliver letters weighing more than 350 grams. They demanded a change, and finally succeeded. There are many other examples of private companies attempting to bring about legal changes in their own interests; these have concerned certain Labor Law stipulations and the Labor Contract Law,

---

[121] Some of our respondents were not very optimistic about the effectiveness of collective lobbying on the part of entrepreneurial deputies to PCs and PPCCs or their willingness to cooperate in the first place. For instance, one Beijing-based entrepreneur contended that '90 percent of entrepreneurs in the PCs are just focused on the interests of their respective businesses and hardly consider anything else'. He also claimed that 'a PPCC deputy is just a false name, it hasn't any content' (interview, 8 September 2015).

for example,[122] or the rules for determining emission levels in the auto-mobile industry.[123] In another prominent case, entrepreneurs lobbied for lifting the ban imposed by the National Development and Reform Commission (*Fagaiwei*) in 2001 on producing plastic dishes. Ten leading private enterprises in this industry spent some 4.5 million RMB toward lobbying for the abolition of this regulation. They mobilized their respective business associations in light industry and the plastics processing industry, commissioned public relation firms to propagate the social and ecological usefulness of plastic dishes, recruited retired high officials for support, and hired lawyers, promising to pay them four million RMB if successful. With the help of the media, scientific reports, expert assessments in favor of plastic dishes and meetings with PC and PPCC deputies, they finally succeeded and the Commission lifted the ban in 2013.[124]

Wang Shaoguang and Fan Peng have described lobbying activities by the Chinese Pharmaceutical Association as extensive media coverage, pharmaceutical conferences attended not only by entrepreneurs but also by decision-makers from the respective authorities, research reports directed to the Ministry of Health, and the leveraging of personal relations with PC and PPCC deputies (Wang and Fan, 2013). Particularly, young,

---

[122]The Labor Law came into effect in 1 January 1995, and was amended in 2009; The Labor Contract Law went into effect on 1 January 2008, and amendment took effect on 1 July 2013. When the draft of these laws were discussed in local PCs before being submitted to the national legislature, both business associations and the ACFIC attempted to influence its content (Cho, 2009: 32–35).

[123]See e.g.: '*Youshui zai Zhongguo: Zhongguo shangye youshui baitai*' (Lobbying in China: all kinds of forms), http://finance.sina.com.cn/g/20060928/13182954856.shtml (accessed 20 February, 2016).

[124]*Zhongqingbao xiang du sheide zui? – Ping xin Zhongguo di yiqi hefa youshuo an* (Whose mouth will the Chinese Youth Daily shut? – On the first legal lobbying case in new China), http://www.guancha.cn/MaPing/2013_03_31_135470.shtml (accessed 22 February 2016); Dalu youshui jituan diaocha (Study on Mainland's lobbying corporations), http://www.360doc.com/content/13/1111/12/88761_328347055.shtml (accessed 22 February 2016). Detailed report of various lobbying cases: *Zhongguo minjian fuxian youshui jituan, duo qudao xiang Renda suqiu quanyi* (Emerging of Chinese private lobbying companies, multi-channel to submit interest proposals to the People's Congresses), http://zazhi.meide.org/2009/0313.htm#MAILLISTDOC2 (accessed 22 February 2016).

well-educated, and globally-oriented entrepreneurs understand lobbying as a legitimate strategic instrument of entrepreneurial behavior. A 28-year-old businessmen in the food industry told us:

> We have to lobby in order to develop. For instance, I saw in foreign countries that kitchens in restaurants are not separated from customers by a wall but by being transparent through a large window. Every customer can watch how meals are prepared and whether the kitchen is clean. This, however, does not suit China's fire prevention regulations. Therefore, we had to lobby among local officials to change the rules. We organized workshops with academic experts, informed them about the advantages of transparent kitchens and the effects for our restaurants, showed them restaurants with transparent kitchens, and finally succeeded in convincing them to change the rules.[125]

Time and again, entrepreneurs have demanded changes to guard against the monopolies developed by state-owned firms and measures against the exclusion of private investment in state-controlled industrial sectors. In other instances, they complained about the negative consequences of the Labor Contract Law for their businesses. Concerning the latter, one of our respondents informed us that this law would soon be revised due to lobbying in the National PC and the National PPCC.[126] Just two days later, major Chinese newspapers reported that the then-minister of finance had criticized this law and demanded revisions due to its one-sided protection of workers' interests, its detrimental effects on enterprises, and its negative effects on enterprise development.[127] Another interviewee commented that entrepreneurial action had resulted in less discrimination against the private sector under the 13th Five-Year Plan (2016–2020).[128] Surprisingly, the 'Proposal of the 13th Five-Year Plan' decided upon by the Central Committee of the CCP in October 2015 emphasized that private enterprises should be permitted to enter and invest in industry sectors previously off-limits to them — thus conceding, at

---

[125]Interview, Beijing, 25 March 2016.
[126]Interview, Beijing, 18 February 2016.
[127]See e.g. *Beijing Qingnian Bao* (Beijing Youth Newspaper), 20 February 2016.
[128]Interview, Beijing, 26 September 2015.

least on a declaratory level, this long-held demand of entrepreneurs and entrepreneurial organizations.[129]

Lobbying via business associations

Deng and Kennedy (2010), Yu *et al.* (2014) and Shen (2014)[130] have all argued that privately established associations have less access to state agencies and lobby less frequently than those which are created from the top down and thereby have 'privileged access' to decision-making bodies due to their good *guanxi* with the government. As a result, the former, lacking such channels and mechanisms, are less successful. In fact, the close relationship of some business associations with local governments facilitates individual lobbying by small- and medium-sized enterprises. Larger firms, in turn, lobby through their own 'public relations departments' (*gongguan bumen*) or 'Departments for Government Relations' (*zhengfu guanxi zhuguan*). Increasingly, such in-house public relations are being outsourced to separate agencies which offer professional lobbying services.[131] These agencies develop public relations strategies for enterprises, act as company spokespersons, organize conferences in order to lobby government officials, arrange visits by leading officials, and work to ensure a positive in-company environment.[132] Generally speaking, as the Chinese business environment increases in complexity, establishing *guanxi* with government officials no longer suffices and is increasingly being replaced by the *guanxi*-building activities of external agencies.[133]

---

[129] *Zhonggong Zhongyang guanyu zhiding guomin jingji he shehui fazhan di shisange wunian guihua de jianyi* (Proposal on the 13th Five Year Plan on economic and social development), http://news.xinhuanet.com/fortune/2015-11/03/c_1117027676.htm (accessed 28 December 2015).

[130] Shen (2014) even speaks of 'strategic interaction' between governments and business associations without, however, clarifying the strategic component of that interaction.

[131] See '*Gongguan gongsi yu qiye gongguan bumen de 5 dian qubie*' (Five differences between PR agencies and enterprises' inhouse PR), https://www.prnasia.com/blog/archives/4563 (accessed 1 February 2016).

[132] Interview, Beijing, 3 March, 2015.

[133] See *Gongguan anli yu saishi* (Public relation cases and competition), http://pr.shisu.edu.cn/s/19/t/38/0b/68/info2920.htm (accessed 2 February 2016).

According to the 2014 'Chinese Report on the Public Relations Industry in China', the turnover of this industry grew by 11.5 percent to 38 billion RMB in 2015.[134]

The Shandong Chamber of Commerce in Guangdong Province provides a good example of constructing multiple channels through which to conduct lobbying activities. In 2015, for example, the annual meeting of its members was attended (on invitation) not only by representatives of the provincial government (e.g. from the provincial Civil Affairs Office) but also by the head of the Shandong Province representative office in Guangdong and — as a special guest — the political commissar of the Guangdong Military Region, a three-star general and leading figure at the provincial level. A report on the meeting noted that at the beginning of the conference the deputies sang the national anthem. The chairman's report pointed out that the members of the chamber had not only heavily invested in both Guangdong and Shandong, but also that they were involved in large-scale welfare and charity projects. In doing so, and through their lobbying activities in Guangdong's PPCC and Federation of Industry and Commerce, the chamber had significantly extended its political influence and gained more political support from the governments in both provinces.[135] As one of our interviewees at the Shandong Chamber of Commerce in Guangdong noted:

> Policy results from a *guanxi* relationship and embodies a process of strategic action. The knowledge of how to use this *guanxi* is crucial for achieving one's strategic goals.[136]

Lobbying and policy/institutional change

Policy and institutional change resulting from individual and collective lobbying by private entrepreneurs comes in various forms: new laws and

[134] *Zhongguo gongguan guanxi hangye 2014 niandu diaocha baogao* (Research Report on China's public relation sector in 2014), http://www.chinapr.com.cn/templates/T_Second/index.aspx?nodeid=97andpage=ContentPageandcontentid=9590 (accessed 1 February 2015).
[135] Guangdong sheng Shandong shanghui 2015; interview, Shandong Chamber of Commerce in Guangdong Province, Guangzhou, 7 March 2017.
[136] Interview, 7 March 2017.

regulations, new formal communication channels, and bargaining platforms for state–business interaction (e.g. the China Entrepreneurs Forum or the Yabuli Entrepreneurial Forum (*Yabuli Zhongguo Qiyejia Luntan*), established in 2001),[137] new informal institutions (e.g. private credit cooperatives or crowdfunding schemes), new access for private enterprises in state-dominated economic sectors, private sector innovations informing new policies (e.g. the campaign to map water quality by the Alibaba Group), the introduction and expansion of corporate social responsibility in private enterprises and SOEs, corporate commonwealth, new lifestyle patterns, and social values among the group of private entrepreneurs which influence their economic behavior.[138] Once again, individual lobbying can, and often is, beneficial to the interests of the whole group in terms of new policies and institutions that it can bring about.

An interesting case that illustrates the nexus between individual lobbying and policy change is that of Alibaba, China's biggest e-commerce company. Alibaba has established a 'Taobao University'[139] which offers specific e-commerce courses for leading county cadres. These courses are held within party schools. By the end of 2015, 1,572 leading county cadres had already been trained in issues of e-commerce.[140] This example

---

[137] For an overview see http://www.cefco.cn/ (accessed 25 July 2018).

[138] It is quite striking to see an increasing trend among private entrepreneurs to develop a new value system based on traditional Confucianism, which seeks to enrich (if not challenge) 'Western' entrepreneurial and management values. Humanity and considerateness shown to customers, passion and empathy for employees and their families, engagement in local charity projects, financial support for 'weak social groups' and an overall commitment to poverty alleviation 'to pay back to society' are promoted as values to be honored by a modern Chinese entrepreneur, which should become part and parcel of their identity (Niedenführ, 2018). In 1999, the China Scholar Merchant League was established which has almost 22,000 member entrepreneurs and is organized in many regional associations across China (see https://baike.baidu.com/item/percentE4percentB8 percentADpercentE5percent8DpercentE8percentE5percent84percent92percentE5percent 95percent86percentE6percent80percentBBpercentE4percentBCpercent9A/10914992 (accessed 24 May 2018).

[139] Taobao refers to Alibaba's 'Taobao online shopping service'.

[140] Interview, Beijing, 20 February 2016. Details of this program: *Qianming xiangguan Alibaba peixun ji: you guanyuan zhi erweima wen zhe shi sha* (On training a thousand county officials: Some officials ask what QR code is), http://www.guancha.cn/society/ 2016_02_04_350362.shtml (accessed 19 February 2016).

shows that influential private enterprises can harness existing structures (e.g. party schools) to find acceptance within the party state leadership and thus enhance their own business interests and influence. Through these activities, Alibaba reaches many local leading cadres and helps to deepen their technical expertise and their awareness of private enterprise operations. This in turn not only helps Alibaba but also helps promote official acceptance of the private sector (in terms of laws, regulations, policies, etc.) to the benefit of the whole private sector.

Certainly enough, lobbying by private entrepreneurs does not seek to change the political system, but rather to bargain with governments at all administrative levels in such a way that creates favorable conditions for private sector development and better legal protection for private businesses. Private entrepreneurs are well aware that their success and political destiny in China's socialist system are strongly predicated on the party's private sector policies. Although private enterprises are overall much more innovative and efficient than SOEs, the party state hovers between protecting a less efficient public economy (which remains an important employment sector) and developing the private sector. As our interviews have clearly demonstrated, private entrepreneurs feel that they are still acting on politically uncertain ground. Therefore, any political engagement on their part remains risky. Most entrepreneurs are not interested in challenging the party state, but frame their collective action as the quest to contribute to the development of the nation. They want to — and must — gain party state support in order to improve the institutional environment in which they have to operate.

Party Membership and Party Organizations in Private Enterprises as Strategic Tools

For entrepreneurs, party membership and setting up party organizations in private enterprises are considered valuable strategic tools to establishing close links and communication channels between themselves and local governments. As one respondent told us:

> The existence of a party branch is positively looked upon by local party state authorities. It makes it easier for us to communicate with party and

government officials and to address higher party levels to help us get through bureaucratic procedures more easily, to accomplish our goals and to be acknowledged as an 'advanced' organization. You are only able to become a strong enterprise if you have a mighty father at your side [i.e. a strong party organization, the authors].[141]

From the perspective of the party state, establishing party branches in private enterprises fulfils three objectives: (a) recruiting new members for the local party apparatus, particularly since privatization processes and labor migration have made such recruitment very difficult over the years; (b) recruiting younger and better educated party members over time; (c) and establishing close links between the local government and enterprise management.[142] To our understanding, the success of this policy is ambivalent at best. In localities where entrepreneurs had been party members for a rather long time, such as Jiangyin and Enshi (where many private businessmen had previously been managers of state-owned enterprises which had later been privatized), they were keen to prove themselves responsible party members and eager to establish party organizations within their company. Here, the recruitment of new party members proceeded rather smoothly. In Wenzhou and Jinjiang, however, where most entrepreneurs were not party members, 'party construction' (*dangjian*) was protracted and seriously criticized by some local cadres.

As our fieldwork in Jilin, Shandong, Hubei, and Jiangsu showed, many entrepreneurs became party members early in their professional careers

---

[141] Interview, entrepreneur, Hangzhou, 3 April 2018.

[142] The establishment of party organizations in state-owned and private enterprises is not obligatory according to Chinese law. Article 19 of China's Company Law only requires that all domestic and foreign-invested enterprises provide the 'necessary conditions' for the activities of party branches. Chapter 5 of the CCP Constitution requires the establishment of a party organization in companies with three or more party members, but the party constitution has no legal authority, at least formally, within the government system. Concerning private enterprises, the CCP Constitution stipulates that party branches shall ensure law-abiding behavior and oversee the trade unions and the Communist Youth League, whereas no prescriptions are made for a company's corporate governance. See Fact Sheet: Communist Party Groups in Foreign Companies in China, *China Business Review*, 31 May 2018. https://www.chinabusinessreview.com/fact-sheet-communist-party-groups-in-foreign-companies-in-china/ (accessed 1 February 2019).

when working as managers or even directors in state or collective enterprises. In Guangdong, Fujian, and Hainan, however, only a minority of native private entrepreneurs were party members. Some local cadres even labeled 'party construction' in private companies as 'fake' (*xujiade*). In fact, in Jinjiang (*Fujian*), some party branches were 'highjacked' by the families of private entrepreneurs. In one case, the father of the company boss served as the secretary of the party committee, the younger brother as chairman of the trade union chapter within the enterprise, and the boss himself was head of the Communist Youth League chapter.[143] In another case, the vice-president of one of the largest companies in Jinjiang concurrently acted as secretary of the party committee, while the president's brother was vice party secretary.[144] These are just two of many examples highlighting our observation in many places that a firm's boss and some of his family members indeed control the party and mass organizations within their enterprise. Local officials insisted that this 'clanization' of party organizations within private enterprises, of which they were well aware, should not happen, but apparently such an outcome seemed better for them than having no party organization at all (see also Schubert and Heberer, 2015).

Overall, we found that, in most of the larger private enterprises, party organizations were frequently headed by the founder and boss of the company or by a leading manager. This was particularly the case in southern Jiangsu's Jiangyin city, where private entrepreneurs had often worked as managers or technicians of former state-owned companies or collectively-owned TVEs, or had held positions in local government bureaus during the early stage of 'reform and opening'. When privatization began in the 1990s, these people used their party connections to jump-start a private business, so their affiliations to the local party apparatus had always been close. Among party members, there were many university graduates 'classified' by our respondents as more committed to party work and more able to take on the role of moderators in case of labor conflicts. Mostly, entrepreneurs responded to questions on the role and significance of a company's party organization in a general and abstract manner. Party members were said to figure as role models and were considered particularly competent and

---

[143] Interview, entrepreneur, Jinjiang, 6 September 2012.
[144] Interview, Jinjiang, 3 September 2012.

capable employees. In general, entrepreneurs contended that party organizations would have a positive impact on the workforce, and they insisted that party branches would not meddle in the affairs of company management. However, many of our respondents were either awkward or outright sarcastic when asked about the specific activities and significance of the party branches in their companies, displaying a sense of indifference or uneasiness. Since the local CCP Organization Departments regularly evaluate the activities of these bodies and their secretaries, party state control of private enterprises is tight. Obviously, if an enterprise party committee's interests differ from those of the management, this may create tensions. At the same time, however, it is clear that the former serves as an important transmission belt linking a private enterprise to the local party state.

Party branches in private enterprises are directly subordinated to superior party committees, for example, in development zones to the party committee of that zone. This, arguably, facilitates communication between private entrepreneurs and local party authorities, as well as supporting the implementation of local development policies at the firm level. Party organizations also help to discipline the workforce in times of strained labor-relations by mediating intra-firm conflicts. They also strengthen company management by recruiting technicians and skilled workers as party members and encouraging them to 'maintain peaceful ties' between the employer and employees. Finally, party branches assume a number of social service functions and organize activities for the workforce, which solidifies intra-firm harmony. As a manager of a large sportswear manufacturer in Jinjiang explained to us:

> The party organization in our enterprise is a kind of a charity foundation (*aixin jijinhui*) for workers who have problems. They also organize sports activities, and we have facilities for treating psychological problems. We've shown you, for instance, a room where female workers learn how to cope with domestic violence. In this room, we have punching balls in the form of a male, so females learn to hit back if they are facing violence at home. This is accompanied by professional advice. In addition, for outstanding party members the party organizes 'red tourism' journeys.[145]

---

[145]Interview, Jinjiang, 7 September 2012.

Local cadres are quite often officially dispatched (*guazhi*)[146] to a private enterprise in order to strengthen communication links between the enterprise and the local government (see e.g. Zhonggong Jinjiang Shiwei Zuzhibu, 2012). As a matter of fact, 'party-building' in private enterprises is one of the most important policy objectives of the central government, aiming to institutionalize contemporary state–business relations in China. For instance, the head of the party committee in the sportswear company just mentioned was the party chief of the local town and had been assigned to take over this position by his superiors in order to overlook 'party-building' in this important enterprise. Naturally, this job came with meaningful remuneration.[147] In another case, the party secretary of a township under the jurisdiction of Jinjiang city (Fujian Province) concurrently acted as party secretary and trade union head of a large private company, assuming responsibility for land acquisition, disciplining the workforce and, naturally, further developing the company's party branch.[148] During our fieldwork in Wenzhou in 2013, the Wenzhou government dispatched more than 10,000 local cadres for *guazhi* purposes to local private enterprises in order to help, as it was announced, local authorities to better understand the problems of private enterprises, to support these enterprises in solving their most urgent problems in a particularly difficult economic environment, and improving their contacts to local government bureaus.[149] As these examples illustrate, dispatching local officials to private enterprises for a certain time period serves several purposes: helping to solve problems between promising enterprises and local authorities, constructing CCP branch organizations within these enterprises, and dis-

---

[146] 'Guazhi' in official 'party speak' means the temporary affiliation of party or government cadres with another work unit, such as an enterprise or a local government bureau, during which their original position is kept.

[147] Interview, Jinjiang, 7 September 2012.

[148] Interview, party secretary, 6 September 2012.

[149] This decision followed a serious collapse of the Wenzhou export industry as a consequence of low-price competition from North America and Europe in the wake of the 2008 global financial crisis and a subsequent increased urgency for restructuring and upgrading the local economy. *Zhejiang Xinwen* (*Zhejiang News*), 13 September 2013, Interviews, Research Bureau of the Party Committee of Wenzhou, 23 September 2013, and with the Wenzhou Federation of Industry and Commerce, 24 September 2013.

ciplining local workers. A cadre who was assigned to work in a tea oil factory (an important local enterprise in terms of tax generation and employment) in Enshi, Hubei province, for a full year told us:

> My main function is to educate the workers. They should understand both the importance of this enterprise, its business operations, and the leadership function of the CCP. I help to educate them in understanding and completing the objectives of this enterprise. (...) The party branch in this company acts as a bridge between the enterprise and the local CCP leadership and between enterprise management and the workers. In case of conflicts between the management and the workers, the party organization acts as a mediator in order to ensure the smooth running of the production process. The objective of my stay here is to guarantee the steady development of the enterprise.[150]

At the same time, party branches can help private entrepreneurs engage in strategic lobbying *vis-à-vis* local governments, as dispatched or retired cadres working in a private company are able to provide useful access to local government bureaus and officials to overcome business problems or help it in any possible way. Even though party organizations in private enterprises are a tool of ideological control for local party state authorities they may also serve as an important mechanism through which the management can steer intra-firm labor relations and an instrument of strategic lobbying for private entrepreneurs in their daily struggle to speak and be heard by local officials, and thereby receive preferential treatment.[151]

In fact, being a party member or actively promoting a party organization in one's company can and does help private entrepreneurs safeguard their wider strategic and economic interests. As one of our respondents noted:

> Actually, People's Congresses, Political Consultative Conferences, the Federation of Industry and Commerce, business organizations — they are all controlled by the government. To be frank, only the Communist

---

[150]Interview, Enshi, 9 September 2013.
[151]This was, for instance, confirmed in an informal talk with private entrepreneurs and local officials in a township in Enshi, Hubei province, 9 September 2012.

Party can really represent the interests of businessmen. Being a party member and establishing a party organization in your enterprise, as much as earning the reputation of model party member, are the most promising ways to secure influence.[152]

A leading member of the Organization Department of Jiangyin's Party Committee stated:

We now urge private enterprises without a party branch to set up such an organization. If they do not have any party members, we ask them to suggest people from their enterprises to become members. At least three members are needed to establish a branch. If entrepreneurs are CCP members they enjoy quite a lot of advantages. For instance, they are entitled to attend training courses at our local party school. There are regular courses for private entrepreneurs. These courses are organized by the local Organization Department that covers all the expenses and brings entrepreneurs into contact with leading local party bodies. Party membership can also assist entrepreneurs in solving business problems. Party membership is just like a name card and shows that you are a member of China's most important, most powerful and most progressive political organization.[153]

Becoming a CCP member is, however, not always a desired choice for private entrepreneurs. In Jinjiang, for instance, some of our respondents argued that they 'had no time' for such activities.[154] Several indicated that they would not place much emphasis on party membership in the first place, though they all were very careful in not explaining any further. Some of them did not seem to think very highly of their respective party organizations neither, as mentioned above, though all of them displayed big billboards in some room or alleyway at the company's headquarters

---

[152] Interview, entrepreneur, Beijing, 2 March 2017.
[153] Interview, 24 August 2012. Similarly, interview, entrepreneur, 7 September 2012.
[154] Interview, entrepreneur, Jinjiang, 3 September 2012.

with detailed charts of the party cell structure and the names and responsibilities of its different members.[155]

Arguably, there are regional differences which trigger divergent strategies by private entrepreneurs in terms of establishing party branches in their companies. For instance, in Jiangyin city (Jiangsu Province), where private entrepreneurs had, in most of the cases, previously been managers of state-owned or collectively-owned enterprises party membership among entrepreneurs was widespread. In fact, entrepreneurs tried to use them as bridgeheads to the local authorities in order to safeguard their business interests. In contrast, in Jinjiang city (Fujian Province), entrepreneurs counted less on party relations and party membership and more on clan or kinship relations to local officials. Accordingly, in Jiangyin there existed a higher percentage of party committees in private enterprises than in Jinjiang.

All in all, our interviews suggest that party organizations within private enterprises embody the symbiosis between state and business in the current regime coalition. They highlight the party's political control of private entrepreneurs, but also that allowing this control can serve as a strategic tool through which to engage local party state authorities, and thus safeguard the business interests of private entrepreneurs. This observation corresponds to Ma and He (2018) who found that the interrelationship between private entrepreneurs and the party state is not asymmetrical, as common wisdom among China scholars holds, but is rather characterized by mutual dependency or even collusion.[156] The party needs to both control and nurture private entrepreneurs, and private entrepreneurs need the party's protection and support. It may be an uneasy relationship but one in which both sides are doomed to maintain a precarious equilibrium.

---

[155] Most private entrepreneurs we interviewed in Jinjiang und Wenzhou were not CCP members, albeit party organizations had been established in most companies we visited there.

[156] Strictly speaking, this is not a contradiction. The relationship between the state and private entrepreneurs can be — and actually is — asymmetric and characterized by mutual dependency and collusion at the same time.

References

Aldrich, Howard, and Staber, Udo H. (1988). Organizing business interests: Patterns of trade association foundings, transformations, and death. In Glenn R. Carroll (Ed.), *Ecological Models of Organization* (pp. 111–126). Cambridge, MA: Bullinger.

Beida Guofayuan Caijingfa Jingjiang Xuejinban zonghe ketizu (Development School of Peking University, Finance and Economic Law Scholarship Comprehensive Project Group). (2016). *Fanfu fengbaoxia de qiyejia mingyun* (The fate of entrepreneurs under the thunderstorm of the anti-corruption drive). http://news.ifeng.com/a/20160426/48590100_0.shtml (accessed 5 May 2018).

Chen, Minglu. (2015). From economic elites to political elites: Private entrepreneurs in the people's political consultative conference. *Journal of Contemporary China* 24(94), 613–627.

Chen, Yi. (2014). Jiti xingdong, wangluo yu Wenzhou qiyejia qunti (Collective action, networks and entrepreneurial groups in Wenzhou). *Wenzhou Daxue Xuebao, Shehui kexue ban* (Journal of Wenzhou University, Social Sciences) 1, 56–62.

Chen, Zhao, Lu, Ming, and He, Junzhi. (2008). Power and political participation of entrepreneurs: Evidence from Liuzhou, Guangxi, China. *Journal of the Asia-Pacific Economy* 13(3), 298–312.

Cho, Young Nam. (2009). *Local People's Congresses in China. Development and Transition*. Cambridge: Cambridge University Press.

Deng, Guosheng and Kennedy, Scott. (2010). Big business and industry association lobbying in China: The paradox of contrasting styles. *The China Journal* 63, 101–125.

Development and Reform Commission. (2017). *Guanyu jin yibu guifan hangye xiehui shanghui shoufei guanli de yijian* (Opinion on further regulating the management of fees). http://www.gov.cn/xinwen/2017-12/01/content_5243785.htm (accessed 23 May 2018).

Dolata, Ulrich, and Schrape, Jan-Felix. (2014). Masses, crowds, communities, movements. collective formations in the digital age. *SOI Discussion Papers* 2, University of Stuttgart, 18.

Gao, Yongqiang and Tian, Zhilong. (2007). How firms influence the government policy decision-making in China. *Singapore Management Review* 28(1), 73–85.

Geertz, Clifford. (1963). *Peddlers and Princes*. Chicago: University of Chicago Press.

Getz, Kathleen A. (1997). Research in corporate political action: Integration and assessment. *Business and Society* 36(1), 32–72.

Gongshanglian (National Federation of Industry and Commerce). (2009). *Di baci quanguo siying qiye chouxiang diaocha* (The 8th National Survey on Private Enterprises). http://www.china.com.cn/economic/txt/2009-03/26/content_17504790.htm (accessed 20 March 2016).

Guangdong sheng Shandong shanghui huanjie da hui ji di erjie huiyuan dahui di yici huiyi yuanman zhaokai (First session of the second membership meeting after reelections, and plenary session of the Shandong chamber of commerce in Guangdong). (2015). *Shandong Ren* (Shandong People). *Journal of the Shandong Chamber of Commerce* 5–6, 82–83.

Guangzhou FIC (Guangzhou Federation of Industry and Commerce). (2016). Chongfen fahui hangye shangxiehui zuoyong, goujian gaoxiao xingzheng guanli tizhi (Fully develop the function of industry associations and chambers of commerce, establish a system of administrative management courses at institutions of higher learning). Guangzhou Federation of Industry and Commerce (Ed.). *Zong Shanghui di 14jie zhiweihui diaocha yanjiu yu canzheng yizheng chengguo huibian 2011–2016* (Collection of the results of the Executive Committees 14th report on research and political participation), pp. 55–61.

Hengyang huixuan yin gaoceng zhennu. Xi Jinping zhuiwen 'Gongchandangyuan nar qule' (The election fraud in Hengyang renders the elite furious. Xi Jinping asks 'Where have the Communist Party members gone'). (2014). http://news.ifeng.com/mainland/detail_2014_02/25/34146829_0.shtml (accessed 25 July 2018).

Hou, Yue. (2019). *The Private Sector in Public Office: Selective Property Rights in China*. Cambridge: Cambridge University Press.

Hu, Kun. (2018). Liu Yonghao: Minying qiye jintian zhongyu dedaole rentong (Liu Yonghao: Today private enterprises are finally acknowledged). *Zhongguo Qiyejia* (China's entrepreneurs), 6 March, pp. 78–81.

Huang, Dongya. (2013). Qiyejia ruhe yingxiang difang zhengce guocheng. Guanyu guojia zhongxin de anli fenxi he leixing jiangou (How do entrepreneurs impact upon local policy processes. Analysis of the type and structure of our countries crucial cases). *Shehuixue Yanjiu* (Sociological Studies) 5, pp. 172–196.

Huang, Dongya and Zhang, Hua. (2018). Minying qiyejia ruhe zuzhi qilai? Jiyu Guangdong gongshang lianxi xitong shanghui zuzhi de fenxi (How do private entrepreneurs organize themselves? An analysis of the industrial and commercial connections in Guangdong's Chambers of Commerce organization. *Shehuixue Yanjiu (Sociological Studies)* 4, 28–55.

Huang, Dongya, and Chen, Minglu. (2017). From 'State Control' to Business Lobbying. The Institutional Origin of Private Entrepreneurs' Policy Influence in China. *Working Papers on East Asian Studies* 118, November. Duisburg (Institute of East Asian Studies, University Duisburg-Essen) with a preface and an introduction written by Thomas Heberer. https://www.uni-due.de/imperia/md/content/in-east/about/publications_green_series/paper118-2017.pdf (accessed 7 February 2019).

Huang, Shaoqing, and Yu, Hui. (2005). Minjian shanghui de jiti xingdong jizhi (Collective action mechanism of private chambers of commerce). *Jingji Shehui Tizhi Bijiao (Comparison of Economic and Social Systems)* 4, 66–73.

Huang, Ye. (2013). *Jin 10nian shang baiming minying qiyejia luoma: chengzheng zhi boyi xishengpin* (In 10 years almost 100 private entrepreneurs fell from grace: victims of political games), http://finance.people.com.cn/stock/n/2013/0827/c67815-22703236.html (accessed 25 February 2016).

Jahns, Christopher. (1999). *Integriertes strategisches Management. Neue Perspektiven zu Theorie und Praxis des strategischen Managements* (Integrated strategic management. New perspectives on theory and practice of strategic management), Sternenfels: Verlag Wissenschaft und Praxis.

Ji, Yingying. (2015). Dangdai Zhongguo hangye xiehui shanghui de zhengce yingxiangli: zhidu huanjing yu cengji fenhua (The influence of business associations on policy in contemporary China: The institutional context and stratification). *Nanjing Shehui Kexue (Nanjing Social Sciences)* 9, 65–72.

Ji, Yingying. (2018). Emerging state–business contention in China: Collective action of a business association and China's fragmented governance structure. *China Information* 32(3), 463–484.

Kennedy, Scott. (2008). *The Business of Lobbying in China*. Cambridge/Mass.: Harvard University Press.

Kung, James Kai-sing. and Ma, Chicheng. (2018). Friends with benefits: How political connections help to sustain private enterprise growth in China. *Economica* 85(337), 41–74.

Lang, Peijuan. (2015). Qiyejia Renda daibiao canzheng guancha (Observation of political participation of entrepreneurs in People's Congresses). *Renmin Luntan (People's Tribune)* 5, 22–25. https://max.book118.com/html/2015/0707/20620988.shtm l (accessed 13 August 2019).

Li, Hongbin, Meng, Lingsheng, Wang, Qian, *et al.* (2008). Political connections, financing and firm performance: Evidence from Chinese private firms. *Journal of Development Economics* 87(2), 283–299.

Li, Jianguo. (2013). Tan shanghui ruhe yu shudi zhengfu goujian hexie de guanxi (On how the chamber of commerce can establish harmonic relations to local governments). *Lushan Meng (Dream of Shandong Businessmen)* 1, 74–75.

Li, Junjie. (2010). Jiedu guonei shoufen qiyejia fanzui baogao (Report on crimes of leading entrepreneurs in China). *Fazhi Zhoubao* (Legal System Weekly), 8 January. http://news.sina.com.cn/c/sd/2010-01-08/101719426623.shtml (accessed 13 June 2018).

Li, Kecheng. (2013). Minying qiyejia "huixuan" fansi (Rethinking vote-buying by private entrepreneurs), *Nanfengchuang* (Southern Window), May 5. http://c.chinaelections.com/wap/article.aspx?id=228567 (accessed 15 February 2020).

Li, Yuejun. (2014). Lixing xuanze zhiduzhuyi shijiao xia de 'Hengyang huixuan sheng Renda daibiao an' (The 'Hengyang People's Congress deputies vote-buying case' seen from the perspective of rational choice institutionalism). *Renda Yanjiu (People's Congress Studying)* 270(6), 9–20. http://www.rdyj.com.cn/Home/Books/detail/id/331.html (accessed 2 January 2018).

Lin, Ping. (2018). *Qiyejia fubai fanzui niandu baogao: 150 ren mian xingfa, wuren pei pan sixing* (Annual Report on Corruptive Criminal Behavior of Entrepreneurs: 150 people avoid punishment, nobody sentenced to capital punishment). https://www.thepaper.cn/newsDetail_forward_2089899 (accessed 7 February 2019).

Liu, Juanfeng, and Zhang, Jianjun. (2018). Regional business associations in China: Changes and continuities. In Zhang, Xiaoke and Zhu, Tianbiao (Eds.), *Business, Government and Economic Institutions in China*. Basingstoke: Palgrave Macmillan, 105–131.

Luqiu, Luwei Rose, and Liu, Chuyu. (2018). A 'new social class' or old friends? A study of private entrepreneurs in the National People's Congress of China. *Journal of East Asian Studies* 18(3), 389–400.

Lüzhi jinze gongyuan Zhongguo meng – fang quanguo zhengxie changwei, Zhengtai jituan dongshizhang Nan Cunhui (Diligently perform one's duty to realize the Chinese dream — Interview with the chairman of the board of Zhengtai Company and member of the Standing Committee of the PPCC). (2016). http://www.chintelc.com/news-view.asp?id=126 (accessed 26 February 2017).

Ma, Jun and He, Xuan. (2018). The Chinese Communist Party's integration policy towards private business and its effectiveness: An analysis of the ninth national survey of Chinese enterprises. *Chinese Journal of Sociology* 4(3), 422–449.

McNally, Christopher A., Guo, Hong, and Hu, Guangwei. (2007). Entrepreneurship and Political Guanxi Networks in China's Private Sector. *East-West Center Working Papers: Politics, Governance, and Security Series* 19. Honolulu: East-West Center.

Mahon, John F. (1989). Corporate political strategy. *Business in the Contemporary World* 1, 50–63.

Niedenführ, Matthias. (2018). Managementinnovation aus China? Der Emerging Trend des 'Confucian Entrepreneur' (Management Innovation from China? The Emerging Trend of the 'Confucian Entrepreneur'). In Deutsch-Chinesische Wirtschaftsvereinigung (German-Chinese Economic Association) (Ed.), *DCW Yearbook 2018* (pp. 67–76). Cologne: DCW.

Pang, Jiaoming. (2005). *Xiufa xin liliang: Ge liyi jituan youshui gongsifa* (Strength through amending a new law: Interest groups lobbying for the company law). http://finance.sina.com.cn/g/20050430/17041565752.shtml (accessed 18 February 2017).

Pei, Minxin. (2016). *China's Crony Capitalism. The Dynamics of Regime Decay.* Cambridge: Harvard University Press.

Provincial Party Committee and Government. (2011). *Guangdong shengwei sheng zhengfu wenjian 'Cujin minying jingji fazhanshang shuiping de yijian'* (Opinion of the Provincial Party Committee and Provincial Government on 'Promoting the Development of the Private Sector Economy'), Guangzhou: internal publication.

Qingdaoshi Gongshang Lianhehui (Ed.). (2012). *Qingdao shi shanghui (hangye xiehui) fazhan zhuangkuang fenxi yu duice jianyi* (Analysis and policy suggestions for the development situation of Qingdao's chambers of commerce (industry associations)). Qingdao: Qingdao Federation of Industry and Commerce and Qingdao General Chamber of Commerce.

Qingdaoshi Gongshang Lianhehui (Ed.). (2015). *Guanyu wo shi minying qiye fazhi shengtai huanjing de xianzhuang ji duice jianyi* (On the environment of the legal system for private entrepreneurs in our city). Qingdao: Qingdao Federation of Industry and Commerce and Qingdao General Chamber of Commerce.

Schubert, Gunter and Heberer, Thomas. (2015). Continuity and change in China's 'local state developmentalism'. *Issues and Studies* 51(2), 1–38.

Schubert, Gunter and Heberer, Thomas. (2017). Private entrepreneurs as a 'strategic group' in the Chinese polity. *China Review* 17(2), 95–122.

Shen, Yongdong. (2014). *Biandong huanjing zhong hangye xiehui yu zhengfu zhijian de celüexing hudong yanjiu* (The strategic interaction of business associations and government in the changing environment of China), PhD thesis, Hangzhou (Zhejiang University).

Shen, Yongdong and Song, Xiaoqing. (2016). Xin yilun hangye xiehui shanghui yu xingzheng jiguan tuogou gaige de fengxian ji qi fangfan (Risks and preventive measures of the new round of decoupling industry associations and chambers of commerce from administrative bodies). *Zhonggong Zhejiang Shengwei Dangxiao Xuebao* (*Journal of the Zhejiang Provincial Party School*) 2, 29–37.

Sun, Rongfei. (2014). Minying qiyejia zhengzhi shenfen kuozhang luxian tu (Roadmap of the enhancement of the status of private entrepreneurs). *Qingnian Shibao* (Youth Times), 29 April.

Sun, Xin, Zhu, Jiangnan, and Wu, Yiping. (2014). Organizational clientelism: An analysis of private entrepreneurs in Chinese local legislatures. *Journal of East Asian Studies* 14(1), 1–30.

Tang, Xinjun. (2016). *Qianruxing zhili: guojia yu shehui guanxi shiyu xiade hangye xiehui yanjiu* (Embedded governance: research on industry associations seen from the threshold between state and society). PhD thesis, Shanghai (Huadong Normal University).

Ten Brink, Tobias. (2013). *Chinas Kapitalismus. Entstehung, Verlauf, Paradoxien* (China's Capitalism. Origin, Process and Paradoxes). Frankfurt/M.: Campus.

Tian, Zhilong and Deng, Xinming. (2007). The determinants of corporate political strategy in Chinese transition. *Journal of Public Affairs* 7(4), 341–356.

Tse, Edward. (2016). *China's Disruptors. How Alibaba, Xiaomi, Tencent and other Companies are Changing the Rules of Business*. London: Portfolio Penguin.

Wallis, Cara. (2013). *Technomobility in China: Young Migrant Women and Mobile Phones*. New York and London: New York University Press.

Wang, Jinjun, and Zhang, Changdong. (2014). Cong xiangheng xiang wangluo zhongde shehui zuzhi yu zhengfu hudong jizhi (Social organizations and mechanisms of government interaction from the perspective of vertical and horizontal networks). *Gonggong Xingzheng Pinglun* (Journal of Public Administration) 7(5), 88–108.

Wang, Shaoguang and Fan, Peng. (2013). *Guonei liyi tuanti yingxiang yigai zhengce zhiding de jiben qudao yu fangshi* (Channels and methods of domestic Chinese interest groups to influence health policies). http://www.guancha.

cn/WangShaoGuang/2013_08_24_160893.shtml (accessed 18 February, 2016).

Wang, Zhongxin. (2014). *Jingti fuhao huixuan zhadui 'lianghui' shi quanmian duoqu zhengquan* (Be vigilant of rich persons buying votes in the two 'legislatives' to fully capture political power). http://www.cwzg.cn/html/2014/guanfengchasu_0818/6953.html (accessed 25 February 2016).

Williams, Colin C. (2008). Beyond necessity-driven versus opportunity-driven entrepreneurship: A study of informal entrepreneurs in England, Russia and Ukraine. *International Journal of Entrepreneurship and Innovation* 9(3), 157–166.

Wu, Jinglian. (2017). *Zhongguo shanghui zuo bu hao, genyuan shi mei gaoqing ding le* (China's chambers of commerce do not work well, the root causes are not clearly defined). http://www.sohu.com/a/210504691_378279 (accessed 1 May 2018).

Wu. Wei. (2006). The relationship among corporate political resources, political strategies, and political benefits of firms in China: Based on resource dependence theory. *Singapore Management Review* 28(2), 85–98.

Xing, Jianhua. (2013). *Fujian siying qiyezhu jiecengde zhengzhi canyu* (Political participation of the class of private entrepreneurs in Fujian). Peking: Shehui kexue wenxian chubanshe.

Xu, Hai. (2017). Gongmin qiyejia zhan zai shizi lukou (Citizen entrepreneurs standing at a crossroad). (2013). *Nanfang Renwu Zhoukan* (Southern Personalities Weekly), 2 August 2013. http://www.nfpeople.com/story_view.php?id=12329 (accessed 29 September 2017).

Yan, Xiaojun. (2012). 'To get rich is not only glorious': Economic reform and the new entrepreneurial party secretaries. *The China Quarterly* 210, 335–354.

Ye, Tan. (2018). Zhege hangye zhi neng fangjia xiuxi (This industry sector can only go on vacation and rest). *Caijing* (Finance and Economic), 6 August. http://www.cb.com.cn/yetan/2018_0808/1250582.html (accessed 8 August 2018).

Yu, Jianxing and Zhou, Jun. (2013). Local governance and business associations in Wenzhou: A model for the road to civil society in China? *Journal of Contemporary China* 22(81), 394–408.

Yu, Jianxing, Yashima, Kenichiro, and Shen, Yongdong. (2014). Autonomy or Privilege? Lobbying intensity of local business associations in China. *Journal of Chinese Political Science* 19(3), 315–333.

Yu, Xie and Sidney Leng. (2018). Tech entrepreneurs replace real estate tycoons as political advisors in China's push for IT edge. *South China Morning Post,* 4 March.

Zhang, Chandong. (2017). Re-examining the electoral connection in authoritarian China: The local People's Congress and its private enterprise deputies. *China Review* 17(1), 1–27.

Zhang, Lei, and Ma, Bin. (2008). *Minjian shanghui: xinxing de shehui zhili zuzhi* (Non-state chambers of commerce: rising organizations of social governance). http://xyblw.com/1/view-327871.htm (accessed 1 May 2018).

Zhang, Ting, and Stough, Roger R. (Eds.) (2013). *Entrepreneurship and Economic Growth in China.* Singapore: World Scientific.

Zhang, Xiaoke, and Zhu, Tianbiao. (2018). Understanding business-government relations in China: Changes, causes and consequences. In Zhang, Xiaoke. and Zhu, Tianbiao. (Eds), *Business, Government and Economic Institutions in China* (p. 346). Basingstoke: Palgrave Macmillan.

Zhao, Lijiang. (2006). *Zhongguo siying qiyejia de zhengzhi canyu* (Political participation of Chinese private entrepreneurs). Peking: Zhongguo jingji chubanshe.

Zhonggong Jinjiang shiwei zuzhibu. (2012). *Zhonggong Jinjiang shiwei zuzhibu tongzhi 'Guanyu yinfa Dao feigongyouzhi qiye guazhi ganbu (2012–2014 niandu) guanli banfa' de tongzhi* (Notification of the Organization Department of the CCP Party Committee of Jinjiang on the operational method of dispatching cadres to private enterprises). Jinjiang: internal publication.

Zhonggong Zhongyang Guowuyuan yingzao qiyejia jiankang chengzhang huanjing, hongyang youxiu qiyejia jingshen geng hao fahui qiyejia zuoyong de yijian (Central Committee of the CCP and State Council on creating an environment for the healthy growth of entrepreneurs, promoting a spirit of outstanding entrepreneurship so that they can play a still better role). (2017). *Renmin Ribao,* 26 September. http://cpc.people.cn/n1/2017/0926/c64387-29558638.html (accessed 3 April 2018).

Zhonghua Renmin Gongheguo Gongye he Xinxihua Bu (Ministry of Industry and Information Technology of the People's Republic of China). (2011). *Guanyu yinfa zhong xiao qiye huaxing biaozhun guiding de tongzhi* (Notification of the decree on criteria for classifying small and medium-sized enterprises), http://www.miit.gov.cn/n1146285/n1146352/n3054355/n3057511/n3057521/n3057523/c3544211/content.html (assessed 15 March 2018).

Zhonghua Renmin Zhengzhi Xieshang Huiyi Quanguo Weiyuanhui ti'an gong-zuo tiaoli (Regulation for motions of the national PPCC). (2011). http://

www.cpPPCC.gov.cn/2011/09/06/ARTI1315304517625107.shtml (accessed 21 March 2016).

Zhonggong Zhongyang Zhengzhiju. (2018). Zhonggong Zhongyang Zhengzhiju zhaokai huiyi (Meeting of the Political Bureau of the CCP). http://politics. people.com.cn/n1/2018/0801/c1024-30181880.html (accessed 8 August 2018).

Zhu, Jiangnan, and Wu, Yiping. (2018). Chinese private entrepreneurs' formal political connections: Industrial and geographical distribution. In Zhang, Xiaoke and Zhu, Tianbiao (Eds.), *Business, Government and Economic Institutions in China* (pp. 165–194). Basingstoke: Palgrave Macmillan.

Zhu, Xi. (2018). *Shizhang tu dai ni kanqing 2017 he 2018 lianghui zhongde shangbang qiyejia hangye fenbu he renyuan biandong* (10 charts clearly show the professional distribution and personnel changes of the two sessions). https://www.qianzhan.com/analyst/detail/220/180308-d1cdf529.html (accessed 1 May 2018).

Chapter 5

Informal and 'Connective' Strategic Action

Aside from formal organizations, private entrepreneurs engage in manifold patterns of collective strategic action in informal settings. As we will show, informal networks constitute an 'organizational grid...a type of associational life that remains outside the surveillance of the state' (Singerman, 2004, 156, *op. cit.* in Diana Fu, 2017, 501). In this chapter, we will first discuss their political strategies via participation in social networks, such as alumni networks and entrepreneurial clubs. We then turn to a specific new form of entrepreneurial agency which we call 'connective action', which here refers to entrepreneurs making use of digital technology for the purposes of strategic action.

Social Networks

Networks link individuals, groups, or organizations together in a social relationship. Network resources, i.e. resources benefitting network members, constitute a particular form of social capital. Mark Granovetter differentiates between strong ties and weak ties in networks. The difference lies in the amount of time that members of a group spend with one another, the emotional intensity of the relationship, levels of mutual trust and intimacy, and the type of reciprocal assistance offered between members. Granovetter conceives strong ties, which tend to cut a group off from others, as less effective with regard to pursuing a network's strategic goals than weak ties.[1] In areas such as Jinjiang, Fujian province, where many private enterprises are family or clan enterprises (*jiazu qiye*), the members of a clan as a 'strong ties' organization are socially obliged to provide mutual assistance and support. These obligations do not only apply to clan members within a given enterprise but also to the social relationship between entrepreneurs and local officials who belong to the same clan; or to the relationship between different lineages that ally with one another in a locality. In contrast, business associations or entrepreneurial clubs as a rule are characterized by weak ties, however they figure as important 'local bridges' (*qiaotoubao*) between entrepreneurs and local governments. In the case of alumni networks, their effectiveness depends on how 'strong' the above-mentioned ties are. Networks are essential resources through which private entrepreneurs engage in strategic action and must be carefully observed in order to gauge the potential of entrepreneurs to influence policy-making.

Collective strategic action by private entrepreneurs is reinforced by their parallel and overlapping membership in different *guanxi*-networks. These networks can facilitate access to important information, help to set up communication channels to local party state officials and assist the coordination of policy initiatives across business sectors and government bureaucracies, arguably contributing to the strengthening of group-awareness and identity-formation among private entrepreneurs.

Table 1 illustrates the embeddedness of private entrepreneur F one of our respondents, into a multitude of different network structures including political, entrepreneurial, alumni, and hometown organizations. Depending on the issue at stake, as this female entrepreneur told us, a certain network will be activated to satisfy specific business needs.[2] Figure 1, meanwhile, highlights how the networks of this respondent are inter-linked so that she can also reach out to very different organizations for the same purpose.

As a leading member of the Qingdao branch of the 'China National Democratic Construction Association', she has access to the provincial

---

[1] On strong and weak ties, see Granovetter (1973).
[2] Interview, Qingdao, 3 March 2016.

Table 1:   Organizational Affiliation of Entrepreneur F in Qingdao: Multilayered Networks

Educational alumni networks	Political networks	Entrepreneurial networks	Others
Primary School 'October 1ˢᵗ', Peking	Political Consultative Conference Qingdao City	Qingdao Federation of Industry and Commerce	Fujian Hometown Association
Alumni Qinghua University	Member of the 'China Democratic National Construction Association'	Qingdao Chinese Enterprise Confederation	
Changjiang MBA Network		Qingdao Association for Promoting Small and Medium Enterprises	
	Chinese Youth Federation member	Qingdao Fujian Chamber of Commerce	
		Quanzhou Chamber of Commerce in Qingdao	
		Qingdao Entrepreneurs' Association	
		Qingdao Association of Privately-Run Enterprises	
		Qingdao Association of Young Chinese Entrepreneurs	
		Qingdao Female Entrepreneurs Association	
		Qingdao Entrepreneurs Exchange Association	
		Qingdao Textile and Garment Industry Association	
		Qingdao Entrepreneurs Club	

Source: Personal information by an entrepreneur, Qingdao, 3 March 2016.

and national leadership of her party. Through her membership in the Qingdao Federation of Industry and Commerce, she was elected as a member of Qingdao's PPCC and thus has access to the city's United Front Department.[3] Hence, entrepreneur F has access to Qingdao's party leadership, too. As a member of the city's PPCC, she can liaise with both the

---

[3]The Federation of Industry and Commerce is affiliated to the CCP United Front Department. United Front Departments (*tongyi zhanxian gongzuobu*) exist at all

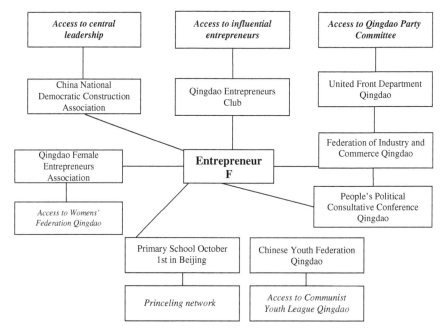

Figure 1: Multilayered Networks of Private Entrepreneur F in Qingdao

Source: Personal information provided by an entrepreneur, Qingdao, 3 March 2016.

provincial leadership of the PPCC and the city government. Moreover, as an active member in the city's branch of the Chinese Youth Federation (*Zhonghua Qingnian Lianhehui*) and the Womens' Federation, she can easily contact the local branches of these organizations. As an alumni of October 1st Primary School in Beijing,[4] she is further affiliated to the '*hong erdai*' or members of the 'second red generation' ('princelings', as they are called in the Western literature),[5] who belong to a tightly-knit

administrative levels — from center to township — under the party committee on the respective level, in this case the party committee of Qingdao city.

[4]This school (primary and middle school) was founded in 1952 for children of high-ranking military cadres.

[5] 'Second red generation' or 'princelings' refers to the children of veteran communist leaders holding high-ranking offices before 1966, be it in politics or in the armed forces.

network among themselves.[6] Finally, membership in the 'Qingdao Entrepreneurs Club' provides her with communication channels to other influential local entrepreneurs. This network constellation illustrates the opportunity structure that any entrepreneur can make use of for strategic action, which is in many instances more important for them than engaging with formal organizations.

The activation of networks and *guanxi* plays a crucial role in the minds of all entrepreneurs as it helps in all kinds of situations they encounter in life. As one of our respondents, an entrepreneur from Beijing, noted:

> There are several *guanxi* networks which I approach if I need help in solving problems: First, school, university, and EMBA classmates (*tongxue*). Second, business partners (*shangye huoban*). Third, friends within the government. Particularly in these times of economic stress I need the help of these networks to solve business challenges.[7]

Particularly in smaller locations in the central and western parts of China, where business associations are not so well developed, entrepreneurs told us that they solve problems by means of their own informal ties and networks which often connect them to local political power as well:

> I was born here and have many good contacts through my various networks of relatives, friends, and former classmates (*tongxue*). Since we know each other here, I am also well-connected to the local government and its leadership.[8]

Often enough, informal network-building stems from, and is often actively encouraged by, local governments in their strategy to foster and intensify private sector development. In Jinjiang, we were told that the local government invited groups of promising entrepreneurs to attend management courses at renowned universities. One entrepreneur noted

---

[6] Interviewees conceived of the latter rather as a 'strong tie' network.

[7] Interview, entrepreneur, Beijing, 8 September 2015.

[8] Interview, entrepreneur, Mile County, 15 March 2017.

that 'this not only helped us to broaden our management skills. It also brought us into contact with other entrepreneurs and thus contributed to our network building'.[9]

In the following, we will look more in detail at alumni networks, entrepreneurial clubs and circles, and finally cyberspace connections as manifestations of informal strategic action by private entrepreneurs.

Alumni networks

Private networks as channels of communication and transaction are particularly salient in the case of former MBA or EMBA graduates from high-profile institutions such as Beijing University's Guanghua School of Management or the Changjiang Business School,[10] which have campuses in Beijing, Shanghai, and Guangzhou. According to one study, graduates of such renowned schools gain higher incomes than they had earned prior to studying there.[11] These schools only accept well-known entrepreneurs with a good reputation. Their programs are particularly aimed at creating peer bonds between them, which is to mutual benefit to both the entrepreneurs and the school: While the former profit from these connections for the rest of their business lives, the school may attract further well-off students in the future for its particular nodal position in these networks.

As a rule, an MBA or EMBA training program takes two years. One of our respondents noted that the Guanghua School prefers to take individuals who have more than 8 years of enterprise experience and whose companies produce an annual total output value of more than 50 million RMB. Until 2014, one-third of admissions were reserved for high-status or promising officials (party secretaries, mayors, ministers, vice ministers), who were normally provided with a scholarship and did not have to pay tuition fees. After graduation they remained esteemed members of the alumni networks. The rationale behind this policy was to connect

---

[9] Interview, Jinjiang, 7 September 2012.

[10] Such schools provide expensive MBA or EMBA training courses for private entrepreneurs.

[11] See e.g. http://daxueconsulting.com/business-schools-in-china/ (accessed 16 August 2019).

important entrepreneurs and high-ranking officials and thereby facilitate mutual understanding and long-lasting relationships. However, the anti-corruption drive initiated by Xi Jinping in 2013 has prohibited this kind of networking between private entrepreneurs and promising officials. Now, the latter are no longer permitted to attend such programs.[12]

An entrepreneur from Qingdao described his *Changjiang* class network as follows:

> Foremost this network is based on trust. Each day we exchange ideas about issues of daily life, hobbies, problems of our enterprises, and how to solve them through *Weixin*. We even help each other if one of us needs specific contacts to high officials or authorities. The level of mutual help and trust is tremendous between us entrepreneurs.[13]

Along the same lines, a Beijing-based entrepreneur from Yunnan Province, who also served as vice-chairman of the Yunnan Chamber of Commerce in Beijing, told us:

> MBA programs in China are organized by an educational institution to create an atmosphere for constructing connections. First, the age of the 'students' in these programs is around 40. In this age you have already developed specific habits, and you have relatively pronounced values. (…) Accordingly, right from the beginning of the program the school endeavored to foster exchanges and connections between us. Second, there exists a multitude of alumni clubs such as in Beijing, Yunnan and other locations which we can attend after graduation and contact in the case of need.[14]

Interestingly, this entrepreneur classified the relationships within his MBA alumni circles as more important than those within his chamber of commerce. To speak from Granovetter's perspective, the ties to one's alumni (*tongxue*) seem to be more effective and deeper than those within

---

[12]An entrepreneur told us that, prior to 2015, officials who were alumni gladly helped on requests of other alumni. Interview, Beijing, 16 February 2016.

[13]Interview, Qingdao, 19 February 2015.

[14]Interview, entrepreneur, vice-chairman of Yunnan Chamber of Commerce in Beijing, 8 September 2015.

the chamber and could be classified as 'strong ties', even though these alumni networks do not constitute a closed group.

Another entrepreneur noted that membership of a Changjiang School MBA alumni community can help to establish social contacts and connections beyond one's own classmate group:

> If I am looking to contact a leading entrepreneur or an opinion leader such as Alibaba's Ma Yun, I would first ask my classmates whether anybody has contact to him or knows someone who is close to him. If not, I'll approach our former teachers asking whether they can arrange for such a contact. If this also fails I'll ask the school's wider alumni network for help. Normally, this network can help me in getting access to such a person as Ma Yun.[15]

Other alumni networks are no less important for strategic action. An entrepreneur in Shenzhen, who returned from the US, runs private educational and training programs similar to UBER models providing education on demand. He is not only in close contact with his former classmates at Tsinghua University, but is also a leading member of the 'Europe–America Fellow Student Association' (*Oumei tongxuehui*), the 'Europe–America Fellow Student Association's Entrepreneurial Society' (*Oumei tongxuehui qiyejia lianyihui*),[16] and the 'Qinghua Entrepreneurs Society (*Qinghua qiyejia xiehui*)'.[17] As he told us, his position in the second and third organization gives him and his fellow entrepreneurs convenient access to the political leadership of Shenzhen and Guangdong Province,

---

[15] Interview, Qingdao, 19 February 2015.

[16] The *Oumei tongxuehui* or 'Europe-America Fellow Student Association' was founded in 1913 and acts under the guidance of the United Front Department of the CCP. It is an important group, as demonstrated when General Secretary Xi Jinping gave a talk at its 10th anniversary in 2013. The *Oumei tongxuehui qiyejia lianyihui*, which was founded in 1994, acts as a branch organization under the *Oumei tongxuehui*. Both primarily serve networking purposes.

[17] The Qinghua Entrepreneurs Society (*Qinghua qiyejia xiehui*), founded in 2001 in Silicon Valley by a group of Tsinghua University alumni, aims at promoting innovation and entrepreneurship in high tech industries. It is a network organization affiliated with Tsinghua University.

connections extremely helpful for pursuing their own or collective business interests.[18]

The 'Zhejiang Regional Economic Cooperation Promotion Association' (*Zhejiang sheng quyu jingji hezuo qiye fazhan cujinhui*)[19] is an association jointly established by the alumni of the 'Advanced Industry and Commerce Director-General Research and Training Classes of Zhejiang University' and the 'Zhejiang University's Management Training Centre'. Its members are private entrepreneurs who have all attended training courses at Zhejiang University. At the time of our visit in March 2017, the organization had more than 7,000 members. It portrayed itself as a network organization for private entrepreneurs operating under the 'Zhejiang Federation of Industry and Commerce'. Originally, it was founded as an entrepreneurial alumni club. Later, its name was changed to make it more attractive for collaboration with government authorities. They claimed to have an excellent relationship with the provincial government and that due to their good relations with provincial and local authorities, members of this group could directly bargain with them if necessary. Trust among members is based on their shared experiences while studying at Zhejiang University, a relationship which permits joint collective action. They see themselves as an 'interest group' (*liyi tuanti*) with a shared identity (as private entrepreneurs and alumni), who pursue their interests by means of long-term strategies (*changqi zhanlüe*):

> Single entrepreneurs are unable to work out long-term strategies for private enterprise development. This can only be done by a group (*qunti*). These strategies refer to long-term objectives for the private sector, particularly in Zhejiang Province, to push ahead development of the provincial economy, engage in charity activities, strengthen the legal rights of private entrepreneurs, and even to train the second and third generation of entrepreneurs.'[20]

---

[18] Interview, Shenzhen, 22 September 2015.
[19] For more information on this association see: http://www.ceoclub.zj.cn/web/MT_B0003. asp?FirstKind=MT_00002_100015247&KindID=MT_00002_100015249 (accessed 5 August 2018).
[20] Interview, 22 March 2017.

Entrepreneurial clubs and private circles

There are also many elite clubs and so-called *quanzi* (cliques or circles of friends), i.e. informal membership associations with shared interests and strict membership rules figuring as tools of strategic action. Some of these provide hobby and leisure activities for entrepreneurs connected by common industry affiliations, shared experiences, social interests (e.g. concerning the environment), and so on. Among the most prominent clubs are the 'Taishan Association' (*Taishanhui*), the 'Chinese Entrepreneurs' Club' (*Zhongguo qiyejia julebu*), 'Zhenghe Island' (*Zhenghedao*), and the 'Chang'an-Club' (*Chang'an julebu*). Their core members are renowned entrepreneurs. The exclusive 'Taishan Association', for instance, was founded in 1993 as the 'Taishan Industrial Academy' (*Taishan Chanye Yanjiuyuan*) by four prominent entrepreneurs in order to discuss business issues at least once a month. It invites only a few people per year to become new members. In addition, famous scholars and politicians such as economist Wu Jinglian or Hu Deping, the influential son of the former CCP chairman Hu Yaobang, act as senior advisors to this club.[21] The annual membership fee amounts to several hundred thousand RMB; social status and professional experience are important for becoming a member. Under the impression that the number of members had increased too much, diluting exclusivity, a group of 16 big-company entrepreneurs established a new, separate organization in 2005, the above-mentioned 'Taishan Association' (*Taishanhui*) (Zhang, 2009).[22]

Zhenghedao is probably the most influential private internet platform and social network of the Chinese business elite. It was founded in 2010 by Liu Donghua, who used to be the chief editor of the journal 'Chinese Entrepreneurs' (*Zhongguo Qiyejia*). In 2017, the club had more than 6,000

---

[21] Hu Deping is the former vice chairman of the All-China Federation of Industry & Commerce and Secretary of the National Association of Industry & Commerce (both under the United Front Work Department of the CCP). As such, he is very familiar with the problems of the private sector. Both his former positions and the fact that he is the eldest son of the late Hu Yaobang, provide him with considerable prestige and influence.

[22] See also the overview of China's 10 biggest entrepreneurial circles and clubs (Zhongguo shida shangye quanzi gaikuang — lanbiao), http://blog.sina.com.cn/s/blog_6143757701 02uz7z.html (accessed 6 March 2019).

members. On its website, *Zhenghedao* calls itself the 'top high-end social networking platform for entrepreneurs in China'. As its core values it emphasizes trust-building, 'bringing together' (*ju zai yiqi*) and cooperation.[23] To gain admission, an entrepreneur must come from a company with an annual turnover of at least 100 million RMB and must have made substantial contributions to society. In addition, membership is given only after a highly selective approval process. Members constantly exchange views and news in the form of blogging and at gatherings, conferences, and banquets which bring together politicians, scholars, and opinion leaders.[24] The network focuses not only on issues related to poverty alleviation, climate change, improvement of the environment, and ecological sustainability. Prominent members of the network have also campaigned against the ivory trade.[25] In addition, as we were told, they initiate 'activities through the media' and 'help the people to understand and trust the social group of entrepreneurs, thus changing public opinion vis-á-vis private entrepreneurship':

We attempt to make our demands for policy improvement public and to explain the problems the private sector is facing, not only to the government but also to the wider public. A better understanding of the private sector by both the government and society is crucial for policy improvements.[26]

Trust is conceived as a specific precondition for creating strategic interest coalitions among entrepreneurs:

Only if entrepreneurs trust our organization they will approach us. Therefore, we try to reinforce trust by means of various activities such as workshops, our journal etc. These activities must be closely related to the interests of our membership. Otherwise it will be impossible to create trust.[27]

---

[23] Website of *Zhenghedao*: http://www.zhisland.com (accessed 26 September 2017).
[24] Interview with members, Beijing, 23 February 2016.
[25] Interview, Beijing, 3 March 2015.
[26] Interview, Zhenghedao, 23 February 2016.
[27] Interview, Zhenghedao, 23 February 2016.

Zhenghedao's internet platform shifted in a more political direction in 2013 when it promoted the emergence of 'citizen entrepreneurs' to encourage active citizenship and the development of civil society.[28] In 2015, *Zhenghedao* promoted a new value system of 'civilized' business behavior among its members, i.e. refraining from corrupt practices, unfair competition, and immoral behavior. As Liu Donghua explained, the basic idea of *Zhenghedao* is to assure the general public that entrepreneurship acts in the interests of a progressing society, is dedicated to the education of globally-oriented entrepreneurs, and supports the government in public goods provision.[29] Again, trust-building is crucial. Both the government and the public should respect and trust private entrepreneurs, which facilitates their endeavors to influence and shape public policies. But trust is also indispensable for group coherence and strategic action which *Zhenghedao* performs on behalf of its members.[30]

A cursory perusal of *Zhenghedao's* member journal 'References for Strategic Policy Decisions' (*juece cankao*) reveals that leading entrepreneurs are ready to express their personal views and how much they are concerned not only with business issues but also with social and political developments in contemporary China. Articles in the December 2014 issue, for instance, discussed steps to be taken in the realm of private sector reform (limiting local governments' interference in company activities, granting private enterprises more leeway and flexibility, etc.) and demanded tax reductions for Chinese enterprises, pointing out that many Chinese dynasties were overthrown due to extremely high tax rates. The January 2012 issue emphasized that entrepreneurs seek reforms but not revolution and that revolution can only be prevented by reforms.[31] Asserting that activities of private entrepreneurs are in China's national interest, including private sector development, is a 'meta strategy' of

---

[28]This objective has since been dropped, however, as the term 'civil society' became politically sensitive after 2014, when the central government published a list of terms of be avoided by officials and the media. See Xu Hai (2017).

[29]Interview, Beijing, 23 February 2016.

[30]Interview, Zhenghedao, 23 February 2016.

[31]Due to the political climate in China after 2015, the journal focused primarily on issues of enterprise philosophies, technical innovations, management issues or creating brand products.

private entrepreneurs, highlighting that private entrepreneurship and the well-being of Chinese society are closely intertwined.[32]

Another important entrepreneurial club, the 'China Entrepreneurs Forum' (*Zhongguo Qiyejia Luntan,* CEF), launched in 2000, organizes a famous annual meeting of private entrepreneurs in the winter resort of Yabuli, Heilongjiang province. These events bring together hundreds of the most influential Chinese entrepreneurs to exchange ideas and to discuss issues concerning sustainable development and corporate social responsibility.[33] During the 2013 meeting, Wang Weijia, President of Mtone Wireless (*Meitong Wuxian*), a company providing internet services, emphasized proudly that China's private sector accounted for two-thirds of China's GDP, 60 percent of its tax income and almost 9 out of 10 jobs, thus pointing to the decisive role of the private sector and its rising significance in the Chinese polity. However, as he stated, to proceed further, a 'transformation in governance is necessary', i.e.

> (…) a clear transition toward the rule of law and the development of a civil society with multiple voices and points of views. In this scenario, the government would no longer be the sole authority determining how China was run, but would be guided by social entrepreneurs, think tanks, and mature non-government organizations (NGOs), both from China and overseas (cited in Tse, 2016, 145–146).[34]

Edward Tse, Founder and CEO of Gao Feng Advisory Company, a global strategy and management consulting firm with roots in China, remarked that Wang's statement had been received by other entrepreneurs in an 'enthusiastic way'. At the same time, Tse argues that these entrepreneurs have developed both a deep love for their country and genuine

---

[32] Official statements by this club and the content of '*Juece Cankao*' have meanwhile been tuned down considerably due to the increasing ideological rigidity under Xi Jinping. Interview, Beijing, Zhenghedao, 23 February 2016.

[33] Interview, entrepreneur, Beijing, 4 March 2015.

[34] Previous meetings discussed 'Sustainable Growth (2014)', 'One Belt One Road' (2015), 'China's Economy under Macro-History' (2016), and 'China's Economic Transition and Entrepreneurial Innovation' (2017), 'New Spirit of Entrepreneurship in the New Era' (2018), 'Facing up to Challenges with Firmness and Confidence. The New Trajectory of China's Reform and Opening-Up' (2019).

respect for the Communist Party and do not intend to bring about political change. Rather, they feel a strong responsibility toward their country and believe that China can only prosper if the private sector is flourishing (Tse, 2016: 146–149). Since the beginning of the Xi Jinping era, as Tse claims, any political engagement on the part of private entrepreneurs has become very risky, many would rather abstain from making the slightest connection between private entrepreneurship and the construction of civil society as a counterweight to the party state.

When establishing networks and increasing their social capital, Chinese entrepreneurs are quite inventive. One respondent told us that he was a member of an association with the surname Wang (*Wangshi xiehui*). Only people with a reputation of being 'influential' are qualified to attend. Nominally, the association is primarily concerned with genealogical research, but, in practice, it is part of a huge networking operation with many locally important people (officials, lawyers, entrepreneurs, etc.) as members.[35] One entrepreneur spoke about his motorcycle club consisting primarily of entrepreneurs and self-employed academics (such as lawyers) and classified this as a 'strong network of friendship and mutual support';[36] another mentioned his golf club, the members of which are again mostly private entrepreneurs. The interviewee argued that such clubs form part of his network-building efforts. As elsewhere in the contemporary world, and particularly in China's privileged strata of successful entrepreneurs, golf clubs are an important platform of multilayered networks which provide personal contact to a multitude of 'important' people including other entrepreneurs and, not least, powerful party state cadres. Engaging in a costly leisure activity, golf club members discuss issues related to both their individual businesses and overall private sector development, but also to cooperation (collective strategic action) among entrepreneurs.[37]

Tightly knit entrepreneurial networks also establish credit cooperatives or advisory bodies for entrepreneurs.[38] A more recent development

---

[35]Interview, Qingdao, 26 March 2017.
[36]Interview, Hangzhou, 21 March 2017.
[37]Interview, Qingdao, 19 February 2015.
[38]See e.g. '*Pengyou quan' shengji xinyong lianheti* (Circles of friends turn into credit alliances), *21Shiji Jingji Baodao* (Economic Reports in the 21st Century), 6 July 2014.

has brought about different types of local credit cooperatives established by private entrepreneurs which, for instance, figure as 'Foundations' or 'Federations' to provide mutual assistance for privately-owned companies (*Minying qiyejia huzhu jijinhui* or *Minying qiye huzhu lianhehui*). Because private enterprises often face difficulties getting access to bank loans, these self-organized cooperatives put together crowdfunding schemes in which each member deposits a certain amount of money which may then be lent out to other members in case of need.[39] Networks undergirded by strong ties and mutual trust also provide members with long-term interest-free loans or flexible bridging loans and often mobilize investments in member enterprises.[40] They also function as advisory bodies which support their members in solving major business or management problems, at times even establishing a 'private board of directors' (*siren dongshihui*), made up of experienced club or *quanzi* members, who counsel an entrepreneur at confidential meetings.[41] Patterns of mutual assistance between private entrepreneurs are an important part of entrepreneurial strategic action. Such activities raise the self-awareness of private entrepreneurs as members of a social constituency who often must, and are able to, pursue objectives beyond — though not against — the party state. This arguably inspires a level of self-confidence that serves to encourage further collective strategic action, which often enough targets the shortcomings of official policy-making concerning private sector development, particularly with respect to access to credit, taxation, regulatory inconsistencies, and the manifold instances of discrimination against private companies in comparison to state-owned enterprises.

While it is hard to measure the policy impact of these entrepreneurial clubs, some of them are clearly very influential due to their direct access to high-level government and party leaders and their opening up of new informal channels for political lobbying and strategic action. However, as mentioned earlier, entrepreneurs have to be cautious and avoid being seen as 'too' political. If this happens, as in the case of billionaire

---

[39] Interview, entrepreneur, Hangzhou, 26 February 2015. See also the various contributions in Cumming *et al.* (2015).

[40] Interview, entrepreneur, Qingdao, 19 February 2015.

[41] Interview, Beijing, 3 March 2015.

Wang Gongquan who launched and financed the 'New Citizens Movement'[42] or the liberal blogger Xue Biqun, they are quickly silenced.[43] As a leading member of an entrepreneurial club noted, 'We must be careful, since we know that we are closely watched and monitored by the authorities for dissident tendencies.'[44] Another of our respondents noted:

> If an entrepreneur acts too politically from the perspective of the officials, it is easy to put him out of action: they may accuse him of tax fraud or corruption. Hence, our leeway for exerting influence is rather limited.[45]

As mentioned above, the political and ideological climate for nonconformist voices in China has greatly deteriorated. As such, entrepreneurial clubs and private networks try hard to keep politics and business separate. At times, this leads to conflict among private entrepreneurs, since many believe that they should become more politically active.[46] In fact, some well-known entrepreneurs have dared to criticize government policies in public repeatedly, ignoring the danger such behavior implies. In February 2016, for example, Ren Zhiqiang,[47] a retired, outspoken real-estate tycoon and party member, used his blog to argue that the increasing restrictions

---

[42] Wang Gongquan was detained in 2013. The 'New Citizens' Movement' (*Zhongguo Xin Gongmin Yundong*) was a civil rights movement working for a peaceful transition towards constitutionalism and the formation of an autonomous civil society. For more information see 'New Citizens' Movement', (https://ipfs.io/ipfs/QmXoypizjW3WknFiJnKLwHCnL72 vedxjQkDDP1mXWo6uco/wiki/New_Citizens'_Movement.html (accessed 26 September 2017).

[43] Xue Biqun was arrested in 2013 for sharing his ideas about corruption and political reform on his blog with 12 million followers. See South China Morning Post 13 January 2014. http://www.scmp.com/news/china-insider/article/1403009/four-months-after-prostitution-arrest-influential-investor (accessed 26 September 2017).

[44] Interview, Beijing, 23 February 2016.

[45] Interview, Beijing, 16 February 2015.

[46] Interview, Beijing, 3 March 2015.

[47] On Ren Zhiqiang and his independent thinking see Hurun Baifu, 11/2015, 36–39. In early May 2016, Ren Zhiqiang's Communist Party membership was put on a one-year probation by party authorities. In the end, he was permitted to keep his party membership.

on media reporting are dangerous for China's further development. At his instigation, a meeting of prominent entrepreneurs complained that the actions of the party leadership reminded them of 'a new Cultural Revolution'. As a result, the newspaper of the Communist Youth League demanded that Ren Zhiqiang's party membership be revoked. Some days later, the Chinese Cyberspace Administration closed down his blog, which had more than 38 million followers. The incident shocked China's business elite, reminding them how much the political climate had reduced the leeway for raising critical entrepreneurial voices (Black and Mitchell, 2016). Ren Zhiqiang reemerged in public in June 2016, when the Chinese media reported that he gave a talk at a forum on environmentally-friendly enterprises, arguing that products of polluting industries should no longer be purchased. He called on the government to deepen market reforms, suggesting that he was now willing to follow the general party line (Choi, 2016).[48] However, many private entrepreneurs still believe that they should have a more pronounced say in politics, as this influence is important for their business success. As a renowned journalist wrote in one of his books on private entrepreneurship:

> Politics is just like the weather. If entrepreneurs do not understand this weather — how will they be able to do a good job? (…) They have to act as politicians in the market. Therefore, I call them 'market politicians' (*shichang zhengzhijia*) (Zhang, 2006: 155).

---

[48] Another example is the prominent businesswoman Wang Ying who, after her resignation from all business functions, strongly criticized official plans to amend the constitution with regard to the term limits of China's head of state on her messenger service 'Weixin' (Goldkorn, 2018). See 'Nü qiyejia gongkai qiang Xi' (A Chinese female entrepreneur publicly irritates Xi), *Zhongguo She* (China Gate), 4 March 2018. http://www.wenxuecity.com/news/2018/03/04/7032126.html (accessed 24 July 2018). Entrepreneurs increasingly figure as 'public intellectuals', who critically comment on scandals and government failures. See e.g. the statements of the billionaire and leading e-commerce industry leader Liu Qiangdong, who demanded severe punishment of persons responsible for a huge vaccine scandal in China in July 2018 and asked for a rapid explanation to the public, see 'What they say', China Daily, 24 July, 2018. http://www.chinadaily.com.cn/cndy/2018-07/24/content_36632069.htm (accessed 24 July 2018). He also asked family members and friends to demand public accountability.

Connective action

Collective action organized by means of internet blogging or digital messenger services has been classified by scholars as 'connective action'. 'Connective action' is based on 'individual engagement using technologies to carry personal stories' and functions as a platform for creating new types of networks (Bennett and Segerberg, 2013: 196). These networks are sometimes labeled as 'E-communities of interest' (Dolata and Schrape, 2014: 16), referring to groups of people linked by shared interests and digital translocality. Arguably, online chat networks are 'flexible organizations' which provide 'online meeting places', coordinate 'offline activities', and are based on 'interpersonal trust' (Bennett and Segerberg, 2012: 753; see also Liu Jun, 2016), as only trusted peers are invited to join.

The Chinese cyberspace is composed of multiple platforms that include websites, microblogs, e-news threads, online shops, chat-rooms, forums, Bulletin Board Systems (BBS), virtual communities, and more. Statistics for 2016 show that WeChat (*Weixin*) is the most frequently used platform (with a usage rate of 78.8 percent), followed by QQ-space and Weibo microblogging services (akin to Twitter or Facebook) with 67.4 percent and 34 percent usage rates, respectively (Zhongguo Hulian Wangluo Xinxi Zhongxin, 2016). At the end of 2018, the usage rates of these three platforms amounted to 83.4 percent, 58.8 percent, and 42.3 percent respectively (Zhongguo Hulian Wangluo Xinxi Zhongxin, 2019). Meanwhile, public discourses occur increasingly through MMS (multimedia messages) and voice messaging services (*Weixin* or *WeChat*) (de Lisle *et al.*, 2016). Social media have arguably spawned an alternative participative culture engendering new socio-political dynamics and changing power relations (Guobin Yang, 2009; Schäfer, 2011; Jenkins *et al.*, 2016). This has brought about new patterns of collective strategic action on the part of private entrepreneurs in contemporary China.

In this context, the smartphone is the most effective tool connecting people with each other, creating a digital turn in social communication as much in China as elsewhere. Cara Wallis argues that smartphones are a central tool for networking without boundaries, for constituting 'selfhood, friendship and group solidarity', generating and maintaining communities and 'a sense of belonging' or exclusivity, enabling 'immobile mobility' in the sense of 'surpassing spatial, temporal, physical, and structural boundaries' (Wallis 2013: 5–16). Activities conducted via these new social media platforms help entrepreneurs to organize as communication communities. In this sense, smartphones do not only act as personal digital assistants but also contribute to the emergence of a sense of selfhood, group solidarity, a sense of belonging or exclusivity and allow for extended networking (Wallis, 2013).

Our fieldwork among Chinese entrepreneurs has shown that new social media provide a broad venue for personalized communication and information which can help entrepreneurs to articulate and strategically solve individual business problems without state interference. Interviewees told us that the members of each branch organization of their entrepreneurial association are interconnected by *Weixin* chat groups, so that they can quickly receive or exchange news relevant to their businesses, including new government policies and regulations. This communication is not only understood in terms of a business relationship but also as part of a social network and intra-group identity building.[49]

Guan Yanhui (2017) has shown that entrepreneurs use the internet not only to pursue their economic interests, but also to promote their contributions to China's development and charitable activities, clearly an effort to enhance their social standing and prestige. Thus, the internet provides entrepreneurs with the opportunity to communicate their views and proclaimed public responsibility to society. Several interviewees emphasized the significance of the internet in providing 'more objective news' on China's private sector, entrepreneurship in general and the social role of private entrepreneurs.[50] Along the same lines, a Chinese professor told us:

> The internet offers private entrepreneurs the opportunity to express their interests under conditions where only limited channels for interest expression exist and where traditional media don't care much about their

---

[49] Interview, Zhejiang Provincial Association of Regional Economic Promotion (*Zhejiang sheng quyu jingji cujinhui*), an entrepreneurial association founded by graduates of Zhejiang University, Hangzhou, 22 March 2017.

[50] Interview, Qingdao, 26 March 2017; Hangzhou, 21 March 2017; Guangzhou, 5 March 2017.

problems. Moreover, if an entrepreneur becomes an influential 'da V' with many followers, i.e. an internet celebrity, he can impact on public opinion and thus enhance the policy influence of entrepreneurs. In such a case, even the traditional media will take notice of him and his opinions.[51]

Entrepreneurial clubs like those mentioned above do engage heavily in such activities. According to Liu Donghua, the founder of *Zhenghedao*, social media work is highly important for his organization in terms of engendering trust in private entrepreneurship:

> We use it for generating societal trust in private entrepreneurs. We hope we can succeed in generating trust in private entrepreneurship and to change public opinion and prejudices (…) Our club is a platform for trust-building. This requires information equality (*xinxi pingdeng*). We need a platform (*pingtai*) to introduce our ideas and intentions. This is an important mission of this club.[52]

For their part, private entrepreneurs use the internet extensively and participate in chat groups of various sorts at both local and national level. Government cadres are sometimes invited to join these chat groups (a means of ensuring both state control and cooperation), thus providing a broad network structure which serves, among other things, to facilitate the dissemination of information and the organization of offline activities by private entrepreneurs. A high percentage of our respondents argued that, in this context, entrepreneurial interests are best represented by entrepreneurs themselves. Digital interaction has become crucial for pursuing their interests, more so than relying on 'distant representatives' in business organizations or parliamentary bodies (PPs, CCPPs).[53] This finding has several implications: (1) Entrepreneurs (like other netizens) are not only

---

[51] Interview, professor at Zhejiang University, Hangzhou, 1 April 2018. 'Da V' is a combination of the words 'big' (*da*) and VIP. The term refers to internet bloggers with many followers or digital 'opinion leaders'.

[52] Interview, Beijing, 23 February 2016.

[53] Interviews: Beijing 2 March 2017; Kunming 9 March 2017; Hangzhou 22 March 2017; Qingdao, 26 and 28 March 2017.

consumers but also producers of blogs, messages, news, etc. Therefore, their online interaction is not only part of an individualizing process but also serves to constantly intensify contact with their peers. (2) Private entrepreneurs take their fate into their own hands via personalized connective action, distancing them from their party state representatives (see also Say and Castells, 2004). Hence, connective action creates a distance between private entrepreneurs and party state elites in the current regime coalition. (3) Business operations via digital networking without state interference are conceived by private entrepreneurs as 'self-organized'. Accordingly, digital networks such as *Weixin* chat groups not only create new patterns and modes of strategic behavior and political agency of entrepreneurs — i.e. connective action — but also enhance their entrepreneurial identity. For example, the members of digital networks support each other in solving a vast array of problems related to their enterprises, allowing them to act as mutual guarantors for bank loans and to exchange views on how to work through business associations, peoples' congresses, or political consultative conferences.

One private entrepreneur told us that he had set up his own internet platforms which could host as many as 800 chat groups (including digital chambers of commerce) with fixed membership, operating independently of government organizations. He himself regularly and actively participates in just four of them, which, he told us, have their own member-elected boards and codes of conduct. The discussions among chat group members primarily focus on business-related problems, such as finding loans, building relationships with politicians, consulting experts and business leaders, and seeking general business advice.[54] Another respondent pointed out that younger entrepreneurs more than any other group are increasingly selling their products via the internet and therefore have less interest in developing *guanxi* to local governments:

> By means of the internet, we can regulate more issues among ourselves at a distance from the government. Our online networks also promote mutual support and collaboration in terms of investment, marketing, enterprise mergers, business advice and credits. We like to take things

---

[54] Interview, Beijing, 7 September 2015.

into our own hands and represent our interests by ourselves (*daibiao women ziji*).[55]

Connective action is therefore also a strategy through which entrepreneurs can gain more autonomy from the government without alienating it. Moreover, it has a positive effect on strengthening collective identity among private entrepreneurs: As one respondent emphasized by commenting on his alumni group of 52 classmates, graduates of the Changjiang Business School in Shanghai, and their chat group communication:

> There is a strong we-group feeling and distinct trust existing among us. Through *Weixin*, we are communicating with each other about everything important on an almost daily basis: our grievances, life experiences, hobbies, entrepreneurial problems and how to solve them. It is a kind of an internal IT and advisory club. We grant each other loans, even without interest, invest in classmates' companies and collaborate wherever possible. If a member of the network is looking for a prominent entrepreneur or a leading figure of a bank, he or she will first of all approach the members of its personal MBA network. If this fails, we ask the professors of the school to establish such contacts via the school's large-scale network. Therefore, these schools are not only training organizations but rather life-long network platforms of cooperation, not only in reality but also virtually.[56]

Entrepreneurs also engage in collective action in 'digital campaigns' initiated and hosted on *Weixin*.[57] For instance, as demonstrated in Chapter 4, Hangzhou entrepreneurs collected 600 signatures of renowned private entrepreneurs via such an online campaign in 2012, thus putting pressure on the provincial government to support entrepreneurs in gaining easier access to credit.[58]

---

[55] Interview, Qingdao, 2 March 2016.
[56] Interview, Beijing, 18 February 2015.
[57] A Chinese report on the internet activities of private entrepreneurs found, however, that even though some 62 percent frequently or sometimes use WeChat, just one-third of the respondents actively participate in blogging activities (Lü and Fan, 2016).
[58] Interview, Hangzhou, 1 March 2015.

Another case illustrates how cyberspace can be used to mobilize public support and pressure local governments to address entrepreneurial grievances: In 2018, one of the largest and most influential entrepreneurs in the city of Dezhou (Shandong Province) published an open letter to the local party secretary via his public *Weixin* account (*gongzhong hao*) that all his followers could read. He explicitly criticized government officials for breaching a promise given by the local leadership many years ago to actively support private enterprise development. Local entrepreneurs and citizens responded well to this criticism and discussed it widely online. The local leadership responded positively by contacting the entrepreneur and promised to solve the issues he had raised as soon as possible.[59]

Certainly enough, local authorities are normally reluctant to listen to any criticism of their policies or attempt to constrain or even suppress those critical voices. However, the fact that the above-mentioned case was also made public in the national print media, thus leaving cyberspace and entering into 'real world politics', confirms a number of observations which we have made across all our fieldwork locations, thus being valid for both connective and real world strategic action by private entrepreneurs: (a) it is quite likely today that the grievances of large entrepreneurial players attract the attention of higher authorities, which would then advise local governments to respond positively; (b) public discussion of grievances by private entrepreneurs is welcomed, at least if it remains restricted to specific localities; (c) only large, renowned and innovative entrepreneurs vital for local private sector development — in the Dezhou case, the complaining entrepreneur was the owner of a large company producing solar energy equipment — can raise such grievances (while the voices of smaller and less important entrepreneurs are often ignored); (d) outspoken entrepreneurs speak up not only for themselves, but also for the interests of other entrepreneurs, pinpointing their significance as members of a core elite within the whole constituency of private

---

[59] 'You you qiyejia wangluoshang biaoda liyi suqiu jubao shiwei shuji lanzheng' (Once again an entrepreneur raised interest demands by denouncing political idleness before the city's party secretary), *Xinjing Bao* (*New Capital Newspaper*), 20 February 2018; http://news.sina.com.cn/c/nd/2018-02-20/doc-ifyrqwkc8433004.shtml (accessed 9 March 2019).

entrepreneurs; (e) party state leaders are interested in solving tangible problems for private sector development at the local level, all the more so as private entrepreneurship has been declared crucial for accomplishing the government's goal of making China a developed country by 2050.[60]

Essential for our discussion here is the observation that connective action can mobilize public support both online and offline, resulting in political pressure on party state authorities that must be addressed in one or another way. Again, all our respondents stressed that 'connective action' does not intend to antagonize the government or to change the political system, but limits itself to ensuring stable and smooth private sector development. As one entrepreneur noted:

> We use the internet also to disseminate ideas on how private entrepreneurs think and how they feel. We need not always talk about the government. We have to create our own space. We have to rely on our own strength to solve our problems.[61]

This, however, does not mean that private entrepreneurs attempt to shield themselves from or avoid the current regime. Most of them feel rather embedded in it and, generally speaking, see no contradiction between their interests and the interests of the party state. Accordingly, one private entrepreneur, when referring to the significance of digital chat applications like *Weixin*, remarked:

> Such kind of networks do not challenge the system but rather change the public perception of it (…) In up to 98 percent of all cases, the Chinese government and private entrepreneurs have the same objectives; they differ only in 2 percent (...) Thus conflicts between the government and entrepreneurs are few (…). In the end, the internet contributes to the

---

[60] A nation-wide strike by private truck drivers against rising costs, bad labor conditions and arbitrary fines in June 2018 was organized via the instant messaging tool service QQ, illustrating how connective action is not bound locally but can be organized on a nation-wide basis. See 'Why protests by China's truck drivers could put the brakes on the economy', *South China Morning Post*, 24 June 2018, https://www.scmp.com/news/china/policies-politics/article/2152196/road-warriors-strike-back-why-protests-chinas-truck (accessed 14 July 2018).

[61] Interview, entrepreneur, Beijing, 2 February 2018.

survival of the system, since the government provides us with assistance and support.[62]

Overall, connective action has become an important component of private entrepreneurs' 'strategic arsenal' for engaging the government at all administrative levels, but it does not (yet) destabilize the regime coalition. Discussing issues of private sector development or solving business problems through messenger services like *Weixin* facilitates day-to-day communication between private entrepreneurs and raises their self-awareness as members of a social constituency that can work around the government, even though it needs the government in many instances. Since private entrepreneurs are members of many chat groups at the same time, connective action can spread like wildfire, thus multiplying the effects of offline strategic action and identity-building among private entrepreneurs.

This chapter has shown that private entrepreneurs are embedded in a multilayered structure of offline and online networks which help them to engage in collective strategic action with their peers. Social networks, as we have called them generically, serve entrepreneurial interests by reproducing favorable connections (*guanxi*) to party and government officials. Public welfare initiatives (charity donations) and lobbying activities, such as inviting leading officials to conferences to discuss policy issues, are important strategies of private entrepreneurs' collective action in today's China. A major feature of such action is, as one entrepreneur explained, to act in a 'discreet but goal-oriented' way and to 'influence the awareness' of important officials in order to change their minds with regard to helping the development of the private sector.[63] In fact, changing the minds of officials is considered to be more effective than any attempt to challenge their political authority. Nevertheless, informal and connective strategic action, much like formal strategic action, gradually allows private entrepreneurs to become critical actors in policy-making in China. Even though they walk a thin line to avoid alienating the party state and are under constant pressure to adhere to the party line, private entrepreneurs have become a strategic group that changes the current regime. This raises the

---

[62]Interview, Beijing, 7 September 2015.
[63]Interview, Hangzhou, 21 March 2017.

question of the direction and quality of that change. We are going to address this question in our concluding chapter.

References

Alchian, Armen A. (1950). Uncertainty, evolution and economic theory. *The Journal of Political Economy* 58(3), 211–221.

Bennett, W. Lance and Segerberg, Alexandra. (2012). The logic of connective action. *Information, Communication and Society* 15(5), 739–768.

Bennett, W. Lance and Segerberg, Alexandra. (2013). *The Logic of Connective Action. Digital Media and the Personalization of Contentious Politics.* Cambridge and New York: Cambridge University Press.

Black, Ben and Mitchel, Tom. (2016). Beijing muzzles tycoon critic known as the Cannon, *First FT* (Financial Times), 28 February. http://www.ft.com/intl/cms/s/0/e9cdc8ce-de0e-11e5-b67f-a61732c1d025.html#axzz41WYCF8A4 (accessed 29 February 2016).

Cho, Young Nam. (2009). *Local People's Congresses in China: Development and Transition.* Cambridge: Cambridge University Press.

Choi, Chi-yuk. (2016). Outspoken tycoon makes first public appearance since Communist Party slapped him with probation. *South China Morning Post,* 6 June. http://www.scmp.com/news/china/policies-politics/article/1966413/outspoken-tycoon-makes-first-public-appearance), accessed 4 August 2016.

Chu, G.C. (1985). The changing concept of self in contemporary China. In Marsella, A.J., DeVos, G., and Hsu. L.F.K. (Eds.), *Culture and Self: Asian and Western Perspectives* (pp. 141–166). New York: Tavistock Publications.

Cumming, Douglas, Firth, Michael, Hou, Wenxuan, and Lee, Edward (Eds.). (2015). *Sustainable Entrepreneurship in China. Ethics, Corporate Governance, and Institutional Reforms,* New York: Palgrave Macmillan.

deLisle, Jaques, Goldstein, Avery, and Yang, Guobin (Eds.). (2016). Introduction: The Internet, social media, and a changing China. In deLisle, Jacques, Goldstein, Avery, and Yang, Guobin (Eds.), *The Internet, Social Media, and a Changing China* (pp. 1–27). Philadelphia: University of Pennsylvania Press.

Fu, Diana. (2017). Disguised collective action in China. *Comparative Political Studies* 50(4), 499–527.

Goldkorn, Jeremy. (2018). Don't talk about the constitution in China. *Supchina Sinica,* 27 February. https://supchina.com/2018/02/27/dont-talk-about-the-constitution-in-china/ (accessed 4 May 2018).

Granovetter, Mark. (1973). The strength of weak ties. *American Journal of Sociology* 78(6), 1360–1380.

Guan, Yanhui. (2017). *Wangluo meijie zai minying qiye liyi bioda zhong de zuoyong yanjiu* (Study on the Role of the Internet Media Used by Private Entrepreneurs to Express Their Interests). Master thesis. University of Inner Mongolia, Hohhot. http://www.doc88.com/p-7058690560826.html (accessed 5 August 2018).

Heberer, Thomas and Shpakovskaya, Anna. (2017). The digital turn in political representation in China. *Working Papers on East Asian Studies*, 119, November. University of Duisburg-Essen: Institute of East Studies.

Jenkins, Henry, Ito, Mizuko, and Boyd, Danah. (2016). *Participatory Culture in a Networked Era*. Cambridge, Malden: Polity Press.

Kennedy, Scott. (2009). Comparing formal and informal lobbying practices in China: The capital's ambivalent embrace of capitalists. *China Information* 23(2), 195–222.

Liu, Jun. (2016). Credibility, reliability, and reciprocity. Mobile communication, guanxi, and protest mobilization in contemporary China. In Lim, Sun Sun, and Soriano, Cheryll R.R. (Eds.), *Asian Perspectives on Digital Culture: Emerging Phenomena, Enduring Concepts* (pp. 69–84). London and New York: Routledge.

Lü, Peng, and Fan, Xiaoguang. (2016). 2015 nian Zhongguo siying qiyezhu hulianwang xingwei diaocha fenxi baogao (Internet behavior characteristics and preferences among private business owners). In Li, Peilin, Chen, Guangjin, and Zhang, Yi, Beijing (Eds.), *2016 nian Zhongguo shehui xingshi fenxi yu yuce* (Analysis and Forecast of China's Society in 2016) (pp. 319–328). Beijing: Shehui Kexue Wenxian Chubanshe (Social Science Academic Press).

McNally, Christopher A. and Wright, Theresa. (2010). Sources of social support for China's current political order: The 'thick embeddedness' of private capital holders. *Communist and Post-Communist Studies* 43(2), 189–198.

Niedenführ, Matthias. (2018). Managementinnovation aus China? Der Emerging Trend des 'Confucian Entrepreneur' (Management Innovation from China? The Emerging Trend of the 'Confucian Entrepreneur'). In Deutsch-Chinesische Wirtschaftsvereinigung (German-Chinese Economic Association) (Ed.), *DCW Yearbook 2018* (pp. 67–76). Cologne: DCW.

Popovic, Emina. (2017). *Lobbying Practices of Citizens' Groups in China. Sage Open. Special Issue on Interest Groups in Developing Countries*. http://

journals.sagepub.com/doi/full/10.1177/2158244017713554 (accessed 1 May 2018).

Say, Araba and Castells, Manuel. (2004). From media politics to networked politics: The internet and the political process. In M. Castells (Ed.), *The Network Society: A Cross Cultural Perspective*. http://econpapers.repec.org/bookchap/elgeechap/3203_5f16.htm (accessed 28 July 2017).

Schäfer, Mirko T. (2011). *Bastard Culture! How User Participation Transforms Cultural Production*. Amsterdam: Amsterdam University Press.

Schubert, Gunter and Heberer, Thomas. (2015). Continuity and change in China's 'local state developmentalism'. *Issues and Studies* 51(2), 1–38.

Schubert, Gunter and Heberer, Thomas. (2017). Private entrepreneurs as a 'Strategic Group' in the Chinese polity. *China Review* 17(2), 95–122.

Singerman, Diane (2004). The networked world of Islamist social movements. In Wiktorowicz, Quintan (Ed.), *Islamic Activism: A Social Movement Theory Approach* (pp. 143–163). Bloomington: Indiana University Press.

Tian, Xiaoli. (2018). Face-work on social media in China. The presentation of self on RenRen and Facebook. In Kent, Mike, Ellis, Katie, and Xu, Jian (Eds.), *Chinese Social Media. Social, Cultural, and Political Implications* (pp. 92–105). New York and London: Routledge.

Tse, Edward. (2016). *China's Disruptors. How Alibaba, Xiaomi, Tencent and other Companies Are Changing the Rules of Business*. London: Portfolio Penguin.

Tu, Wei-ming. (1985). Selfhood and otherness in Confucian thought. In Marsella, Anthony J., DeVos, George, and Hsu, Francis L.K. (Eds.), *Culture and Self. Asian and Western Perspectives* (pp. 231–251). New York and London: Tavistock Publications.

Wallis, Cara. (2013). *Technomobility in China: Young Migrant Women and Mobile Phones*. New York and London: New York University Press.

Yang, Guobin. (2009). *The Power of the Internet in China: Citizen Activism Online*. New York: Columbia University Press.

Yu, Haiqing. (2018). Social media and the experience economy in China's microphilanthrophie. In Kent, Mike, Ellis, Katie, and Xu, Jian (Eds.), *Chinese Social Media. Social, Cultural, and Political Implications* (pp. 9–21). New York and London: Routledge.

Zhang, Jingping. (2006). *Zhejiang fashengle shenme. Zhuangui shiqi de minzhu shenghuo* (Democratic life in the transformation period). Shanghai: Dongfang chuban zhongxin.

Zhang, Youhong. (2009). *Taishanhui: Lishi de beiying* (Taishan Association: Background of its history), http://www.chinaweekly.cn/bencandy.php?fid=63&id=4614 (accessed 5 July 2016).

Zhongguo Hulian Wangluo Xinxi Zhongxin (China Internet Network Information Center). (2017). *Zhongguo hulian wangluo fazhan zhuangkuang tongji baogao* (Statistical Report on the development of the Internet in China), July 2016. http://www.cnnic.cn/hlwfzyj/hlwxzbg/ (accessed 24 July 2018).

Zhongguo Hulian Wangluo Xinxi Zhongxin (China Internet Network Information Center). (2019). *Zhongguo hulian wangluo fazhan zhuangkuang tongji baogao* (Statistical Report on the development of the Internet in China), February 2019. http://www.cac.gov.cn/wxb_pdf/0228043.pdf (accessed 16 August 2019).

Conclusion

In this volume, we have argued that private entrepreneurs constitute a 'strategic group' within the Chinese polity. By definition, strategic groups pursue their interests and goals in a strategic way. As we have explained in detail in Chapter 3, the strategic group concept does not require that each member of a group is in contact with all other members of that group (Berner, 2005). As such, strategic action is often uncoordinated in its evolution. This is especially evident between different localities and when members of a strategic group collectively respond to state policies or try to initiate such policies in order to safeguard their group-specific interests — an idea inspired by the work of James C. Scott (1985). Scott has convincingly shown that many small events in different places — uncoordinated collective strategic action, as we call it here — combine to exert hard pressure on the state to change existing policies and institutions. The limitation of previous studies on private entrepreneurship in China is a result of the enduring assumption that entrepreneurs are an atomized social constituency unable to engage in collective action, and therefore easily coopted or controlled by the party state. This assessment neglects the invisible impact of 'everyday forms' (Scott, 1989) of entrepreneurial action on the regime's internal power configurations and performance capacity. In fact, the significance of private entrepreneurs within China's political system has been underestimated due to the fact that they have never become open challengers of its authoritarian nature. Although our study confirms this observation, we would add that their formation as a strategic group within the current regime coalition of party state elites and private entrepreneurs bears the potential to change the political system considerably over time — especially in those policy areas where the interests of the coalition parties strongly differ. This relates, for example, to the current tension between the central government's support of the public sector and the preferential treatment of state-owned enterprises at all administrative levels on the one hand and the many political obstacles for sound private sector development on the other. This tension may sooner or later evolve into a fundamental conflict in today's China, which would naturally be of paramount importance for the sustainability of Communist rule.

Our fieldwork has revealed that private entrepreneurs increasingly pursue their overarching interests and shared objectives in uncoordinated yet strategic ways by working through both formal and informal organizations and communication channels. Their strategic action is multidimensional: They often approach party state officials individually, articulating policy demands that actually express a 'we-intention', as these demands are relevant to more, if not all, private entrepreneurs. They often negotiate with and lobby the central state and local governments via People's Congresses, People's Political Consultative Conferences, business associations, informal networks, and 'connective' action. Making use of their economic capital, they buy off party state elites in order to secure and expand their respective business interests, nurturing a Chinese variant of 'crony capitalism' (Pei, 2016), which has led to serious persecution of many entrepreneurs since the launch of the anti-corruption campaign by Xi Jinping in 2013. As a consequence, China's private entrepreneurs have become even more cautious in their dealings with the party state than they have been before. Challenging it may quickly result in social defamation, political exclusion, and legal punishment. Nevertheless, private entrepreneurs in today's China should not be considered tame and obedient allies of the state, but rather persistent and powerful partners who, though accepting party state supremacy, negotiate resolutely to get their way. Avoiding any open confrontation with the government and committing themselves to the party state does not indicate submissiveness but is a strategy by itself to ensure the party state still acts as an indispensable 'helping hand' to protect and develop the private sector, particularly those industries crucial for China's economic and technological aspirations.

The 'large number effect' is highly relevant to understanding how private entrepreneurs act as a strategic group. On the one hand, entrepreneurial delegates in PCs and PPCCs across the country raise similar issues and demand similar policies to solve problems the private sector is facing. On the other, the diversity of their strategic action, playing out in a plurality of formal and informal settings, eventually converges as an 'aggregate of organizations' and similar strategic behavior that often brings about substantial policy and institutional change to the benefit of private sector development.[1] This is especially relevant in regards to accessing credit, land and markets, government subsidies, protection of property rights, and the reining in of arbitrary and discriminating bureaucratic behavior.

Institutional change initiated by private economic actors first came about in the late 1970s when surplus laborers in rural areas engaged in what was later acknowledged as 'individual economic activities' and the formation of an 'individual economic sector'. Eventually, in 1988, 'private enterprises' were officially recognized (see Chapter 1). By running 'red hat enterprises' (*dai hongmao de qiye*), private entrepreneurs obscured the real character of their economic activities for the sake of political acceptance. Particularly in the 1980s and early 1990s, when the private sector was still ideologically suspect and operated under conditions of legal and institutional uncertainty, this was a viable strategy of legitimation (Pearson, 1999: 100–115; Dickson, 2003).

Kellee S. Tsai, among many others, has argued that it is difficult to verify the influence of private entrepreneurs on policy-making in China. At the same time, however, she has suggested that the 'cumulative effect of entrepreneurial actions' and 'adaptive informal institutions engendering formal institutions' have contributed to the acceptance and protection of this sector (Tsai, 2006: 139–140). Against this background, our empirical

---

[1] Powell and DiMaggio (1991, 64–66) argue that organizations operating in the same 'organizational field' are very close regarding their strategic behavior, intentions, interests, values, etc. and therefore operate in similar, though uncoordinated, ways. This relates to Bourdieu's social field theory which we have engaged for our theoretical framework on strategic groups (see Chapter 3).

data and the many examples given in Chapters 4 and 5 illustrate by which means, or 'weapons', private entrepreneurs attempt to shape the policy process and bring about institutional change in China.

Whereas 'cultural' institutions (social norms, beliefs, attitudes, and values) may alter rather slowly and incrementally (North, 1990: 83), other institutions, particularly political ones, may change much more quickly. In Chapter 1, we showed that the institutional setting in which entrepreneurs are acting has changed rather rapidly over the last few decades: Jiang Zemin's propagation of the 'Three Represents' (*sange daibao*) in 2001, allowing entrepreneurs to become CCP members, and the amendment of the constitution in 2004 to protect private property rights are the two most salient examples of institutional changes triggered by the rise of the private sector.[2] Add to this the vast number of central documents, speeches by party and government leaders, enacted laws and legal provisions to protect the private sector, the increasing activism of entrepreneurs in China's parliaments and advisory bodies, the widespread collusion of entrepreneurs and local officials, the recent decision to accept more than one business organization in an industrial or trade sector, new tax regulations, and the opening up of new industry and service sectors for private investment, all of which point at the party state's exposure to private sector pressure and ensuing institutional change. Other examples are the 'dilution' of the state-dominated banking system through the creation of alternative (informal) patterns of lending and corporate finance, the expansion of private businesses in sectors previously the exclusive domain of state-owned enterprises (such as logistics, delivery networks, smart TV production, entertainment, educational institutions, health care, medical services, aerospace, weapons technology, etc.); the establishment of private internet and IT companies; and the

---

[2]Article 11 of the constitution now reads as follows: 'The non-public sectors of the economy such as the individual and private sectors of the economy, operating within the limits prescribed by law, constitute an important component of the socialist market economy. The State protects the lawful rights and interests of the non-public sectors of the economy such as the individual and private sectors of the economy. The State encourages, supports and guides the development of the non-public sectors of the economy and, in accordance with law, exercises supervision and control over the non-public sectors of the economy' (see Constitution, 2014).

successive improvement of the legal system to protect private property rights. Such institutional changes are unlikely to be the product of an 'enlightened' political elite, but rather the result of strategic action on the part of private entrepreneurs.[3]

Huang (2014: 138–140) has argued that the impact of entrepreneurs on policy-making is bigger than that of any other social group in contemporary China. Entrepreneurs endeavor to safeguard the group's overall interests by engaging in different forms of collective (including 'connective') strategic action and bargaining. Based on the available evidence, though difficult to measure, we argue that the vast multiplicity of the 'weaponry' available to China's private entrepreneurs, used to assert and expand their influence within the existing regime coalition, has been effective and is becoming increasingly more so. Political participation — both formal and informal — has intensified over the years, though it tends to turn to informal channels in order to circumvent restrictions in formal participation. Interaction with party state authorities has become more negotiation-driven, arguably resulting in more business-friendly policy-making and policy-implementation, especially at the local level where state–business relations are particularly close. Finally, as our interviews have shown, private entrepreneurs in China increasingly consider themselves members of a distinct social group whose membership share a common set of interests and values. Put differently, they have begun to entertain a collective identity, driven by their (uncoordinated) collective action and a similar habitus that increasingly informs much of their thinking about themselves and their political behavior within the Chinese polity. Hence, the balance of power between the party state and private entrepreneurs has changed significantly in recent years. Today, private entrepreneurs pursue their interests strategically by working through both formal organizations and informal networks. They are increasingly turning to collective action to improve the institutional environment of their business operations and to protect their commercial interests. Large entrepreneurs are forerunners and trendsetters of strategic action at the

---

[3]For more details on institutional change affected by private entrepreneurs, see Kshetri (2007), Nee (2009), and Jun *et al.* (2017); in a more general sense see Beckert (1999), Elert and Henrekson (2017). See also Tse (2016, pp. 221–225).

national, provincial, and local level. Joint action in PCs and PPCCs, business associations, entrepreneurial clubs, and chat groups pushes the development of both the collective identity of private entrepreneurs and their collective capacity to engage in strategic action.

At the same time, a healthy development of the private sector has become increasingly critical for leading officials in local governments to achieve positive performance evaluations and thus to enhance their career prospects. As a consequence, over the last decade, the state–business relationship has shifted from 'leadership' (*lingdao*) to more market-driven 'guidance' (*yindao*) and 'service provision' (*fuwu*). Today, the voices and interests of private entrepreneurs is the most important source of GDP development, tax generation, employment, and innovation. As such, they must be taken into account by local governments in order to achieve their development goals and perform acceptably in the eyes of their higher-ups. At the same time, private entrepreneurs who are economically significant for the development of a certain jurisdiction can exert substantial political pressure by threatening local officials with transferring their enterprises to other locations if their requirements and expectations concerning public services and support are not satisfactorily met. Larger and more important companies are particularly powerful in this regard. If a major enterprise moves to another location, its suppliers often follow suit, thus causing tremendous economic damage within a locality and, again, jeopardizing the chances of leading local cadres receiving a positive performance assessment. Hence, these officials and private entrepreneurs clearly share a common interest in successful private sector development within a city, county, or township, and are 'doomed' to close cooperation, given the particular institutional environment they face.

However, state–business relations are always exposed to political 'climate change'. Over the course of the Xi Jinping era, private sector policies have become increasingly rigid in an attempt to merge state and privately-owned enterprises or to control private enterprises through public sector investment. Moreover, many private companies have been forcefully shut down in conjunction with the party state's prerogative to restructure the economy, often by claiming to provide for a cleaner environment. Our interviews revealed that conditions are particularly deteriorating for small- and medium-sized businesses.[4] A debate in 2018 over whether the private sector should be nationalized, combined with frequent politically-motivated government inventions into legal proceedings against large entrepreneurs, resulting in unfair verdicts (Tang, 2018), plus official support of high-tech enterprises at the expense of low-tech companies (Chan and He, 2019) all serve to foster a decline of confidence in government policies, and nurture among private entrepreneurs a sense of lacking legal protection. The case of tycoon Chen Tianyong who left China by complaining about the harsh environment for entrepreneurs is an expression of this declining confidence in private sector development in today's China (Chen, 2019; Li Yuan, 2019).

It is the declared 'mission' of the current CCP leadership to make the country an 'overall-modernized entity' on an equal footing with the United States by 2050, which requires systematic steering of the private sector into innovation and technical upgrading. The fundamental tension in state–business relations resulting from the regime's economic dependence on sound private sector development on the one hand and its simultaneous quest for a strong public sector and political control over the private sector on the other do not bode well for the future harmony within the present regime coalition.

The strategic action of private entrepreneurs may not always be effective or successful, but, as we argue, their large number across the entire country, even when uncoordinated, definitely has political impact at local and national level. 'Connective' action based on the dynamic development of digital technologies and social media will most substantially alter state–business relations in the near future. It has already created new patterns of collective strategic action in which each member of the strategic

---

[4] See e.g. the complaints of an entrepreneur, who returned from the US, about the enormous difficulties and obstacles of small- and medium sized enterprises: 'Zhizaoye da taowang, qingzhule liunian xinxue de gongchang, jintian xuanbu pochan daobile!' (The great flight of the manufacturing industry, I have thrown my heart blood into my factory for six years, today I announce its bankruptcy and close down). https://dushi.singtao.ca/toronto/财经-分类/创业故事-分类/制造业大逃亡%ef%bc%8c倾注了6年心血的工厂%ef%bc%8c今天宣布破/ (accessed 15 February 2020).

group of private entrepreneurs can participate, hence widening the scope of such action and strengthening group coherence, self-representation, and identity. This brings more distance between private entrepreneurs and party state elites. In the words of one entrepreneur, quoted earlier:

> By means of the internet, we can regulate more issues amongst ourselves, at a distance from the government. Our online networks also promote mutual support and collaboration in terms of investment, marketing, enterprise mergers, business advice, and credits. We like to take things in our own hands and to represent our interests by ourselves.[5]

This viewpoint reflects the rising significance of new social media. Smartphones, for instance, do not only act as personal digital assistants but also constitute selfhood, self-organization, group solidarity, a sense of belonging or exclusion and extended networking (Wallis, 2013: 5–6). The self-representation of private entrepreneurs does, in the perspective of many of our respondents,[6] not only mean self-portrayal through personal websites. It rather means that they need to take their fate in their own hands by solving problems via online (and offline) networks instead of working through distant representatives in party state bodies or business associations. Accordingly, the internet has developed into a strong instrument of self-organization and autonomous expression transcending the political system (Say and Castells, 2004)[7], although the party state attempts by every means to bring the internet under its control. Put differently, by engaging in 'connective' action, private entrepreneurs take representation into their own hands which, arguably, emancipates them gradually but incessantly, from the political supremacy of the party state.

At the same time, the party state continues with its attempts to co-opt private entrepreneurs by their incorporation into formal organizations (such as the CCP, PCs, PPCCs, and business associations). But such incorporation may become increasingly tricky in the future, as private

---

[5]Interview, Qingdao, 2 March 2016.
[6]Interviews: Beijing 2 March 2017; Kunming 9 March 2017; Hangzhou 22 March 2017; Qingdao, 26 and 28 March 2017.
[7]Eugenia Siapera called this 'connected autonomy' (2008: 59).

entrepreneurs become more unyielding in negotiating with the party state. Ding Xueliang (1994) has shown early on, in the example of business associations, how entrepreneurial interests infiltrate party state organizations in a way that makes them susceptible for new policy initiatives that serve private sector interests. Whereas business associations are closely connected to the party state, sometimes to the point of 'institutional parasitism' (in the sense that their financial and personnel resources have been widely controlled by and deeply embedded in the party state structure), party state institutions are also gradually changed by these organizations in a process of 'institutional manipulation and conversion' in Ding Xueliang's terms. Along the same logic, the heightened pressure on private enterprises to establish party branches to furnish a new type of 'intimate' state–business relations, as propagated by the government of Xi Jinping, is a Janus-faced matter for the CCP regime: It brings more party oversight into the private sector but, at the same time, the party becomes more exposed to private sector demands, which may result in more responsiveness.

For the time being, however, private entrepreneurs remain firmly 'embedded' in the Chinese political system as they are still bound to the party state by an asymmetric relationship which they cannot, and do not (yet) want to, challenge.[8] As summarized above, they have been and are agents of policy and institutional change, but not regime change. They are foremost interested in improving the environment for their business activities; they expect that the party state acknowledges their crucial role in the development of the nation and protects their legitimate interests. The fact that private entrepreneurs are supportive of the current political order in China results from (1) the institutional environment in which they must operate; (2) the intensive competition between jurisdictions that makes it advisable for private entrepreneurs to cooperate closely with local governments in order to gain market leverage; and (3) the

---

[8]The asymmetric relationship is carefully guarded by the party state. As Changdong Zhang (2017) argues, monitoring private enterprises by means of a discriminating tax system maintains their dependency on the party state and contributes to the resilience of the political system. From the perspective of the party state, institutional reform has its limits where they constrain its position as the gatekeeper of vital economic resources.

party state's enduring power to rein in any effort to challenge the authority of the current regime. Only by acknowledging the power of the party state is it possible for private entrepreneurs to enjoy privileges and opportunities to do business in China. Hence, the sharpening of their 'weapons' notwithstanding, private entrepreneurs do not challenge the power of the CCP but rather focus on making it commit to business-friendly policies.

It follows that grievances and discontent in the Chinese business world are frequently concealed behind 'politically correct' language and alleged conformity. As one private entrepreneur expressed metaphorically:

> The Communist Party does not provide you with food and drink. The only thing it can provide for entrepreneurs is a good environment. It permits you to emerge and to perish on your own. If your enterprise runs well, you are respected. If not, you will be appreciated by no one. Only the Party provides the environment and policies for entrepreneurs.[9]

Most of our respondents emphasized that as 'patriots' they are strongly interested in developing their country. In fact, patriotism is an important sentiment that makes private entrepreneurs identify with the Communist Party's mission to rejuvenate the Chinese nation and, in case they have made a business career abroad, to return to their 'motherland' to help its further rise. As two of our respondents noted respectively:

> Meanwhile I have a US passport. I could of course remain in the US and live an easy and prosperous life as an entrepreneur. But I returned since I want to contribute to China's development and modernization. It is my home country, which I deeply love, despite the difficult environment in which we entrepreneurs have to operate.[10]
>
> In general, it is often easier to do business in a Western country where entrepreneurs, no matter if they are big or small, are legally equal. Many things would be easier there. I was trained in Europe and speak

---

[9] Interview, Changchun, 11 September 2015.
[10] Interview, Beijing, 18 February 2016.

several foreign languages. What the people in the West are lacking, however, is knowledge on how to properly handle the culture of human relations (*renwen*). In China, the legal system is still underdeveloped. The culture of human relations is more important. And I understand this culture, I know how to handle it, am familiar with the Chinese market and the ways you have to behave here. Also, we have many friends who can and would help us.[11]

Moreover, renowned Shanghai entrepreneur Chen Jianming cloaked the same stance in the following words:

> The fate of [private] enterprises is strongly bound to the development of the country (*guojia*). Only if the country is strong can enterprises flourish, and only then individuals can achieve a beautiful future (Chu, 2018: 84).

This reiterated the above-made point that, at least for the time being, private entrepreneurs as a strategic group remain loyal to the existing regime coalition in partnership. There is not much interest in openly demanding political change:

> The driving-force of our entrepreneurship is not money but rather a kind of self-fulfillment. We like challenges. An enterprise is like a kind of game. We don't fear anything but just do it. In fact, we are not interested in such abstract things as 'democracy'. The party and the government are not our opponents. And if we need support we turn to our networks of friends, classmates, co-entrepreneurs. Thus, we are happy with this society in which we feel at ease.[12]

While the strategic group of private entrepreneurs is obviously content with backing the existing political system, there are also worrying signs of intensifying 'crony capitalism' which suggest that they may also contribute to its erosion. The rigor of the anti-corruption campaign seems to suggest that the party state is strong enough to control such

---

[11] Interview, Qingdao, 26 March 2017.
[12] Interview, Beijing, 25 March 2016.

entrepreneurial misconduct. The long-term consequences of (yet unco-ordinated) strategic collective action by private entrepreneurs across China to make the political system more compatible with their economic interests are, however, much harder to gauge. Moreover, whether or not the new generation of private entrepreneurs will acquiesce to remaining agents of the party state and 'forever go along with the party' is still an open question. China's young entrepreneurs have often been trained at institutions of higher learning abroad, are self-conscious, and possesses a different world view and a stronger sense of entrepreneurial indepen-dence than their forerunners. The party state will strive hard to maintain control over this modern segment of Chinese society.[13] It remains to be seen to what extent these efforts will continue to be successful.

Finally, scholars should carefully observe the evolving state–business relationship against a background of rising party state dependence on private sector development. This is vitally important in order to continue China's economic transformation and bring about a 'New Normal', thus safeguarding the power monopoly of the Communist Party in times of domestic and global economic change and restructuring.

---

[13]Note, for example, the training courses organized by the United Front Departments of the CCP and its new 'Colleges of Socialism'. These colleges have been set up under the auspices of the 'united front departments' of the CCP from the central level down to the county level; see Zhonggong Zhongyang yinfa 'Shehuizhuyi Xueyuan' gongzuo tiaoli (Working regulation of the Central Committee of the CCP for 'Socialist Colleges')], 25 December 2018, http://www.gov.cn/zhengce/2018-12/25/content_5352099.htm (accessed 17 March 2019). They are classified as special 'party schools' in which members of the Chinese non-Communist parties and the 'new social classes' (see Chapter 1) are trained in the interest of tying them more closely to the political system and its leading ideology. See e.g. the website of the 'Central College of Socialism' (*Zhongyang Shehuizhuyi Xuexuan*), http://www.zysy.org.cn/a1/a-XDI2ZW3589101058940F20 (accessed 17 March 2019). As we were told by a representative of the college in Qingdao city they also offer courses for the second and third generation of entrepreneurs, start-up entrepreneurs or 'promising' people who want to turn to self-employment (interview, 'College of Socialism' in Qingdao, 27 March 2017).

References

Beckert, Jens. (1999). Agency, entrepreneurs, and institutional change. The role of strategic choice and institutionalized practices in organizations. *Organization Studies* 20(5), 777–799.

Berner, Erhard. (2005). *Networks, Strategies and Resistance: The Concept of Strategic Groups Revisited* (Working Paper No. 218). Bielefeld: University of Bielefeld.

Chan, Elaine and He Huifeng. (2019). China's private firms in traditional low-tech sectors struggling without government support. *South China Morning Post*, 21 April. https://www.scmp.com/economy/china-economy/article/3006995/chinas-private-firms-traditional-low-tech-sectors-struggling (accessed 16 July 2019).

Chen, Tianyong. (2019). *Wo weishenme likai Zhongguo. Yige qiye jingyingzhe de linbie zhengyan* (Why I am leaving China. An entrepreneur's farewell admonition). https://botanwang.com/articles/201901/我为什么离开中国%EF%BC%9F.html (accessed 18 August 2019).

Chu, Ruiya. (2018). Chen Jianming: Hulianwang shi gaizao qiye de buerzhixuan (Chen Jianming: The internet is a tool for enterprise transformation*). Zheshang (Zhejiang Business People)* 239, 15 August, pp. 83–84.

Constitution of the People's Republic of China. (2014). http://english.gov.cn/archive/laws_regulations/2014/08/23/content_281474982987458.htm (accessed 23 August 2018).

Dickson, Bruce J. (2003). *Red Capitalists in China. The Party, Private Entrepreneurs, and Prospects.* New York: Cambridge University Press.

Ding, Xueliang. (1994). Institutional amphibiousness and the transition from Communism: The case of China. *British Journal of Political Science* 24, 293–318.

Elert, Niklas and Henrekson, Magnus. (2017). Entrepreneurship and Institutions: A Bidirectional Relationship. IFN Working Paper No. 1153, Stockholm: Research Institute of Industrial Economics. http://www.ifn.se/wfiles/wp/wp1153.pdf (accessed 18 August 2018).

Heberer, Thomas. (2017). The resilience of authoritarianism: The case of the Chinese developmental state. In Gerschewski, Johannes and Stephes, Christoph H. (Eds). *Crisis in Autocratic Regimes* (pp. 155–174). Boulder, Colorado: Lynne Rienner.

Huang, Dongya. (2014). Siying qiyezhu yu zhengzhi fazhan. Guanyu shichang zhuanxing zhong siying qiyezhu de jieji xiangxiang ji qi fansi (Private entrepreneurs and political development. Class imagination and reflection of private entrepreneurs in the process of market transformation). *Shehui (Chinese Journal of Sociology)* 4, 138–164.

Kshetri, Nir. (2007). Institutional changes affecting entrepreneurship in China. *Journal of Developmental Entrepreneurship* 12(4), 415–432.

Li, Yuan. (2019). China's Entrepreneurs are Wary of Its Future. *New York Times*, 23 February. https://www.nytimes.com/2019/02/23/business/china-entrepreneurs-confidence.html (accessed 12 April 2019).

Ma, Jun and He, Xuan. (2018). The Chinese communist party's integration policy towards private business and its effectiveness: An analysis of the ninth national survey of Chinese private enterprises. *Chinese Journal of Sociology* 4(3), 422–449.

Ma, Jun, He, Xuan, Zhu, Lina, and Liu, Ye. (2017). How Does the Speed of Institutional Change affect the Allocation of Entrepreneurship in Family Firms: empirical research on the based view of dynamic system. *Nankai Business Review International* 8(4), 447–474. https://www.emeraldinsight.com/doi/abs/10.1108/NBRI-01-2017-0001 (accessed 19 August 2018).

Nee, Victor. (2009). Endogenous Institutional Change and Capitalism in China. Paper submitted to the Conference on '1989': Twenty years after, Laguna Beach, CA, November 5–8, 2009. https://www.democracy.uci.edu/files/docs/conferences/nee.pdf (accessed 17 August 2018).

North, Douglass C. (1990). *Institutions, Institutional Change, and Economic Performance*. Cambridge and New York: Cambridge University Press.

Pearson, Margaret M. (1999). *China's New Business Elite. The Political Consequences of Economic Reform*. Berkeley: University of California Press.

Pei, Minxin. (2016). *China's Crony Capitalism. The Dynamics of Regime Decay*, Harvard: Harvard University Press.

Poletti, Anna and Rak, J. (Eds.). (2017). *Identity Technologies: Constructing the Self Online*. Madison and London: The University of Wisconsin Press.

Powell, Walter W. and DiMaggio, Paul J. (Eds.). (1991). *The New Institutionalism in Organizational Analysis*. Chicago: University of Chicago Press.

Roland, Gérard. (2004). Fast-moving and Slow-moving Institutions. CeS Ifo DICE Report 2, 16–21. https://www.cesifo-group.de/DocDL/dicereport204-forum3.pdf (accessed 25 August 2018).

Say, Araba and Castells, Manuel. (2004). From media politics to networked politics: The Internet and the political process. In M. Castells (Ed.). *The Network Society. A Cross Cultural Perspective* (pp. 363–381). Northampton,

Massachusetts: Edward Elgar Publishing, Inc. http://econpapers.repec.org/bookchap/elgeechap/3203_5f16.htm (accessed 14 August 2018).

Scott, James C. (1985). *Weapons of the Weak. Everyday Forms of Peasant Resistance.* New Haven and London: Yale University Press.

Scott, James C. (1989). Everyday forms of resistance. *Copenhagen Journal of Asian Studies* 4, 33–62.

Siapera, Eugenia. (2008). The political subject of blogs. *Information Polity* 13(1–2), 97–109.

Tang, Frank. (2018). Why China's private firms aren't convinced the law will protect them. *South China Morning Post*, 31 December. https://www.scmp.com/news/china/article/2180129/why-chinas-private-firms-arent-convinced-law-will-protect-them (accessed 22 July 2019).

Tsai, Kellee S. (2006). Adaptive informal institutions and endogenous institutional Chang in China. *World Politics* 59(1), 116–141.

Tse, Edward. (2016). *China's Disruptors. How Alibaba, Xiaomi, Tencent and other Companies Are Changing the Rules of Business.* London: Portfolio Penguin.

Wallis, Cara. (2013). *Technomobility in China: Young Migrant Women and Mobile Phones.* New York and London: New York University Press.

Yang, Keming. (2004). Institutional holes and entrepreneurship in China. *The Sociological Review* 52(3), 371–389.

Appendix

Map of Fieldwork Sites (2012–2018)

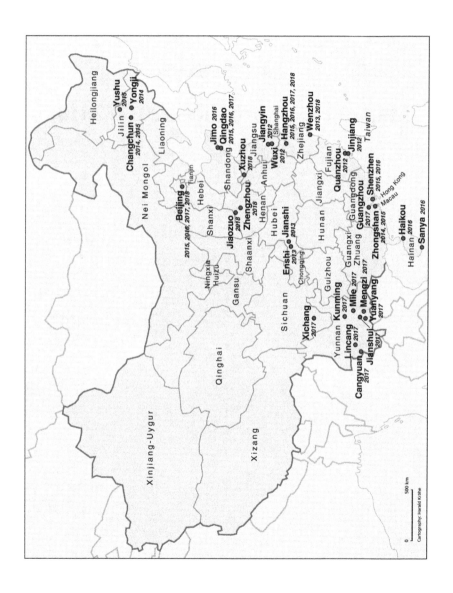

Index

CPSIA information can be obtained
at www.ICGtesting.com
Printed in the USA
LVHW011231230420
653775LV00004B/9